TEACHING ACADEMIC AND PROFESSIONAL ENGLISH ONLINE

Isabel González-Pueyo / Carmen Foz Gil / Mercedes Jaime Siso /
M. José Luzón Marco (eds.)

TEACHING ACADEMIC AND PROFESSIONAL ENGLISH ONLINE

PETER LANG
Bern · Berlin · Bruxelles · Frankfurt am Main · New York · Oxford · Wien

Bibliografische Information Der Deutschen Bibliothek
Die Deutsche Bibliothek verzeichnet diese Publikation in der Deutschen Nationalbibliografie; detaillierte bibliografische Daten sind im Internet über ‹http://dnb.ddb.de› abrufbar.

British Library Cataloguing-in-Publication Data: A catalogue record for this book is available from *The British Library,* Great Britain

Library of Congress Cataloging-in-Publication Data

Teaching academic and professional English online /
Isabel González-Pueyo ... [et al.] (eds.).
p. cm.
ISBN 978-3-03911-582-2 (alk. paper)
1. English language–Rhetoric–Study and teaching (Higher)–Computer-assisted instruction. 2. Academic writing–Study and teaching–Computer-assisted instruction. 3. Language and the Internet. I. González-Pueyo, Isabel.
PE1404.T367 2009
808′.0420785–dc22 2008045512

Cover Illustration and cover design:
Eva Rolli, Peter Lang Bern

ISBN 978-3-03911-582-2

Hochfeldstrasse 32, Postfach 746, CH-3000 Bern 9
info@peterlang.com, www.peterlang.com, www.peterlang.net

Printed in Germany

Contents

Introduction

The integration of ICTs in education is radically transforming second language teaching and learning, and motivating teachers to define new learning models and new teaching strategies. ICTs have brought about changes in the type of learning materials and in the way these materials are accessed by students. They have also led to changes in the type of teacher mediation and in the form of peer interaction. In order to take advantage of the benefits that the new medium may offer for language learning, teachers need to assume the role of facilitator and guide. This includes planning, organising, interacting with students and supporting them in their learning process, and, basically, developing a repertoire of instructional strategies to maximise the benefits of online learning.

Therefore, teachers face the challenge of determining how the Internet can be used for effective language learning. That involves reflecting on several aspects, e.g. which materials are suitable for online delivery, how materials should be adapted for their use online, how interaction between peers and between students and teacher should be structured to yield effective learning. The most important question to address is how the Internet can be harnessed to get students engaged in activities that enhance the learning experience. Teachers of English for Academic and Professional Purposes very frequently design their own materials, in an attempt to adapt to the specific needs of their students. ICTs provide useful tools and resources that facilitate this designing function and enable teachers to create tasks that would be difficult or impossible in the traditional face to face classroom setting. For this reason, many ESP teachers have taken the challenge involved in creating online tasks and materials and designing online courses. However, although the exchange of ideas regarding the design, implementation and management of online innovative learning experiences could be highly illuminating, both for other teachers engaged in online instruction and for those who would like to teach online but need a know-how guide, there is a scarcity of publications reporting experiences in teaching English for Professional and Academic Purposes online.

After developing a website of commercial correspondence in English aimed at small and medium Spanish enterprises, and having had to face various methodological and technical difficulties, we felt we needed to share opinions and concerns with other teachers involved in similar projects. It was in this way that the idea of editing this book took root and finally led to this collection of papers written by 11 teachers of ESP at European universities.

Our aim is to offer an empirical view both of the learning gains and the difficulties involved in developing online teaching materials, designing courses and implementing them using virtual learning environments. This view is made up of the opinions of the participants involved in the courses, both course managers and students. The contents of the book will allow professionals interested in online instruction to assess and compare different course management systems or virtual learning environments, some of which, such as Moodle and WebCT, are universally used, while others have been specially designed and developed by the authors to meet their specific teaching needs.

The volume opens with the paper by Luzón, which serves as a general overview of how online teaching and learning is being integrated into ESP/EAP courses and what ICT can contribute to such courses. It outlines some pedagogical principles for the design of ESP online learning environments and offers an account of several studies reporting experiences with these environments, so as to provide an overview of how ICTs can enhance ESP/EAP teaching and learning. The paper offers theoretical insights which may serve as a background to the practical examples in the subsequent papers.

In the second paper, Trinder redefines the teacher–student roles and that of the entire learning environment, taking into account the new demands on learners in terms of autonomy, learning strategies and self-organisation. Trinder describes how learners perceive the characteristics of both face-to-face and CALL contexts and makes an emphasis on the learner's active role in deciding which elements of each environment are more suitable for their learning requirements.

The following six articles (Arnó et al., Gimeno, Carrió, Bueno, Elia and Mungra) report on several practical experiences where different applications of ICTs as course management systems have been incorporated to the process of teaching-learning Academic and Professional English within university degree studies (e.g. Industrial and Agriculture Engineering, Medicine, Humanities and Foreign Languages). They suggest some guidelines for the selection and development of online material and present the advantages and disadvantages observed in the implementation of their projects.

The design of online teaching activities confronts many ESP teachers with the urgent need of finding and adapting appropriate teaching resources. At the same time, the multitude of target language input available in the electronic format on the Internet opens interesting opportunities, enabling browsing, evaluating, retrieving and adapting texts and recordings from their specialist areas as classroom materials. In this process, corpora and concordancing can be used to assist teachers. In his paper, J. Krajka describes an attempt at the implementation of concordancing procedures to promote discovery learning, using both ready-made corpora resources and custom-made ones, in Moodle-based online courses. The author points out the opportunities and drawbacks of concordancing-based discovery learning approach, and some possible applications of corpora in teaching various language skills.

We are aware that ICTs are constantly evolving and that some of the e-learning tools and course management systems mentioned in the book may have changed or disappeared in a not too distant future, being replaced by new ones which will facilitate use and accessibility. However, we believe that the opinions and ideas presented in the papers of this volume will still remain as helpful guidelines on how to set up and run online English courses. This volume is specially aimed at teachers of English for Academic and Professional Purposes, for whom the Internet has not only become the perfect medium to find valuable authentic resources, but also provides support to the appropriate software for their exploitation as teaching-learning materials. These materials can help learners develop their specific language skills as well as some of the skills required for their professional careers: communication, information management and knowledge construction. It is also hoped that this book will inspire those who intend to explore the possibilities of online instruction and the ways ICTs can be used to help their students learn.

The Editors

This volume has been published with Aragon Government funding to support project H245-123 of the research team *Inglés para Fines Académicos y Profesionales.*

María José Luzón

Learning Academic and Professional English Online: Integrating Technology, Language Learning and Disciplinary Knowledge[1]

1. Introduction

In recent years, as the role of technology in education has gained greater recognition, the use of ICT in language learning has become common in many universities. An increasing number of higher education language teachers are turning to online delivery of language materials and to the computer as a tool for interaction, cooperation and information access, in order to facilitate SLA and to meet some of the challenges posed by traditional face-to-face classrooms.

Computer networking provides useful tools to implement approaches appropriate for ESP learning, e.g. problem-based learning, case-based learning, cooperative learning, project-based learning. Additionally, it makes it easier to solve timetabling problems, so frequent when teaching ESP, and enables students to access a large amount and variety of authentic materials which cater to diverse learning styles and different levels of language competence. In this way, computer networking may contribute to a more personalised instruction, something which is extremely important in ESP classes, usually characterised by the heterogeneity of students. These factors are leading many ESP practitioners to engage in online teaching, either by designing Web-based

1 The research carried out for this paper is part of a project funded by the Aragón Government (Project code: H245-123).

projects or by setting online ESP courses. Most of these courses are part of blended learning experiences, where students complete several tasks to supplement class-based instruction (e.g. Esnawy, 2004).

The purpose of this paper is to provide an overview of how online teaching and learning is being integrated into the ESP/EAP classroom. In the first part of the paper I summarise very briefly the educational and workplace context which frames ESP courses and consider what ICT can contribute to such courses. In the second section I outline some pedagogical principles for the design of ESP learning environments. In the third part I discuss several pieces of research which describe different online environments for learning academic or professional English. This discussion is intended to provide a picture of how online learning is being integrated into ESP courses and to extend ESP teachers' awareness of the pedagogical requirements and the technological possibilities for developing effective online courses.

2. Learning ESP in higher education: The role of ICT

The world is changing economically and socially at a great pace. Therefore, students will need to be able to adapt to new situations, to self-manage their career, and to become life-long learners. The Bologna process (with the student mobility it promotes), globalisation, technological change and the need to cope with new literacies are rapidly transforming education reality and will necessarily affect the way ESP is taught and learnt.

One of the objectives of the Bologna process is to foster mobility within the European Higher Education Area. Students will need to develop a variety of communication and socialisation skills which enable this mobility and allow them to cope in different communicative situations, e.g. understanding both oral and written material or participating in international conferences. ESP instruction must be designed with the purpose of helping students find and carry out a job in a working environment where communicative needs change and evolve continuously. For this purpose, it is essential to prepare students to become autonomous life-long learners and to be able to continue to access education. Autonomous learners are able to take charge of their own learning, to analyse what they need in order to cope in specific situations of language use, and to make decisions as to how to solve their limitations and as to which strategies are most appropriate in a situation. An approach focusing on the development of autonomy emphasises the importance of the students' own pace and developmental processes, learning styles, self-monitoring and control over the learning process. Although technology can help to provide conditions that facilitate autonomous learning, more important than technology itself is the teachers' role in providing support leading to autonomy and in choosing the technological tools appropriate for effective teaching and learning.

Another factor to keep in mind when teaching ESP is that English has become the Lingua Franca of the globalised world in which students will have to follow their professions. Students will, therefore, need to use English to interact in varied communicative situations with people from different first language backgrounds. Considering English as a Lingua Franca has important implications for ESL and for ESP in particular. As Seidlhofer (2002, p. 272) puts it:

> Since ELF is, by definition, not the native language of its users, an ELF model for learners should accordingly not be dictated by any native-speaker language use, but instead its design should be guided by *pedagogical principles* rather than only linguistic ones. That is to say, insights from the psychology of learning should be taken into account, and considerations of learnability and teachability would have to be crucial design features.

The development of technology and its pervasiveness in all spheres of life has also brought about a redefinition of literacy, which has to be taken into account when designing ESP courses. Kasper (2000, p. 106) states that "to be considered multiliterate, students today must acquire a battery of skills that will enable them to take advantage of the diverse modes of communication made possible by new technologies and to participate in global learning communities". She considers that in addition to acquiring linguistic competence in English, ESL students must become functionally literate (i.e. "able to speak, understand, read, and write English, as well as use English to acquire, articulate and expand their knowledge"), academically literate (i.e. "able to read and understand interdisciplinary texts, analyze and respond to those texts through various modes of written and oral discourse"), critically literate (i.e. able to "evaluate the validity and reliability of informational sources") and electronically literate. Kasper draws on Shetzer and Warschauer's concept of electronic literacy as the ability to use electronic tools for communication, construction, research, and autonomous learning (Shetzer and Warschauer, 2000). Electronic literacy also involves multimodal literacy, necessary to be able to construct meaning in current society. Texts, especially online texts, are often multimodal, and meaning is communicated by a combination of words with visual, audio and spatial modes.

Although the increasing prominence of technology as a means of communication and a resource for information in the educational, academic and professional world poses many challenges for ESP teachers, who must help students become electronically literate and master online forms of communication, it also brings promising opportunities to help solve some of the problems of the ESP face-to-face classrooms. Oakey (1999) defines very clearly the limitations of the traditional mode of delivery when he explains why the ESP staff at the University of Hull decided to offer an online course:

- high number of students,
- different levels of English proficiency,
- students' different expectations about the course and about what they can learn from it,
- lack of attendance due to timetabling constraints,
- limited resources and scarce face-to-face contact time,
- difficulty to provide individualised feedback, which seemed to discourage students from doing any independent work,

– lack of time for tasks involving oral communication, such as work on presentation skills and low interaction between students.

Some of these limitations may be met, at least partially, with appropriately designed online learning environments. These environments can offer flexibility, authenticity and interaction. In addition, they help in the acquisition of new literacies and may be designed to promote autonomous learning.

The Internet provides flexibility in many ways. Teachers can create tasks in many formats and link them to any content document they consider useful for the students to complete the tasks. Students can work at their own pace and access multimodal documents (including text, graphics, sound, video, etc.) (Egbert and Jessup, 1996; Oxford et al., 1998; Curtis et al., 1999). Online learning environments can be designed to cater to different learning styles, both including materials in different modes and allowing different routes of accessing the materials. The interactive and hypertextual nature of the Web enables more personalised and individualised teaching and learning, with the provision of activities for different learning styles and different proficiency levels. It is possible to build learners' options into the system by letting them choose their sequence of learning, which task to engage in or which type and degree of support they need (Cummings, 2002). Hypertext enables teachers to design activities where students can get support (e. g., through online dictionaries, clarifications, examples) only when they need it.

Authenticity is also provided in various ways. ESP students can retrieve an enormous range of authentic materials related to their discipline. Additionally, the genres they can access through the Internet (e. g., academic papers and lectures, product reviews, reports) and those they produce when communicating over the Internet are genres used in the real world, outside the limits of the classroom. This facilitates the design of meaningful tasks (i. e., tasks which engage students in thoughtful learning and which are relevant to their academic or professional lives) which lead to the construction of meaningful knowledge by having students link new and old information.

ICT also facilitates the design of activities which rely on interaction and collaboration with authentic audiences and for authentic purposes, thus increasing students' motivation. The capabilities of the Internet as a mode of communication which enables students to interact with their mates or with people from other language backgrounds (including native speakers) seem to promote collaboration and make interaction and negotiation more effective than in face-to-face exchanges (Warschauer, 1998; Lamy and Goodfellow, 1999; Strambi and Bouvet, 2003). Among the advantages of CMC (Computer Mediated Communication) Strambi and Bouvet (2003) mention the following ones: learners have more time for reflection and easy access to reference materials, which improves comprehension and enables them to plan and monitor their input; CMC provides a non-threatening environment where learners can use the target language: they can decide when to contribute and the risk of making mistakes and losing face in front of other students is minimised.

In the context of ESP, one of the main advantages of ICT is its potential contribution to the development of autonomy and higher order thinking. Little (1996, p. 203) argues that

> […] information systems and information technologies can promote the development of learner autonomy to the extent that they can stimulate, mediate, and extend the range and scope of the social and psychological interaction on which all learning depends.

The non-linear nature of hypertexts and the opportunities ICTs offer for collaborative and problem-solving tasks can promote the development of cognitive strategies (Jonassen et al., 1997). Hypermedia and hypertexts make it possible to build complex learning environments, based on a constructivist perspective of information organisation: information does not follow a linear sequence, but can be presented in discrete units, and the user can choose which information to access and when to access it. However, as Villanueva (2006) points out, rather than generating autonomous behaviour, ICTs require new approaches and offer new opportunities for autonomy training, e.g. learning how to manage complexity, learning how to cope in a multimedia environment and developing critical thinking. In line with this view, Levine et al. (2000) investigate the extent to which using authentic tools, tasks and environments in a computer networked EFL academic reading classroom contributes to the development of critical reading skills and strategies. Slaouti (2002) is also concerned with the use of the Internet to develop critical information processing skills as part of an English for Academic Purposes teaching and learning context.

Finally, ICTs are the perfect tool for helping students develop multiliteracies. Capabilities such as multimedia and hypertext can be used to design online learning environments which foster a new model of meaning making, relying on different semiotic clues, not only words, and a new model of teaching and learning based on learner's navigation and linking, interaction with content, and interaction with peers through ICT. Warschauer (2002b) claims that the new forms of written communication deriving from the use of real-time chatting, electronic mail, and the World Wide Web should be taken into account in academic writing courses. One of the greatest advantages of these forms of communication for the ESP classroom is that they can help to create a community (Bowdon, 2005; Giles, 2005). The Internet enables students not only to communicate with other students in different places, making it possible for them to engage in authentic communication tasks, but also to join subject specific discussion lists and to publish for an authentic audience.

3. Pedagogical principles for the design of ESP online learning environments

The starting point when designing online materials or online courses for ESL should be sound pedagogical principles to guide the choice of technological options (Chapelle, 1998; Doughty and Long, 2003). As Felix (2002, p. 3) puts it, we should ask "What do new technologies have to offer us in our search for even more effective teaching and even greater success in passing on to the student appropriate life-long learning skills?" When considering ESP courses, this question should be framed taking account of the specific characteristics of ESP learning and teaching and the needs of ESP students.

Several researchers have put forward teaching methodological principles or conditions for a computer-supported language learning environment (e.g. Egbert and Jessup, 1996; Esch, 1996; Chapelle, 1998; Doughty and Long, 2003). I will focus here on those principles which, in my opinion, are especially relevant for ESP.

1. Activities. Use task as the unit of analysis and promote learning by doing (Egbert and Jessup, 1996; Doughty and Long, 2003). Through task-based language teaching and through learning by doing, ESP students can practice the language they will need in real discipline-related situations and acquire the necessary skills to meet their present or future real-world communicative needs. Egbert and Jessup (1996) posit that learners should get engaged in authentic tasks (i.e. tasks with a real purpose behind) which promote exposure to and production of varied language. Tasks should be based on the communicative needs as perceived by the professional discourse community (e.g., reading or writing a report, understanding a paper) and should reflect the communicative purposes for which this community uses texts. Doughty and Long (2003) mention computer simulations of target environments and tasks as a good example of the promotion of learning by doing.
2. Input. Doughty and Long (2003, p. 59) consider that learners need rich input, that is, "realistic samples of discourse use surrounding NS and NS-NNS accomplishment of target tasks", which usually means "task-specific and domain specific target language use". It is, therefore, important to provide authentic sources of information, related to the students' discipline and future workplace environment. In addition, in order to make input comprehensible for the learners, these should receive help with semantic and syntactic as-

pects (Chapelle, 1998). As a way to provide rich input Doughty and Long (2003) propose constructing a sufficiently large specific-purpose corpus, relevant to a target task, and tagging this corpus for task complexity. This specific-purpose corpus can be used to design tasks intended to make students familiar with the communicative purpose and linguistic features of the genres used by a discourse community and to show how language choices are made to achieve specific communicative goals.

3. Output. Learners need an authentic audience to produce comprehensible target language output, intended to convey meaning (Chapelle, 1998; Strambi and Bouvet, 2003). Strambi and Bouvet (2003, p. 88) suggest that negotiation of meaning and the production of comprehensible output can be achieved through "tasks that require learners' interaction and negotiation with an authentic audience and authentic materials". When asking ESP students to interact for real communication, it is important to develop their understanding of intercultural and workplace aspects which will affect communication. An example of an e-learning project that takes these aspects into account is described by Rogerson-Revell (2003). The aim of the project is to exploit online technology to get students familiar with key aspects of European work culture and develop intercultural business and professional language skills for European managers in the construction industry.
4. Learning processes. Both *focus on meaning* and *focus on form* (Chapelle, 1998; Doughty and Long, 2003) are necessary. Doughty and Long (2003) define *focus on form* as a shift of the students attention from meaning to linguistic code features, in context, but only when students need help and "noticing" as they work on communicative tasks focusing on meaning. Doughty and Long (2003) note that technology offers many coding options to make information perceptually salient, e.g. input enhancement (through highlighting, animations, etc), pop-up windows with brief explanations or lexical assistance. Learners also "need to notice errors in their own output" (Chapelle, 1998, p. 24) and to receive negative feedback, for in-

stance in the form of recasts (Doughty and Long, 2003), which enables them to correct their output.

The interaction in the target language and negotiation of meaning facilitated by computer-mediated communication also result in learners' attention to language and comprehensible input (Egbert and Jessup, 1996; Chapelle, 1998).

5. Learners. Doughty and Long (2003) claim that it is necessary to promote autonomous learning and individualised instruction, in order to cater to individual differences in learning styles and strategies, goals, interests, proficiency levels, etc. and to respect "learner syllabuses"/developmental processes.

McLoughlin and Marshall (2000) state that for effective online learning, teachers must help students develop the following "learning to learn" skills: articulation (being aware of one's own learning), self-regulation (being able to set goals and choose strategies to achieve the goal or complete a task), development of independent learning strategies, self-assessment, reflection and self-monitoring. ESP students need to develop skills to evaluate their own production and become independent life-long learners in the workplace.

Helping students to become autonomous and facilitating individualised learning to respond to student differences involves providing students with scaffolding when needed. This can be achieved in an online learning environment in several ways (Esch, 1996; McLoughlin and Oliver, 1998; Strambi and Bouvet, 2003; Luzón, 2006), i.e.

- by offering opportunities for learner control over the instructional path(s) to follow and rendering the possibility of self-repair and changing of options,
- by providing students with tools to plan and monitor their learning process,
- by giving learners control over a variety of media sources, materials and tasks,
- by letting students interact with hypermedia materials which offer different degrees of assistance through online help,

- by facilitating flexible feedback from peers and teachers,
- by encouraging reflective thinking,
- by providing social support for interaction and the sharing of ideas.

4. Online environments for learning English for Academic and Professional Purposes

Many papers concerned with the role of the Internet in the ESP/EAP classroom describe how different Internet tools can be used for ESP teaching: the use of computer conferencing in ESP/EAP courses (Leppänen and Kalaja, 1995), online discussion forums in college and professional development courses (McIntosh, 2005), MUDs (Multi-User Domain) and MOOs (MUD Object Oriented) as collaborative environments for learning languages (Robbins-Spoonas and Nolan, 2005), teamrooms in the teaching of technical report writing (Pathak and Hoon, 2006), or interactive online databases to learn academic vocabulary (Horst et al., 2005).

Another frequent issue is the description of Internet assignments or tasks for EAP/ESP (Jarvis, 2001; Luzón, 2002; Freiermuth, 2005). Jarvis (2001) provides some examples of Internet-based activities that might be integrated onto EAP courses to help non-native speakers develop skills they will probably need to follow academic courses at a British university. Luzón (2002) proposes using WebQuests as tasks in a content-based approach to ESP instruction. Other papers focus on the use of Internet-based simulations to practice professional writing (Connaughton and Ruben, 2005; Freiermuth, 2005).

Due to space constraints, I will not deal here with the above-mentioned lines or research, but concentrate on research focusing on the design of online environments or online courses for learning English for Academic and Professional Purposes (see for instance, Nesi, 1998;

Oakey, 1999; Canapero, 2004; Chen et al., 2004; Gimeno, this volume).

Most ESP online learning environments have been designed as tools for blended learning, i.e. the integration of e-learning techniques and activities (e.g. online delivery of materials, online discussions) with classroom face-to-face learning experiences. Blended learning can increase the benefits that ESP students can get from both classroom learning and distance learning in many ways, e.g., multimodal and interactive material (sound or video files, simulations, etc) complementing traditional classroom instruction can be uploaded and used by students outside the classroom; class time can be used more effectively and for activities where face-to-face human interaction is more beneficial (e.g. oral activities aimed at improving the students' oral skills, oral presentations).

The first ESP/EAP online learning environments were developed in the late 90s' and focused mainly on online content delivery. Nesi (1998) reports on the development of an EAP self-access centre on the Internet at the University of Warwick. The purpose was to improve content delivery by maximizing materials flexibility and accessibility and to provide some basic electronic literacy. Some of the technological problems and limitations faced when developing this course (e.g. impossibility to include audio and video materials) were solved in later courses. Oakey (1999) describes a component of an EAP module, delivered via Merlin (Multimedia Educational Research into Learning via an Information Network), a web-based learning environment developed at the University of Hull. The central feature of the course, whose main purpose was also to improve content management, was the *Pathway*, an area with tasks supplementing the content of face-to-face classes. Each week students had to submit workpieces to their own private space or *Personal Workbook*. The tutor had his or her own workbook, where he/she received all pieces of work. There was also a *Resource Centre* with links to other parts of the EAP Merlin environment or the World Wide Web, which provided input for some tasks and links to Internet resources such as online dictionaries. The Resource Centre also contained lectures stored in RealPlayer audio format.

With the emergence of CMS (Course Management Systems), e.g. WebCT, Blackboard, Moodle, which greatly facilitate the management and administration of online courses, many ESP teachers have embarked upon the creation of blended learning environments for their classes[2]. The software tools included in these systems make it very easy for teachers to deliver content, provide access to authentic texts adapted to the tasks and set tasks involving collaboration and discussion. Teachers can also get workpieces from students, track students' activity and performance, assess students' work and provide individualised feedback. Baskerville and Robb (2005) provide a good example of the use of Moodle for teaching Business English. In their paper they show how Moodle has been used to provide the interactive element in a Business English course with an emphasis on written communication at Kyoto Sangyo University. The course is a business simulation where students become employees of a company whose president is an English-speaking foreigner. The students must react to the messages forwarded by the president and produce the requested documents (e.g., letters of inquiry, product descriptions).

However, in spite of the advantages of CMS, these systems have some limitations when adopting a learner-centred and autonomising approach to ESP learning. Although they incorporate tools for communication and collaboration, they still seem to be too centred on content management, do not provide for the design of some activities and assessment mechanisms that would be appropriate for language learning (e.g., voice recording, audio feedback), and their multimedia capability is limited. Additionally, learning paths are usually teacher-led, there is little room for the students' choice and the design of the tasks to achieve a specific goal tends to follow a one-size-fits all approach. Integrative CALL (Warschauer, 1996) requires language environments based on the provision of tasks for learning in authentic contexts, which enable students to learn by doing and creating real artefacts (real texts),

2 Some of the papers in this volume report the use of WebCT to implement different types of EAP/ESP courses.

"adaptive tasks" and "open-ended contexts for learning", and "collaborative projects" which allow real world interaction (Ortega and Sánchez-Villalón, 2006, p. 106). Therefore, several ESP practitioners have launched into developing their own systems, specially designed for language learning, with a view to improving general-purpose CMS by incorporating elements which make it possible to realise effectively pedagogically grounded models of language learning.

Some systems intended for the design of language courses are aimed at furnishing a framework which enables teachers to incorporate activity formats appropriate for language learning and at providing flexibility and adaptability to students' varying needs. For instance, the web-based course developed by Chen et al. (2004), *Academic English,* is intended to optimise the language learning process of individual students by designing materials suitable for different language learning goals. The course stores various kinds of multimedia learning materials and information. Students can select materials, participate in question/answer sessions, and receive feedback after each interaction. Communication tools (e.g., a chat tool) also offer opportunities for student-student and student-teacher interaction. In this course the learning style of students is taken into account to select the instructional strategies for a specific instructional goal (e.g. listening comprehension). The contents for each lesson can be generated according to two selection methods, Strategy A and Strategy B. In Strategy A, the lesson is dynamically selected to fit the student's current knowledge level and a particular course strategy (e.g., a step-by-step strategy for students with a sequential learning style). In Strategy B, the students can select the learning tasks suitable for their own learning goals.

Other interesting examples of online systems for language learning are those developed as a result of the *Proyecto InGenio* (Gimeno, this volume) and *AIOLE* (An Interactive Online Learning Environment) (Ortega and Sánchez-Villalón, 2006). The aim of *Proyecto InGenio* was to create a language independent authoring online tool that would enable language teachers around the world to design their own materials, adapted to their students' needs, and create a shared database with these materials. This authoring tool has been used to create the ESP course *Intermediate Online English,* currently being used at the Polytechnic University of Valencia. The course offers diversity of activities, in order to help students develop both receptive and productive skills, and includes tasks which engage the student in using the target language in specific communicative situations in order to achieve a particular outcome.[3] *AIOLE* (Ortega and Sánchez-Villalón, 2006), developed by the CHICO research group, is intended to provide flexibility and adaptability to attend the specific needs of students in different campuses at the university of Castilla La Mancha (Spain) and to cater to the communicative interaction that language courses require. It integrates interactive Web tools for dynamic learning and online communication (e.g. chat channel, discussion forums, AWLA system[4]) to help students develop the skills of writing, reading and listening.

Although most ESP/EAP online courses seem to be designed for blended learning, there are also courses intended for distance learning. This is especially true of EAP courses for academicians who need to improve their communicative competence in academic contexts. An example is the web-based course for academic English learning via a distance tutoring system developed by Chen et al. (2001). In this kind of course, where at no moment can students interact face to face with teachers and ask questions, students need constant online tutor support. Special attention should be paid to the organisation of the tasks, and to the provision of clear guidelines regarding communicative goals and student's activity in order to achieve these goals. In these cases it is of special importance to incorporate teaching techniques which help students develop metacognitive strategies and become progressively autonomous in their learning process.

3 More information and details on the authoring tool and the course are provided in Gimeno (this volume).

4 The AWLA System is a web resource which allows teachers to create tasks where they propose a topic to write about, guide the learner throughout the writing process and correct and evaluate the product.

As a matter of fact, most online ESP courses seek (to a lesser or greater extent) to promote autonomous learning and help students become lifelong learners (e.g. Oakey, 1999; Cummins, 2002; Gimeno, 2002; Arnó et al., 2003; Devaux et al., 2006). That was the purpose of the *Airline Talk project* (Gimeno, 2002), a Leonardo da Vinci Project aimed at promoting continuing learning amongst airline staff in three target languages: English, German and Spanish. Similarly, the online EAP course *English for Academic Purposes: Learning English through the Web* (Arnó et al., 2003) was developed with two main aims: to help students improve their language and communication skills and to foster learner autonomy. Arnó et al. (2003) carried out a research to determine the profile of the students who used this course as autonomous learners and concluded that students are able to perform a number of self-directed learning actions and use metalanguage to reflect on their role as language learners. However, there are studies which suggest that this may not be true with students from all cultural backgrounds. Thang (2004) used Malasyan undergraduates of a public university as subjects for her study and found that they lack autonomy and awareness of language learning and language learning processes. Hence, the need to design online ESP/EAP programmes which offer students opportunities and tools to develop learning strategies and enhance autonomous learning.

As has already been pointed out, in order to develop autonomy in online environments, scaffolding and teacher support play an important role. This is a main concern in the computer programme developed by Cummins and Chascas (Cummins, 2002), *e-Lective Language Learning,* designed to promote students' academic language proficiency. The system enables learners to choose which texts to read and to self-regulate the type and degree of support they require while reading in the target language. Support takes different forms, e.g. students have one-click access to L1 and English dictionary support; the system provides individualized practice to students to help them learn the words they have clicked; students are provided with an environment where they can explore aspects of the meaning, form and use of different words they choose; there is also an environment to support students' writing in response to texts they have read. Devaux et al. (2006) also illustrate how they used several ICT tools to provide scaffolding and help their Asian students engaged in learning ESP to shift from a passive role to being active learners. In order to build the foundation for an effective scaffolding environment they resorted to the following tools: teacher's websites for information and community building; e-mail for communication, individualised mentoring and collaboration; bulletin boards and chat rooms for students to collaborate in primary research and carry out team writing; and, Web-based research to get access to reference material and explore new territory.

To round off this review of research on online ESP learning, it should be pointed out that although the number of ESP teachers engaged in online learning is on the rise, there is still a scarcity of research examining the effectiveness of online models of ESP teaching and learning. An example of such research is that carried out by Harker and Koutsantoni (2006), who analysed the effectiveness of a web-based learning programme of English for Academic Purposes (EAP) for British students from ethnic minority backgrounds. The purpose of the study was to compare distance and blended learning in terms of student retention, achievement levels and satisfaction with the programme. While distance and blended learning resulted in similar students' achievement levels and satisfaction, the blended learning mode was much more effective in students' retention. Chen et al. (2004) also carried research to determine the mode of interaction (i.e., negotiation of meaning in inter-personal versus intra-personal activities) which leads to more effective language acquisition in a Web-based listening environment.

Some studies have also examined ESP students' and teachers' attitudes towards online learning. Pathak and Hoon (2005), for example, investigate users' perceptions and their interaction patterns in the context of teamrooms (collaborative spaces where teams can communicate by posting messages). The results revealed that teamrooms are more suitable for exploratory tasks rather than structured tasks. Moloney and Gutierrez (2006) conducted series of interviews with several university lecturers in order to determine their knowledge, current use, interest, and experiences of working with Moodle. They found that although there was much interest in this CMS, very few lecturers knew how Moodle could help learners to learn online or how to incorporate it in the classroom. This research very clearly illustrates one of the main difficulties for the spread of online models of ESP teaching, the teachers' lack of familiarity with the technology, but also reveals teachers' high interest and willingness to explore how ICT can be used to optimise their students' learning experiences.

5. Conclusions

The rapid emergence of new technologies and their increasing prominence in workplace and education contexts have led many ESP teachers to integrate these new technologies into their classroom. Online learning has the potential to deliver great benefits in the ESP learning context by providing opportunities for flexible and collaborative learning, for more personalised instruction and for the development of learner autonomy, and by facilitating content management and delivery.

In this paper I have presented an overview of how online teaching and learning is being integrated into the ESP/EAP classroom, with a view to providing a general picture which can help ESP practitioners to become aware of the pedagogical requirements and the technological possibilities for developing effective online courses.

The different research discussed here shows that the implementation of innovative online environments for ESP learning is the result of the interrelation between sound pedagogical principles, students' learning needs and technological opportunities. In the current educational and workplace context, one of the fundamental needs of ESP students is to develop autonomy strategies, and to be able to learn on their own after the course has finished, in order to adapt to new communicative situations. Therefore, when designing online environments for ESP, it is of paramount importance to use technology to create a supportive environment for learner autonomy, i.e. an environment characterised by flexibility, adaptability to the varying needs of students and opportunities for reflection and shareability (Esch, 1996).

Most of the ESP teaching and learning experiences discussed here are concerned with blended learning, since, in an attempt to enhance the students opportunities for learning, most ESP teachers design online courses that do not replace face-to-face courses but which complement them. This way they can achieve a blend of independent learning, teacher-led activities and group collaboration. Although blended learning is an optimum way of learning that may contribute to solving some of the problems of the face-to-face ESP classroom, its design requires thoughtful reflection on how to combine online and classroom instruction, asynchronous and synchronous modes, to achieve the best environment for language teaching and learning. Being able to use technology for achieving this optimum environment is the main challenge of ESP teachers. In this sense, Warschauer (2002a, p. 472) points out, "the essential role of a body of teachers with the knowledge, skills, and attitude for innovatively designing, adapting, and applying technology in the classroom, appropriate to local context". And he adds that "at the professional level, that implies developing networks of innovators with expertise in technology-enhanced teaching, teacher development, and educational reform".

References

Arnó, E., Rueda, C., Soler, A., & Barahona, C. (2003). Developing Learner Autonomy through a Virtual EAP Course at University. *BELLS: Barcelona English language and literature studies*, 12/1, 100–114.

Baskerville, B., & Robb, T. (2005). Using MOODLE for Teaching Business English in a CALL Environment. *PacCALL Journal* 1/1, 138–151.

Bowdon, M. (2005). Virtual Networks: Mapping Community-Based Collaboration and Professional Writing. In K. St. Amant & P. Zemliansky (Eds.) *Internet-Based Workplace Communications: Industry and Academic Applications*. Hershey, PA: The Idea Group Publishers.

Canapero, M. (2004). Connecting, motivating and raising awareness via WELL: Developing e-learning environments for science students. *RECALL*, 16, 330–344.

Chapelle, C.A. (1998). Multimedia CALL: Lessons to be learned from research on instructed SLA. *Language Learning & Technology*, 2/1, 22–34. Retrieved June 8, 2007, from http://llt.msu.edu/ vol2num1/article1/.

Chen, J., Inoue, I., & Okamoto, T. (2001). The development of a hypermedia language learning environment on the Web for teaching academic English. In C.H. Lee, S. Lajoie, R. Mizoguchi, Y.D. Yoo & B. du Boulay (Eds.) *Proceedings of ICCE/SchoolNet 2001 Conference* (November 12–15). Seoul, Korea: Incheon National University of Education.

Chen, J., Belkada, S., & Okamoto, T. (2004). How a Web-based course facilitates acquisition of English for academic purposes. *Language Learning and Technology*, 8/2, 3–49. Retrieved June 6, 2007, from llt.msu.edu/vol8num2/pdf/chen.pdf.

Connaughton, S.L., & Ruben, B.D. (2005). Millennium Leadership Inc.: A Case Study of Computer and Internet-Based Communication in a Simulated Organization. In K. St. Amant & P. Zemliansky (Eds.) *Internet-Based Workplace Communication: Industry and Academic Applications*. Hershey, PA: The Idea Group Publishers.

Cummins, J. (2002). The Potential of ICT to Promote Academic Language Learning. In A. Dimitrakopoulou (Ed.) *Proceedings of the 3rd International Conference Information and Communication Technology in Education*. Rhodes: University of the Aegean, 55–64.

Curtis, S.A., Duchastel, J., & Radic, N. (1999). Proposal for an online language course. *ReCALL*, 11/2, 38–45.

Devaux, C., Otterbach, R., & Cheng, Y.Y. (2006). Technology for Trust, Collaboration, and Autonomy: Transitioning Asian Students from the 'Banking Method of Education' to Active Learning. In E. Arnó, A. Soler & C. Rueda (Eds.) *Information Technology in Languages for Specific Purposes: Issues and Prospects*. New York: Springer, 123–138.

Doughty, C., & Long, M. (2003). Optimal psycholinguistic environments for distance foreign language learning. *Language Learning and Technology* 7/3, 50–80. Retrieved June 26, 2007, from llt.msu.edu/vol7num3/doughty/default.html.

Egbert, J.L., & Jessup, L.M. (1996). Analytic and systemic analyses of computer-supported language learning environments. *TESL-EJ, 2*/2, 1–24.

Esch, E. (1996). Promoting learner autonomy: criteria for the selection of appropriate methods. In R. Pemberton, E. Li, W. Or & Pierson, H. (eds) *Taking Control: Autonomy in Language Learning* Hong Kong, Hong Kong University Press, 35–48.

Esnawy, S. (2004). Combining in-class and online in EAP writing. Teaching English with Technology. 4/3. Retrieved July 16, 2007, from http://www.iatefl.org.pl/call/j_article18.htm.

Felix, U. (2002). The Web as a Vehicle for Constructivist Approaches in Language Teaching. *ReCALL*, 13/1, 47–58.

Freiermuth, M. (2005). A Bridge to the Workplace: Using an Internet-Based Simulation in the Writing Classroom. In K. St. Amant & P. Zemliansky (Eds.) *Internet-Based Workplace Communication: Industry and Academic Applications*. Hershey, PA: The Idea Group Publishers.

Giles, T. D. (2005). Creating Community in the Technical Communication Classroom. In K. St. Amant & P. Zemliansky (Eds.) *Internet-Based Workplace Communication: Industry and Academic Applications*. Hershey, PA: The Idea Group Publishers.

Gimeno, A. (2002). E-language learning for the airline industry. *Recall*, 14/1, 47–57.

Gimeno (this volume). Online courseware design and delivery: the *Ingenio* authoring system.

Harker, M., & Koutsantoni, D. (2005). Can it be as Effective? Distance versus Blended Learning in a Web-based EAP programme. *ReCALL*, 17, 197–216.

Horst, M., Cobb, T., & Nicolae, I. (2005). Expanding academic vocabulary with an interactive on-line database. *Language Learning and Technology*, 9/2, 90–110.

Jarvis, H. 2001. Internet usage on English for Academic Purposes courses. *ReCALL*, 13/129–142.

Jonassen, D. H., Dyer, D., Peters, K., Robinson, T., Harvey, D., King, M., & Loughner, P. (1997). Cognitive flexibility hypertexts on the Web: Engaging learners in meaning making. In B. H. Khan (Ed.), *Web based instruction*. Englewood Cliffs, NJ: Educational Technology Publishing, 119–133.

Kasper, L. F. (2000). New technologies, new literacies: Focus discipline research and ESL learning communities. *Language Learning and Technology*, 4/2, 105–128.

Lamy, M. N., & Goodfellow, R. (1999). "Reflective conversation" in the virtual language classroom. *Language Learning & Technology*, 2/2, 43–61.

Leppänen, S., & Kalaja, P. (1995). Experimenting with computer conferencing in English for academic purposes. *ELT Journal, 49*, 26–36.

Levine, A., Ferenz, O., & Reves, T. (2000). EFL Academic Reading and Modern Technology: How Can We Turn Our Students into Independent Critical Readers? *TESL EJ*, 4/4, 1–9.

Little, D. (1996). Freedom to learn and compulsion to interact: promoting learner autonomy through the use of information systems and information technologies. In R. Pemberton, E. S. L. Li, W. Or & H. Pierson (Eds.), *Taking control: Autonomy in language learning*. Hong Kong: Hong Kong University Press, 203–218.

Luzón, M. J. (2002). Internet content-based activities for ESP. *English Teaching Forum*, 40/3, 20–25.

Luzón, M. J. (2006). Providing scaffolding and feedback in online learning environments. *Mélanges, CRAPEL. TIC et autonomie dans l'apprentissage des langues*. 28, 113–122.

McIntosh, S. (2005). Expanding the Classroom: Using Online Discussion Forums in College and Professional Development Courses. In K. St. Amant & P. Zemliansky (Eds.), *Internet-Based Workplace Communication: Industry and Academic Applications*. Hershey, PA: The Idea Group Publishers.

McLoughlin, C., & Marshall, L. (2000). Scaffolding: A model for learner support in an online teaching environment. In A. Herrman & M.M. Kulski (Eds.) *Flexible Futures in Tertiary Teaching. Proceedings of the 9th Annual Teaching and Learning Forum 2000*. Perth, Curtin University of Technology. Retrieved July 18, 2007, from http://lsn.curtin.edu.au/tlf/tlf2000/mcloughlin2.html.

McLoughlin, C., & Oliver, R. (1998). Maximising the language and learning link in computer learning environments. *British Journal and Educational Technology*, 29/2: 125–136.

Moloney, B., & Gutierrez, T. (2006). An Enquiry into Moodle Usage and Knowledge in a Japanese ESP program. *PacCALL Journal*, 2/1: 48–60.

Nesi, H. (1998). Using the Internet to teach English for academic purposes. *ReCALL*, 10/1: 109–118.

Oakey, D. (1999). An EAP module via the Merlin Internet Learning Environment. In B. Morrison, D. Cruikshank, D. Gardner, J. James & K. Keobke (Eds.) *Information Technology & Multimedia in English Language Teaching*. Hong Kong: English Language Centre, Hong Kong, 151–169.

Ortega, M. and Sánchez-Villalón, P.P. (2006). An integrated blended environment for language learning: AIOLE. In *Virtual Campus 2006 Post-proceedings. Selected and Extended Papers*, F.J. García et al. (Eds.) CEUR. Retrieved July 16, 2007, from http://ceur-ws.org/Vol-186.

Oxford, R.L., Rivera-Castillo, Y., Feyten, C., & Nutta, J. (1998). Computers and more: Creative uses of technology for learning a second or foreign language. Paper presented at the conference *Educational Technology in Language Learning, Theoretical Considerations and Practical Applications*, Lyon, France. Retrieved July 15, 2007, from http://www.insa-lyon.fr/Departements/CDRL/computers.html.

Pathak, A., & Hoon, L.H. (2006). Participation In Teamrooms: A Study In Online Academic Collaboration. *PacCall*, 2/1, 61–79.

Robbins-Spoonas, R., & Nolan, J. (2005). MOOs: Polysynchronous Collaborative Virtual Environments. In K. St. Amant & and P. Zemliansky (Eds.), *Internet-Based Workplace Communication: Industry and Academic Applications*. Hershey, PA: The Idea Group Publishers.

Rogerson-Revell, P. (2003). Developing a cultural syllabus for business language e-learning materials. *ReCALL*, 15/2, 155–168.

Seidlhofer, B. (2002). The shape of things to come? Some basic questions about English as a lingua franca. In K. Knapp & C. Meierkord (Eds.) *Lingua Franca Communication*. Frankfurt am Main: Peter Lang, 269–302.

Shetzer, H. and Warschauer, M. (2000). An electronic literacy approach to network-based language teaching. In M. Warschauer & R. Kern (Eds.) *Network-based Lan-*

guage Teaching: Concepts and Practice. New York: Cambridge University Press, 171–185.

Slaouti, D. (2002). The World Wide Web for Academic Purposes: Old Study Skills for New? *English for Specific Purposes*, 21/2, 105–124.

Strambi, A., & Bouvet, E. (2003). Flexibility and interaction at a distance: A mixed-mode environment for language learning. *Language Learning and Technology*, 7/3, 81–102.

Thang, S. M. (2004). Developing a self-directed online programme for an English for Academic Purposes course – exploring and accommodating learner characteristics. *Proceedings of the UNTELE conference*, Universite de Compiegne, France. 17–20 March.

Villanueva, M. L. (2006). ICT paradoxes from the point of view of autonomy training and plurilingualism. *Mélanges, CRAPEL. TIC et autonomie dans l'apprentissage des langues*. 28, 9–27.

Warschauer, M. (1996). Comparing face-to-face and electronic discussion in the second language classroom. CALICO Journal, 13(2), 7–26.

Warschauer, M. (1998). Interaction, negotiation, and computer-mediated learning. Paper presented at the *Educational Technology in Language Learning: Theoretical Considerations and Practical Applications*, Lyon, France.

Warschauer, M. (2002a). A developmental perspective on technology in language education. *TESOL Quarterly*, 36/3, 453–475.

Warschauer, M. (2002b). Networking into academic discourse. *Journal of English for Academic Purposes*, 1/1, 45–58.

Ruth Trinder

The Potential of Blended Learning Environments in Terms of Beneficial Language Learning Conditions

Introduction

Blended learning, understood in the context of this paper as the combination of face-to-face (f2f) and computer-assisted language learning (CALL), is at present being ardently embraced by universities. Reasons for introducing a CALL element range from pedagogical to pragmatic issues: whilst teachers are fascinated by the possibilities of technology to individualise learning, university administrations regard it as a way to gain a competitive edge. And especially now, at a time when the effects of the Bologna process spell reduced teaching hours for many language departments at European universities, the necessity to streamline programmes and to enhance the out-of-class part of learning lends crucial importance to the creation or adoption of suitable e-materials. Inevitably, such a redistribution of balance between teacher-led and self-access learning opportunities must involve a rethinking/redefinition of the roles of teacher, student, and the entire learning environment, placing as it does new demands on learners in terms of autonomy, learning strategies and self-organisation. However, little research has been done so far on how students deal with this remapping of the educational territory. Recent publications on blended learning (e.g. Dewar & Whittington, 2004; Neumeier, 2005; Stracke, 2007) have pointed out the curious fact that despite the quite respectable body of empirical studies focusing on learners' perceptions of the use of technology, only few researchers have broadened their perspective to include the 'traditional' f-2-f component and to gauge the effectiveness of an integrated BL environment. However, since the quality of the learning conditions characterising one mode is bound to impact on students' experience of the other, further research into BL as a whole is needed. The purpose of the present study is to provide information on how learners perceive the characteristics of each learning environment, and how they attempt to match those characteristics with their requirements in the process of developing their own individual 'blend' of learning opportunities.

Background

Ideally, blended learning programmes should not consist of a "traditional" face-to-face (f2f) syllabus on to which self-access CALL elements are added later; rather, the proper distribution of learning content and objectives to the two modes should be carefully considered and planned in advance (see Neumaier 2005). In practice, language departments often find themselves struggling with the brief to customise e-materials to supplement their courses as a way of coping with ever larger class sizes and/or reduced contact hours. This was also the case in the context this study reports on. The pedagogical, rather than the administrative, rationale behind the choice of course delivery was the desire to offer more individualised learning experiences than teacher-fronted large-scale lectures can offer; in other words, the wish to counteract the current 'massification' of university life.

Organisational and curricular context

The investigation was carried out at Vienna University of Economics and Business Administration. It deals with *Business English 1* (BE1), the first class in the Department's Business English program, to which it serves as an introduction. All students who take English as their compulsory foreign language have to register for this class and pass an examination if they want to continue with BE 2. With the introduction of a new program of studies and, concomitantly, the introduction of blended learning, class attendance was made voluntary. Students now have the option of regarding BE 1 as a distance learning course.

Given the fact the department's introductory classes are notoriously heterogeneous in terms of general English proficiency (as well as in terms of learning styles and preferences), it made sense to provide CALL self-study materials which learners could use at their own pace in order to counteract individual weaknesses. The importance of being able to exploit learning opportunities in accordance with individual needs is even heightened in the ESP-context reported on: the problem of heterogeneity is compounded by students' dissimilar backgrounds (i.e. work experience, commercial college vs. other types of school at secondary level), so that whilst some are experienced in business communication and familiar with the terminology, others are complete novices. On the downside, this approach has the disadvantage that no *lead mode* can be established. Neumaier (2005, p. 167) defines lead mode as the setting where learners are familiarised not only with the principles of BL, but also with the sequencing and organisation of content. The lead mode tends to be the setting where learners spend most time, and where there is consequently more opportunity for guidance.

There is yet another caveat. For such curricular parameters to work to best effect, students need to be aware of their own needs as language learners. They consequently have to be adept not only at organizing their learning, but also at self-evaluation. Furthermore, they need to be ready and willing to take on some responsibility for their own learning – without, however, having the freedom of choosing their own learning objectives. In the particular cultural setting reported on, the educational background of the majority of students will have done little to develop their autonomous learning skills. As it is a misconception that the mere provision of self-access learning modes will automatically lead to the development of such skills (see e.g. Little, 2001, 2007; Littlemore, 2001), there is always the danger that the demands placed on inexperienced students in terms of managing their own learning might be too great – or might simply come too early. This point will be taken up again under the heading of 'learner control' and in the discussion section.

CALL materials and distribution of learning content

The online materials *Online English Mentor (OEM)* were created by a team of teachers/material developers and multimedia designers specially recruited for this project. My responsibilities as the project leader, and the only permanent member of staff, included the initial conceptualization and the on-going evaluation of the materials. The pedagogical rationale behind the *OEM* is described in detail elsewhere (Trinder, 2003); suffice here to point out that the CALL materials mirror the linguistic and content focus of each of the ten class units, and offer a wealth of integrated and interactive reading, vocabulary and grammar exercises, as well as an extensive hyperlinked grammar reference section.

As mentioned above, due to this "parallel" distribution of learning content (see Neumaier 2005 on descriptors of BL), students can be given authority over the appropriate composition of the environment. In other words, they can decide if and when their time is best spent on attending f2f classes, working independently, or combining the two modes. How and why they blend the components as they do, will depend on a multitude of interlinking factors, ranging from cognitve and affective learner-internal variables such as learning style, motivation, and aptitude, to factors which are inherent characteristics of the learning environments. It is this latter category that is the focus of this investigation.

Research interest

Elsewhere, I have attempted to explore the intricate web of factors impacting on students' choices in a BL environment in all its complexity (Trinder, 2006). The present contribution has a narrower scope, concentrating on the field of environmental language learning conditions. If it is possible to identify a set of criteria that potentially promote language learning – and Egbert (1993) argues that it is –, students' opinions on how well such conditions can be replicated/fulfilled in either environment would bring us a step nearer to comprehending students' choices, and by extension to developing models of BL that cover as wide a range of students' needs as possible. The main research question framing the present investigation is formulated as follows:

- According to students' perceptions, how do the two learning environments compare in terms of beneficial language learning conditions?

Language learning conditions

Drawing on environment researchers such as Moos (1974) and Fraser (1986), Egbert (1993) posits that a "language learning environment" can be broken down into a number of conditions which, if fulfilled, foster learning. These conditions include the nature of language learning tasks, but also cover affective components like learner attitude towards self and others, atmosphere, and teacher behaviour and expectations. Egbert starts from the premise that the eight conditions she extracted from the SLA and learning theory literatures are the most widely researched and supported constructs and hence qualify as necessary constituents of an ideal learning environment. Rather than relying on one SLA theory to 'prescribe' principles that should inform practice, she formulates a set of guidelines based on a number of diverse theoretical accounts (Egbert, 1993; Egbert, Chao & Hanson-Smith, 1999). From there, she sets out to test to what extent technology-supported learning environments can replicate such conditions, comparing learners' perceptions of two different types of CALL environments ('cooperative' vs. 'traditional'). In the present study, this approach – as well as its survey instrument – has been adapted to fit a blended learning context.

1. Learners have opportunities to interact and negotiate meaning (interaction)
2. Learners interact in the target language with an authentic audience (audience)
3. Learners are involved in authentic tasks (task)
4. Learners are exposed to and encouraged to produce varied and creative language (sources)
5. Learners have enough time and feedback (feedback)
6. Learners are guided to attend mindfully to the learning process (cognition)
7. Learners work in an atmosphere with ideal stress / anxiety level (atmosphere)
8. Learner autonomy is supported (control)

Conditions for optimal language learning environment (Egbert & Jessup, 1996; Egbert, Chao & Hanson-Smith, 1999).

Empirical study: Beneficial learning conditions in classroom and CALL learning environments

The seven 'scales' of the questionnaires employed mirror Egbert's (1993) categorisations of environmental conditions (see above), though a number of questionnaire items had to be adapted to take account of the particularities of the setting. One of Egbert's eight original constructs, "authentic audience", was omitted altogether as it did not apply to the type of self-contained courseware we used.

Procedure

The survey used a non-experimental research design, placing reliance on a mix of quantitative and qualitative data. The questionnaires contained closed questions which required respondents to choose from a five-point Likert scale indicating varying degrees of agreement or disagreement (5 = maximum agreement, 1 = minimum). Numerical data were analysed first descriptively by calculating mean scores, standard deviations, and percentages. Analysis of variance (ANOVA) and *t*-tests were used to establish differences in means between groups (such as comparison of attitudes of more and less proficient learners). The *p*-value reported with *t*-tests represents the probability of error involved. Differences at a level of $p < 0.05$ are considered statistically significant, at $p < 0.005$ highly significant.

The respondents were first-year students studying for degrees in International Business Administration or Economics. The study employed two questionnaires, both of which were distributed during f2f sessions. The environmental factors or learning conditions outlined above were applied to classroom and computer-assisted learning respectively, whenever necessary with slight adaptations to the statements to accommodate the peculiarities of the CALL or the class environment. In order to avoid overloading students with questions, the surveys were conducted on two separate occasions; 90 students took part in the 'classroom-survey' and 60 in the 'CALL survey'. The difference in numbers is due to the fact that attendance rates tend to drop in the course of the semester; yet in order to allow students to become familiar with both environments, I decided to wait until the end of the semester to administer the questionnaires. Another weakness of the procedure is caused by the fact that the sample was self-selected insofar as it included only those students who *had chosen* to attend the 'traditional' classes.

Results

Scale 1: Interaction and Negotiation of Meaning

Originally, the term *interactional modifications* referred to any changes made during verbal interaction in response to signals of incomprehension – later also known as instances of "negotiation of meaning" (Long, 1983; Pica, 1994) – and was researched mainly with regard to learner-learner and learner-native speaker face-to-face conversations. Chapelle (2003) demonstrated how the concepts can be transferred not only to computer-mediated communication (CMC), but also to dedicated CALL materials: input can be made comprehensible through simplification, elaboration, paraphrasing, added redundancy, translations, etc., all of which can be programmed so as to be accessible for the learner at a mouse click.

As for f2f classes, communicative language teaching methods have devised plenty of techniques to promote interaction and negotiation of meaning. However, learner-learner or learner-teacher interaction is more difficult to achieve, and perhaps also considered less important, in large teacher-fronted classes whose main target is the transmission of content-based knowledge. In such settings, simply asking the teacher for clarifications may be a daunting experience for weaker, less confident students as it involves speaking up if front of the class; and such anxiety can easily extend to normally fairly confident learners if they fear they are admitting ignorance of concepts everybody else is familiar with.

Students' readiness to negotiate meaning and clarify linguistic gaps in either learning mode was measured by four items. Two of these as well as the overall scale mean yielded highly significant differences: participants were significantly more likely to use the opportunities provided by the CALL application to find out meanings of unknown linguistic items – by employing online tools such as the glossary for input modification (item I2), or by going over the reading/listening text again (item I4) – than by asking the teacher/fellow students for adjustments. This is an important point, since in the case of content-based teaching, the comprehension and acquisition of specific terminology and relevant phrases is critical to success. The results indicate furthermore that the CALL environment is considered more appropriate for detail-focused language work.

CLASS	mean	SD	OEM	mean	SD	p-value
I1. I use English with my classmates and the teacher during class	3.93	1.04	I feel I'm actively using my English when interacting with the OEM	3.72	0.93	
I2. If there is a word/expression I don't understand, I ask for clarification	2.95	0.99	If there is a word/expression I don't understand, I use the pop-up windows to get an explanation/definition	4.12	1	$p = 0.000$
I3. When my classmates and I do exercises together, we discuss why the answers are right or wrong	3.02	0.93	When I do exercises on the OEM, I try to find out actively why my answers are right or wrong	4.40	0.71	
I4. If somebody speaks in class and I don't understand what they are saying, I ask them to repeat it.	2.14	1.12	If I do listening tasks on the OEM and I don't understand what they are saying, I listen again or read the transcript	3.23	1.31	$p = 0.000$
Overall mean	*3.26*	*0.63*		*3.88*	*0.57*	$p = 0.000$

Scale 2: Tasks

This scale assesses the motivational potential of language learning tasks and activities, looking in particular at intrinsic interest and authenticity of class and CALL activities. 'Authentic', in Egbert's (1993) usage, means transferable to real-life situations, confidence-building, and of meaning to students outside the classroom. Healy (1999), too, stresses this individualistic, learner-centred aspect of authenticity. In a contribution on authentic tasks in CALL environments, she posits that any kind of language learning task, even drills, "are authentic tasks when learners find them useful and look for that kind of practice, as in learning vocabulary, improving pronunciation, or coming up with an irregular past form without having to think about it" (Healy, 1999, pp. 135–6).

As far as tasks are concerned, f2f classes were consistently rated as superior. The differences for items T2 and T4 as well as the overall mean are statistically significant. It is interesting to note how differently respondents assess the future relevance of the language presented in the *OEM*: only about half of them agreed or agreed very much that the English they learnt with the e-learning materials might be important for the future careers. By comparison, the 'classroom questionnaire' yielded only 20% of students who did not perceive the English they learnt in class as relevant.

This result suggests that oral and aural skills are considered of utmost importance – students appear to equate 'surviving' in real Business English situations mainly with being able to speak and listen. In view of the fact that the classes are far from communication or discussion-oriented, it is interesting that the 'nature' of the English acquired there is still viewed as inherently different; after all, also in the f2f setting much time is spent on detail-focused (pen-and-paper) exercises that attend to form as well as meaning. It seems as if the supplementary explanations and asides most teachers automatically tend to provide in the course of discussing, say, a simple type of matching-exercise, are considered more 'real-life' because they are spontaneous and spoken; and as if the limited opportunities students have for speaking or simply for reading aloud are still perceived to be more effective in helping them develop the target language.

CLASS	mean	SD	OEM	mean	SD	*p*-value
T1. The activities I do in class help me improve my English	4.27	0.95	The activities I do on the OEM help me improve my English	4.22	0.79	$p = 0.000$
T2. The English I learn in this class may be important for my future career	4.27	1.50	The English I learn with the OEM may be important for my future career	3.53	1.10	$p = 0.031$
T3. I find the activities we do are interesting	3.95	0.88	I find the activities on the OEM interesting	3.79	0.97	
T4. The activities we do in class make me more confident about using English in the real world	3.90	0.96	The activities I do on the OEM make me more confident about using English in the real world	3.56	0.96	
Overall mean	*4.10*	*0.68*		*3.78*	*0.69*	$p = 0.005$

Scale 3: Sources (input and output)

Teaching methods and theoretical accounts of SLA alike place a great deal of emphasis on the role of input, even if there is no agreement on the ideal level and form it should have to optimally foster language learning. There is common consent – amongst practitioners at least – that exposure to a wide variety of comprehensible and meaningful input is desirable; and it is the *variety* of input and output opportunities that is the focus of this scale.

Somewhat surprisingly, respondents found the mixture of language learning activities offered by the CALL environment more varied. Possibly this indicates that they put quite a narrow interpretation on the term "activity", comparing pen-and-paper exercises to the clearly more colourful *OEM* tasks and disregarding more informal activities such as classroom discussions as opportunities for learning.

CLASS	mean	SD	OEM	mean	SD	p-value
S1. In class I learn English from many different sources (different types of texts, videos, etc.)	3.65	1.01	With the OEM I learn English from many different sources (different types of texts, listening, etc.)	3.65	0.86	
S2. There is opportunity for different types of activities	3.74	0.86	There is opportunity for different types of activities	4.21	0.92	$p=0.012$
S3. During class we have opportunity to listen, speak, read, and write	4.05	0.98	With the OEM I have opportunity to listen, speak, read, and write	4.13	0.97	
Overall mean	*3.82*	*0.68*		*4.10*	*0.69*	

Scale 4: Learner choice and control

At present, dominant SLA paradigms emphasise the importance of learner autonomy that gives students control over the path to the goal. Learner autonomy has even been described as "the key concept in modern language learning and in all humanistically oriented pedagogy" (Wolff 1999, p. 128). Despite its current buzzword status particularly in the domain of technology-supported learning, the concept means different things to different people. Wolff (2007) points out that the term has been variously used to refer to a capacity, an educational objective, a methodological approach and a process which can be promoted by the teacher. Recently, the role of the new media in promoting learner independence has been vaunted somewhat overenthusiastically, prompting researchers such as Little (1991, 1997) to spell out the differences between *autonomous* and *self-organised* learning. Others take issue with the notion that autonomy is an inborn capacity. Esteve (2007) stresses the pre-eminence of 'nurture' over 'nature' by insisting that learners need to be guided towards autonomy. Beatty and Nunan (2003) similarly found that, at least at the beginning of the online learning experience, the majority of learners do not yet have the highly developed learning skills enabling them to deal with choice in an informed way. They come to the conclusion that such learners "need some form of scaffolding to provide a supportive framework for the learning process" (Beatty & Nunan, 2003, p. 180).

The main potential dangers that could prevent learners from taking control in a CALL environment are software-inherent features (opaque, unclear structure; insufficient signposting) and learner-inherent factors (e.g., students disliking ambiguity or with strong closure needs often feel uncomfortable in an open hypertextual environment that lacks clear directions). However, before grappling with the tricky question of how much control and how much choice is ideal for what type of learner, it is necessary to assess the level of control afforded by the two blended learning modes.

Comparing teacher-fronted classes with courseware, students can generally be expected to perceive the CALL environment as more suitable to the granting of choice as far as pace, timing and activity type are concerned. This was confirmed in this study; the issue of control was decided clearly in favour of technology, with respondents indicating that the CALL environment gave them more independence. However, it also became clear that at least in the f2f environment, the majority were content to hand the responsibility back to the teacher (Item C3/ class questionnaire).

CLASS	mean	SD	OEM	mean	SD	*p*-value
C1. My opinion has some effect on what happens in class	2.45	1.13	The OEM helps me take control of my learning	4.19	0.77	$p = 0.000$
C2. Within limits, I can help decide what to work on in class (activities, topics)	3.03	1.01	I can choose what to work on with the OEM (activities, topics)	4.73	0.54	$p = 0.000$
C3. I think the teacher alone should decide on which activities we do and how much time we spend on them	3.22	1.20	Although the OEM provides the structure, the topics and activities, there is enough room for me to choose	3.55	1.06	
Overall mean	*2.89*	*0.59*		*4.00*	*0.45*	$p = 0.000$

Scale 5: Atmosphere

The literature on anxiety suggests that language anxiety has a consistently negative effect on performance (see Dörnyei 2005 for a review); conversely, students who feel at ease in the learning situation are more likely to benefit from learning opportunities ('tasks' and 'sources') and to take control of the learning process. The construct 'atmosphere' gauges how comfortable and confident students feel in the CALL/class modes, and also inquires generally into students attitudes towards independent, technology-supported learning.

The data from the classroom questionnaire confirmed that publicly 'performing' or producing output in a foreign language is a major challenge: 20% admitted to experiencing speaking anxiety (disagreed/disagreed very much with item At1), and 12% were afraid of publicly making mistakes (item At3). Given the fact that the majority of students perceived the classroom atmosphere as friendly and relaxed, this is indeed food for thought, and highlights one of the core advantages of CALL: privacy for practising and making mistakes without fear of any kind of repercussions.

The results attested to a wide range of affective reactions to the use of CALL (see SD item At1/CALL questionnaire), with perhaps a surprisingly large percentage expressing a very positive attitude (40% agreed very much with the statement). Even higher mean values were achieved by item At 4: 77% agreed/agreed very much that they were comfortable when studying on their own. These findings, reflected also in the overall mean values, suggest strongly that the CALL mode is better able to provide an environment with ideal stress/anxiety levels.

CLASS	mean	SD	OEM	mean	SD	p-value
At1. I feel fine about answering questions or giving opinions in class	3.37	1.06	I feel fine about using a computer for language learning	3.75	1.36	
At2. I feel comfortable working with my class-mates and the teacher	4	0.90	I feel confident about finding my way round the OEM	4.02	0.88	
At3. I am not afraid to make mistakes in class	3.65	1.06	I am not afraid to make mistakes when using the OEM	4.52	0.76	$p = 0.000$
At4. The atmosphere is friendly and relaxed	4.22	0.89	I feel fine about working on my own	4.17	1.03	
Overall mean	*3.81*	*0.80*		*4.12*	*0.75*	$p = 0.043$

Scale 6: Feedback

In instructed learning contexts, the prevalent student opinion is that corrective feedback will foster learning; many learners are convinced that only if their mistakes are corrected, their command of the target language will improve. The explicitness of feedback provided will depend on the instructor's methodological affiliation, as well as on the task and on the learning goal; but irrespective of whether it leans towards 'scaffolding' or 'reinforcement', feedback is an expected and integral component of instructed language learning.

In the present study, feedback is understood to include (possibly rule-based) linguistic explanations (items F1 and F2) as well as more general progress assessment (F4). Clearly, the latter is much more encompassing and thus more difficult to achieve in either learning environment; in the f2f mode, class size of course influences how much individual attention can be allocated to the development of each student. Item F3 seeks to establish whether respondents apply context-appropriate strategies, managing to get the answers they need by exploiting the relevant tools in the CALL environment or turning to teachers/peers in class.

The high mean values indicate that the majority of respondents did not consider any environment lacking when it comes to offering feedback in the sense of corrections and explanations. Item F4, relating to 'general feedback' on how well the learner was doing in the course, was the notable exception. A comparison of the two environments showed highly significant differences in ratings even though F4 was also the weakest item in the OEM section. Students seemed to find it considerably easier to extract information concerning their general standing from the immediate and detailed OEM feedback than in class, where large student numbers made it nearly impossible for teachers to keep track of and respond to individual student needs.

CLASS	mean	SD	OEM	mean	SD	*p*-value
F1. In class I get the information I need to help help me speak and write English (e.g., information about pronunciation, spelling, grammar, informal and formal ways of expressing something...)	4.25	0.85	With the OEM I get the information I need to help me speak and write English (e.g., information about pronunciation, spelling, grammar, informal and formal ways of expressing something...)	4.16	0.66	
F2. I get sufficient explanations and feedback on why something is correct/incorrect	4.13	0.92	I get sufficient explanations and feedback on why something is correct/incorrect	4.32	0.67	
F3. I get help from the teacher or my classmates if there is something I don't understand	4.27	0.77	I get help from the OEM if there is something I don't understand	4.06	0.73	
F4. I get feedback on how well I'm doing	2.73	1.03	I get feedback on how well I'm doing	4.02	1.00	$p = 0.000$
Overall mean	*3.85*			*4.14*	*0.57*	

Scale 7: Cognition

Learners need adequate time to notice new linguistic items, to reflect on input and to formulate ideas. The scale intentional cognition is concerned with appropriate pacing on the part of the teacher and 'mindful engagement' (Salomon 1990) on the part of the learner. As far as pacing is concerned, CALL environments can be expected to fare better than classes – after all, the opportunity to spend as much or little time on tasks as individually required is one of the core advantages of self-access. On the downside, CALL applications have been accused of encouraging 'mindless' clicking rather than active engagement. Yet cognitive engagement, considered by many an essential requirement of learning, is not necessarily promoted in f2f environments, either: physical distance to the teacher, large numbers of fellow students, background noise, heat, etc., are all uncongenial conditions that can easily distract students. Thus it seems worthwhile to inquire into student views on the following aspects: which environment makes it easier for learners to concentrate on the task in hand, which allows adequate time on tasks, and which attempts to offer guidance concerning adequate learning strategies.

Interestingly, findings showed no statistically significant differences in students' ratings of the 'cognition' aspect. Mean values were generally high, with classes overall having a slight edge. This is surprising in the case of two items dealing with adequate timing (Co1 & Co2); as pacing is completely in the hands of the users, I am at a loss as to how to interpret this finding. Gratifying, on the other hand, are the results of item Co3, which indicate that both modes manage to generate high cognitive engagement.

This last item (Co4) achieved the lowest mean score. As for classes, teachers cannot realistically be expected to cover the topic of learning skills in any depth – the time simply is not there. The e-learning materials, on the other hand, do provide a section on learning and reading strategies – unfortunately, a feature which apparently went largely unnoticed by students.

CLASS	mean	SD	OEM	mean	SD	p-value
Co1. I have enough time to complete activities and to think about what I do	4.12	0.94	I have enough time to complete activities and to think about what I do	3.92	1.08	
Co2. I have enough time to notice new words and grammar patterns	4	0.83	I have enough time to notice new words and grammar patterns	3.95	0.82	
Co3. I pay attention in class	4.41	0.81	I pay attention when working with the OEM	4.21	0.88	
Co4. I get guidance/tips on how best to approach language learning	3.85	0.86	I get guidance/tips on how best to approach language learning	3.79	0.74	
Overall mean	*4.04*	*0.67*		*3.97*	*0.65*	

Summary of results

Combining the possibilities of CALL and traditional classes in a context where students have authority over the blending of the two major modes leads to a multiplication of learning opportunities that promises to accommodate a wide range of learner requirements. The purpose of this investigation was to find out how the subjects of the learning process experienced the potential of each setting to promote learning.

Both modes were generally well received. Students found they had better opportunities for negotiation of meaning (scale 1) in the CALL environment, but found the classroom setting superior when it came to authenticity and motivational potential of tasks (scale 2). The computer environment again got better ratings for variety of tasks and sources (scale 3). The biggest differences in mean values were manifested in scale 4 (control), where the computer environment far outperformed the f2f mode. Scale 5, atmosphere, assessed how much at ease students felt in either setting, including feeling free to make mistakes. Results were rather mixed, and it was only the latter item which achieved significantly better ratings in the CALL environment. Scale 6 (feedback and help) highlighted, amidst general satisfaction with linguistic feedback and explanations, one shortcoming of the traditional classes – due to class sizes, teacher were unable to provide general feedback on level and progress of individual students. And finally, as far as intentional cognition is concerned (scale 7), both environments encouraged students to mindfully attend to language learning, with classes achieving non-significantly higher mean scores.

Discussion and conclusion

This study was based on the premise that the quality of a blended learning environment can be broken down into a number of constructs generally believed to have a beneficial effect on language learning. These constructs, measured by individual scales, are by no means distinct, but influence each other. For instance, how comfortable and at ease learners feel in either environment (scale 5) obviously hinges on how well the learning tasks (scales 2&3) match their individual requirements.

At least in formal educational contexts, individual requirements, in turn, are partially subject to variation: in the course of a semester, students' main motivation might change from the desire to globally improve (business) communication skills ("real life English") to a concern with very detailed exam-preparation and feedback. The data has shown that students perceive the former need to be better served by classes (scale 2) and the latter by CALL (scales 1&6). Predominance of modes can be expected to shift accordingly.

Records of class attendance and tracking of CALL use confirm this anticipated fluidity: students numbers tend to drop continuously in f2f classes, use of e-materials increases sharply before exam time. The core question, however, is one that cannot be solved by statistics – is this trend due to a well-considered evaluation of strengths and weaknesses of either mode, or to panicky last minutes attempts to make up for earlier lack of dedication/self-discipline?

Common sense and experience suggest that more than likely both extremes will be represented, as well as a whole range of learning behaviours in between. Open questions in the survey aiming at exploring students' attitudes in a qualitative way largely confirmed this hunch. The pedagogical challenge is to shift the balance in the right direction. Obviously, the aim is to increase the percentage of students who deliberately, purposefully and successfully exploit the blended learning opportunities, and to decrease the number of those who fail to do so because they feel overwhelmed by the myriad of choices facing them.

I have mentioned before that our novice students are confronted not with one, but a number of new forms of teaching and learning in this particular BL environment, requiring them to deal maybe for the first time with CALL, content-based teaching, voluntary f2f attendance, shifting levels of responsibility, etc. Again, as pointed out before, it is highly unlikely that all learners are equipped with the necessary autonomous skills to survive in such an environment. A number of steps could be taken in order to decrease drop-out and failure rates. It is beyond the scope of this contribution and the focus of this investigation to discuss far-reaching interventions such as learner training; I will instead briefly address some weaknesses in the organisation of this blended learning setting, and suggest what could be changed in order to provide more active support for students.

The lack of an explicit *lead mode* is an obvious shortcoming. It seems essential to make at least one BL component compulsory so that there is a platform where teachers can be sure to reach all students, and where they have the opportunity to make explicit the demands and necessity of self-regulation, as well as to provide the necessary supportive scaffolding. This could also be the platform where strengths and limitations of the two modes of learning are discussed and made explicit. A follow-up study with students in the second semester, where f2f classes are mandatory, showed that the majority of students appreciated the increased sense of structure and opportunity for interaction established by the f2f lead mode.

Second, the data indicated that CALL is perceived to be more adequate for analysis and detail-focused language work, including acquisition of specialised ESP lexis. Designing a BL environment with clearly demarcated distribution of content and of skill-building tasks according to the strengths of each mode could vastly improve the transparency, and consequently the success, of the BL modes.

And finally, it is paramount to communicate to students what part of learning is best allocated to which environment. Both BL components facilitate cognitive and metacognitive learning strategies, but to different degrees. For instance, the data has shown that the feedback in f2f classes does not enable learners to gauge their general progress. Rather than trying to remedy this, we should invest effort in optimising and promoting the relevant CALL feedback features. If it is made clear that each mode has distinct roles and purposes, students can be expected to avail themselves of the learning opportunities in a more principled way.

References

Beatty, K., & Nunan, D. (2004). Computer-mediated collaborative learning. *System* 32 (2), 165–183.

Chapelle, C. (2003). *English Language Learning and Technology*. Amsterdam/Philadelphia: John Benjamins Publishing Company.

Dewar, T., & Whittington, D. (2004). Blended learning research report. *Calliope Learning*, 2 (1). http://www.calliopelearning.com./resources/index.html#Research_Reports. Retrieved February 2006.

Dörnyei, Z. (2005). *The Psychology of the Language Learner.* Mahwah, New Jersey: Lawrence Erlbaum Associates, Inc.

Egbert, J. (1993). *Learner perceptions of computer-supported learning environments: Analytic and systemic analyses*. Unpublished doctoral dissertation. Tucson: University of Arizona.

Egbert, J. (1999). Classroom Practice: Creating Interactive CALL Activities. In J. Egbert & E. Hanson-Smith (Eds.), *CALL environments: research, practice and critical issues*. Alexandria, VA: TESOL, 27–40.

Egbert, J., & Jessup, L. (1996). Analytic and Systemic Analyses of Computer-Supported Language Learning Environments. *TESL-EJ* 2 (2).

Egbert, J., Chao, C., & Hanson-Smith, E. (1999). Computer-enhanced language learning environments: An overview. In J. Egbert & E. Hanson-Smith (Eds.), *CALL environments: research, practice and critical issues.* Alexandria, VA: TESOL, 1–13.

Esteve, O. (2007). Interaktion und Lernerautonomie. Keynote address at the *Bremer Symposium: Autonomes Fremdsprachenlernen in Hochschule und Erwachsenenbilidung.*

Fraser, B. (1986). *Classroom environments.* London: Croom Helm.

Healy, D. (1999). Theory and research: Autonomy in language learning. In J. Egbert & E. Hanson-Smith (Eds.), *CALL environments: research, practice and critical issues.* Alexandria, VA: TESOL 391–402.

Little, D. (2001). Learner autonomy and the challenge of tandem language learning via the Internet. In A. Chambers & G. Davies (Eds.), *ICT and Language Learning: A European Perspective.* Lisse: Swets & Zeitlinger, 29–38.

Little, D. (2007). Language learner autonomy in practice: a challenge for university and adult education. Keynote address at the *Bremer Symposium: Autonomes Fremdsprachenlernen in Hochschule und Erwachsenenbilidung.*

Littlemore, J. (2001). Learner autonomy, self-instruction and new technology in language learning: Current theory and practice in higher education in Europe. In A. Chambers & G. Davies (Eds.), *ICT and Language Learning: A European Perspective.* Lisse: Swets & Zeitlinger, 39–52.

Long, M. (1983). Linguistic and conversational adjustments to non-native speakers. *Studies in Second Language Acquisition* 5, 177–193.

Moos, R. (1974). *Evaluating educational environments.* San Francisco: Jossey-Bass.

Neumeier, P. (2005). A closer look at blended learning. *ReCALL* 17 (2), 163–178.

Pica, T. (1994). Research on negotiation: What does it tell us about second-language learning conditions, processes, and outcomes?. *Language Learning* 44 (3), 493–527.

Salomon, G. (1990). Cognitive effects with and of technology. *Communications Research* 17(1), 26–44.

Stracke, E. (2007). A road to understanding: A qualitative study into why learners drop out of a blended learning class. *ReCALL* 19 (1), 57–78.

Trinder, R. (2003). Conceptualisation and development of multimedia courseware in a tertiary educational context: juxtaposing approach, content, and technology considerations. *ReCALL* 15 (1), 79–93.

Trinder, R. (2006). *Language Learning with Computers: The Students' Perspective. A Theoretical and Empirical Investigation.* Frankfurt am Main: Peter Lang.

Wolff, D. (1999). Review of Mike Levy: Computer-Assisted Language Learning. Context and Conceptualization. *System* 27 (1), 125–128.

Wolff, D. (2007). Selbstbestimmtes Lernen und Lernerautonomie: Einige Überlegungen zum lernpsychologischen Hintergrund. Plenary talk at the GAL Symposium 2007, Bremen, Germany: *Autonomes Fremdsprachenlernen in Hochschule und Erwachsenenbildung.*

Elisabet Arnó Macià, Carmen Rueda Ramos,
Antonia Soler Cervera

Designing a Virtual Learning Environment for EAP Students: *Quantum LEAP (Learning English for Academic Purposes)*

1. Introduction

In the last few years, as university lecturers in the field of LSP, we have been especially involved in the design and development of teaching materials based on the use of ICT tools for EAP students. We have been working on the creation of a web-based learning environment, *Quantum LEAP (Learning English for Academic Purposes)*, which seeks to help university students improve communication skills in English in an academic context[1]. As part of an inter-university team based at Universitat Politècnica de Catalunya and including lecturers from Universitat de Lleida and Universitat Rovira i Virgili (Tarragona), we have devised a tool for EAP teachers and students in Catalan universities. In this context, EAP students have a variety of proficiency levels, objectives, academic interests, and learning styles. In addition, the new university curriculum adapted to the guidelines of the European Higher Education Area (EHEA) requires students to display learning and communicative competences in different academic situations. It is therefore crucial for

1 *Quantum LEAP* is an ongoing project that has been funded by Generalitat de Catalunya (MQD-2003 and MQD-2005), Universitat Politècnica de Catalunya (UPC-2004, UPC-2006 and *Component específic de la planificació estratègica,* 2006), Universitat de Lleida (UdL-2004 and UdL-2005), and Universitat Rovira i Virgili at Tarragona (URV-2007).

students to develop EAP and learning skills in academic life, and at the same time it is also advantageous for lecturers to be able to collaborate and share materials and effort, which is possible thanks to ICT.

The aim of this project is to develop a flexible ICT tool that can be adapted to different learning modalities. *Quantum LEAP* is based on a hypermedia format, with an interactive online environment that can provide feedback and direct access to different resources. This interaction with the system can also support learner autonomy, which can be further promoted with tools especially designed for *Quantum LEAP*. Another issue considered in the project is the potential of a web-based environment to foster the development of learning and communication skills (Monereo, 2005; Arnó et al., 2006). Through specific tasks, *Quantum LEAP* makes the most of the Internet and the WWW to help learners develop strategies for information management, knowledge construction, communication and collaboration, since we believe that materials design and resource-based approaches are crucial for the development of learner training and autonomy (Benson, 2001; White, 2003). In *Quantum LEAP*, the Internet is also used for the selection of contents, with the WWW as a source of authentic materials in multimedia format. Both oral and written web-based materials have been selected, and specific, meaningful tasks have been designed to cater for different EAP needs and interests (Jordan, 1997). Altogether, *Quantum LEAP* is a flexible virtual learning environment to support distance and mixed-mode courses, as well as self-access learning.

The remainder of this chapter deals with the rationale behind the development of *Quantum LEAP* and addresses several issues regarding online materials for EAP students and the use of the Internet for online course design. The following sections deal with the criteria underlying the development of *Quantum LEAP*, focusing on the organization, the design of the environment, and the selection of contents. Then, a discussion follows about the integration of multiple competences, new literacies, language and study skills, and the promotion of learner autonomy for EAP students. Derived from our own experience in the creation of *Quantum LEAP*, some guidelines for online EAP materials development are suggested. Some final considerations on the innovation of our project and its future developments are also presented.

2. Framework for the creation of the learning environment *Quantum LEAP*

The project *Quantum LEAP* involves the design of an online learning environment which contains a set of materials and tools for the EAP student. Our main aim was to design a learning environment flexible enough to support face-to-face tuition and self-access learning. The need for a versatile tool meant considering how to organize and present the materials so that they could be adapted to different needs, learning styles and competence levels. Thus, the decision to structure the materials into different thematic modules allowed us to achieve not only variety but also the desired flexibility that could enable the design of different learning routes. Integrated in the virtual learning environment, the modules, together with a series of navigation tools and resources, should allow students to work on the materials and monitor their own learning. One of the main considerations in the design was to create a virtual learning environment open to any user who could register individually as a learner or collectively as a group or class. The idea of creating open access materials is in accordance with the current views on shared knowledge and public resources – along the lines of the open courseware movement (see e.g. White, 2003) – and also stems from the very nature of the developing team, composed of lecturers from different universities interested in creating and sharing resources for a variety of EAP students.

The context of the EHEA and the Common European Framework of Reference for Languages, or CEF (Council of Europe, 2001), have been taken into account in developing *Quantum LEAP*. We have adapted the descriptors in the CEF to an academic context, specifying the EAP competences that students need to master, in order to help students become aware of their own linguistic and communicative needs in EAP and, therefore, choose the most appropriate learning path. Another important consideration was to create an electronic portfolio of academic English, which allows students to keep a record of samples of their oral and written production and can demonstrate their communicative competence in EAP.

The point of departure for the creation of a web-based environment was to make a careful selection of topics of academic interest, which would later become the groundwork for the development of materials centered on the four skills. In order to design materials that could meet the needs of university students in general – rather than those of a particular discipline – we established a set of criteria that should help us decide on different topics of general academic interest (Soler et al., 2006):

- They should be addressed to a wide variety of university studies.
- They should be truly interesting for university students, but not closely related to any particular discipline.
- They should allow an interdisciplinary perspective.
- They should be motivating enough so as to promote interaction and thus enable students to make valuable contributions to the topic.

The resulting list of topics to develop fifteen thematic modules can be seen in Figure 1 below. This thematic framework allows us to contextualize the activities and to achieve greater coherence throughout *Quantum LEAP*. Each module is organized into different sections *(Preview, Reading, Writing, Listening, Speaking)* that contain the learning activities, tools to promote learning management *(Study Guide, Personal Log)* and to aid the student with the use of materials *(Glossary, Help)*, and tools for reference materials and language resources *(Online Resources, Tutorial of Pronunciation)*. All the sections and tools, together with the navigation bar that provides instant access to other modules, are always visible to the user, regardless of the module, section or activity the student is working on.

Fig. 1. Screenshot with a map of the modules.

3. Development of online materials in *Quantum LEAP*: Integrating skills and new literacies

When designing *Quantum LEAP*, we took into account the specific needs of our EAP students. Apart from the development of oral, writing and study skills (Jordan, 1997), university students need to acquire specific skills that allow them to carry out tasks in English related to their academic activities, like giving presentations in English or writing academic essays. In the design of EAP activities, attention was paid to students' familiarization with different genres, written and spoken, that are common in the academic world, so that they could recognize and produce effective samples of them. Such activities involved the development and use of appropriate study skills.

With regard to EAP students' needs, Flowerdew and Peacock (2001) relate the skills of EAP students to the development of learner autonomy. Also from a similar general perspective, Waters and Waters (2001, p. 378) identify EAP students' need to develop a general study competence, which refers to the "cognitive and affective capacity for study" involving "self-awareness, logical thinking, critical questioning, self-confidence or autonomy". In other words, students need to develop this general study competence together with the specific skills that are necessary for academic life. Within the same EAP context, Luzón and González (2006) identify the following criteria for web-based activities that can promote autonomy: (i) motivation, (ii) integration of web-based activities with other course activities, (iii) learner-centredness and scaffolding, and (iv) engagement in higher-level thinking and development of strategies. Besides, EAP students also need to develop skills related to new literacies, essential in the 21st century. The demands posed by the digital age call for the development of a wide range of "new multiliteracies" (Kern *et al.* 2004), which include electronic literacy, internet literacy, online literacy, multimedia literacy, information literacy or (inter)cultural literacy. All these terms go beyond the use of computers and new media and, at the same time, overlap with the general EAP skills mentioned above.

This view of the needs of EAP students guided us in the development of the modules that make up *Quantum LEAP* and led us to take a number of decisions in materials design. On the one hand, we aimed at integrating study and new literacy skills in the development of students' competence in reading, writing, listening, and speaking, combining content with language through meaningful tasks. On the other hand, we developed topic-based modules as the framework for such communicative activities, with topics related to university life, which could be approached from an interdisciplinary perspective. The choice of topics was made on the grounds that they could lead to discussion, critical thinking, and the exchange of ideas and opinions. At the same time, these topics were approached in such a way that they could lend themselves to reflection on societal, ethical, technological and cultural issues.

Some of the modules developed for *Quantum LEAP* clearly suggest a societal concern *(Women and Science, Environmentalism, Business and the Media, Emotional Intelligence at Work, Urban Planning)*, whereas others present a technological interest *(Computer Security, Humans and Machines)*, openly have an ethical component *(Medicine and Ethics)*, or distinctly deal with academic life today *(New Challenges at University: The Student of the 21st Century)*. Some of the modules even present a combination of issues, be it ethical and technological *(Internet Piracy, GMOs: Genetically-Modified Organisms)*, or societal and technological *(From Military Uses to Civilian Items, Science Fiction or the Limits of Science in Fiction, The Universe: the Last Frontier?)*. The module on *Globalization and the English-Speaking World* specifically addresses different representations of English-speaking cultures, attitudes towards language and the role of English as a global language.

Therefore, the cultural dimension of language learning, often neglected in the development of language teaching materials in general, has been taken into account in the design of the materials that constitute our online environment. The importance that authors like Kramsch (1993) place on the need to raise cultural awareness has made them regard it as the fifth skill; others like Pulverness (2003, p. 428) even consider it "not the fifth, but the first skill, informing every step of the language learning process". Despite the different attempts to encourage an integration of language and culture in the mid 1990s, this notion has not had the expected effect on materials developers. Pulverness (2003, p. 434) advocates for "the teaching of intercultural awareness in tandem with foreign language", claiming for the role of the teacher or materials designer "as an intercultural mediator". Recently, in online courses and materials, efforts are being made to incorporate intercultural competence (Holmberg et al., 2005).

3.1 Skills development through an online environment

The design of the learning activities in *Quantum LEAP* posed the challenge of integrating the wide range of EAP skills discussed above with the development of students' competence in the communication skills of reading, writing, listening, and speaking. Our aim was that students could communicate fluently and accurately, both in speech and writing. We tried to keep a balance between encouraging students' expression of ideas and paying attention to language forms at different levels (discourse, lexis, grammar, and phonology). These activities were implemented in the web-based learning environment specifically designed for this project, and we used the potential of hypermedia to enhance the development of such skills. Hypermedia refers to the combination of a hypertextual, i.e. non-linear, structure (like that of the Internet) with the use of multimedia, i.e. different sources of input such as texts, graphics, audio, and video. This hypertextual structure, together with the modularity of the system, facilitates the choice of learning routes, from a constructivist perspective, with students taking an active role in making decisions on the syllabus and expected learning outcomes (Felix, 2002). Having an online environment also facilitates the presentation of input in different modalities, combining text, graphics and video or audio files, for example.

In order to characterize this project, it is useful to consider the different types of electronic materials, which range from self-contained multimedia packages with predefined content to open-ended environments that do not provide contents, but facilitate participants' interaction and the construction of materials and tasks (Derewianka, 2003). This learning environment, *Quantum LEAP*, could be placed within this spectrum since it combines the presence of multimedia contents that can be built into the design of a course syllabus with elements of interaction with the system and with other users. Accordingly, in order to provide the essential elements of "learning materials, pathways for learning, and interpersonal communication" (Derewianka, 2003, p. 213–15), we have taken into account the following criteria that this author identifies: (i) flexible, expansible and editable materials, which allow different paths, (ii) guidance for learners and teachers, (iii) balance between macro- and micro-skills and reflection on one's learning, (iv) balance between offering authentic language use and providing scaffolds (v), maximising the use of multimedia and hypertextual features for effective learning, (vi) ease of navigation, fostering the review of contents and skills throughout the materials, (vii) facilities for interaction with the system (getting feedback and keeping track of one's progress) and with the teacher and other learners (exchanging materials and collaborating).

The learning materials in the modules that form *Quantum LEAP* are organized according to skills, with sections on reading, writing, listening, and speaking, together with a shorter preview section which provides an introduction to the module and aims to engage students and help them activate their previous knowledge of the topic. This division into skills, however, does not mean that they are dealt with in isolation, but presented in an integrated manner, as occurs in real life activities. It is in this context of communicative activities that attention is paid to language forms, exploiting the potential of ICT to promote reflection and language awareness (Palfreymann, 2007), following a focus on form approach, whereby attention to form is integrated in a broader communicative activity, which is primarily meaning-oriented (Doughty and Williams, 1998).

3.1.1 Reading

The development of reading skills has traditionally received a lot of attention in EAP. Students should be encouraged to cope with a wide range of texts and develop appropriate strategies to deal with them. The incorporation of ICT into language learning has enabled materials designers to exploit the potential of technology to enhance these skills. For example, emphasis has been placed on the need to help students activate their previous knowledge and use strategies related to predicting and guessing, and nowadays, with the use of multimedia, we can facilitate this through the combination of written texts with graphics and video. Online materials also allow users to focus on different sections of a text – in a non-linear way – to highlight different items, or to navigate through a text and its accompanying tasks and help material. The potential of hypermedia was taken into account in the design of learning activities in *Quantum LEAP*. The Internet was used not only as the medium through which we transmit content and engage in communication, but also as the source for selecting authentic texts for reading activities. The texts were chosen on the basis of their relevance to the topics in the module, so that the set of texts for each module made up a coherent unit. In spite of the university scope of the materials, the texts are not highly specialised, so that they can be approached from an interdisciplinary perspective. The texts selected should also be motivating for students so that they can engage in further activities involving critical thinking and creative language use. In our EAP context, it is also important to look at questions of genre, integrating the development of reading skills with the familiarization of students with different types of genres that they can encounter in university life.

The following example (see Fig. 2), taken from the module on *Computer Security* exemplifies, on the one hand, the use of hypermedia to enhance reading activities and, on the other, the approach to genre in an online learning environment.

As can be seen in the screenshot, first of all, the text is presented on the main screen and the reading activities are presented in independent and movable pop-up windows. This scheme is present in all modules and is intended to facilitate navigation through the texts and the activities, so that readers can focus on the relevant parts of the texts. This particular example illustrates how technology is used for the development of reading skills in combination with work on genres. In this activity, students are asked to contrast two reading texts in the module which exemplify different genres. The questions in the activity in the pop-up (and direct links to facilitate the navigation between the two texts) encourage students to analyse the texts and decide on their features. The hypertextual structure of the environment is used to present

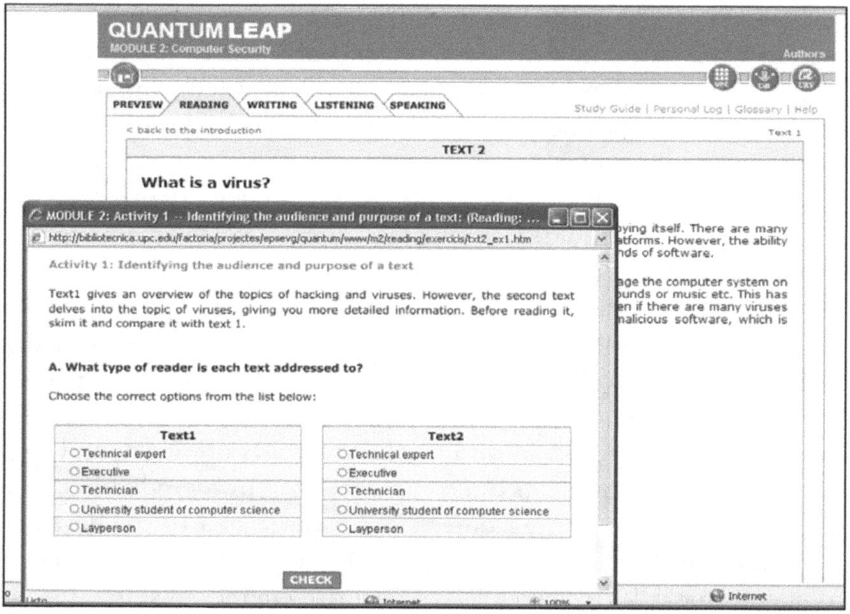

Fig. 2. Reading activity from *Computer Security.*

contents in different steps, through questions that engage students in exploration and analysis, in order to make the most of technology to promote higher-level thinking.

3.1.2 Writing

Our approach to writing for EAP is based on two key concepts, process and genre, which are integrated in the design of these online materials. Considering that this learning environment can be used as a self-access resource, it was particularly challenging to devise meaningful production tasks that provided enough guidance and feedback so that they could be used by students working alone. On the other hand, using hypermedia and computers allows a wide range of possibilities for enhancing writing skills (Hyland, 2003). Input from different sources, such as texts, video and audio materials, can create a meaningful context for a real-world task that requires students' written production.

The online environment also facilitates the development and demonstration of the writing process. Through specific tasks, students can engage in the different stages of the process, with prompting questions, models, and examples that guide them in the production of a text. For example, one of the guided writing tasks focuses on the planning and drafting stages of the process. As students move through different screens, they are asked to gather and select information on a given topic, choose an appropriate organizational pattern, and develop an outline and a draft. In that particular task, whose aim is to familiarise students with the writing process, guidance is provided while students do the task, together with *a posteriori* feedback, which consists of models and suggested answers that students can compare to their own production. The development of the writing process is closely related to the development of language and new literacy skills. Since this is a web-based environment, students are encouraged to use the Internet to search for information or visit language resources, for example. The Internet also plays a key role in such tasks as producing online genres, like e-mail writing, or engaging in collaborative writing that combines online and offline work, such as in a Webquest.

With regard to genre, *Quantum LEAP* provides practice and models of a wide range of relevant genres for EAP students, together with tools for text organization and language development. As with the speaking section of the modules, the aim of the writing section is to encourage production. An advantage that an online environment offers is that it allows us to easily record, store and share not only the final product but also the different stages of the process. One of the tools that have been created within *Quantum LEAP* is an electronic portfolio in which students can store and organize samples of their written and spoken production. Another feature of online writing, as opposed to print materials, is that the Internet offers students the opportunity to publish their own texts and share them with other users. In this sense, students are "[empowered] to develop new ways to find and express a personal voice" (Warschauer et al. 2000, p. 131). In *Quantum LEAP*, this sense of authorship is fostered through tasks that encourage students to contribute their production to Internet sites and forums. Both the portfolio and the guidance for Internet publishing make students' production purposeful, give them a sense of achievement, and spur them to engage in revising and editing, because their production is either displayed to demonstrate their competence (as in the portfolio) or read by real Internet users (as in online publishing).

3.1.3 Listening

In *Quantum LEAP*, the skills of listening and speaking are dealt with in a closely integrated manner, trying to replicate real-world situations in which speakers listen for a purpose and interact with other participants. Whereas the kind of listening activities in most textbooks are based on scripted material, which often do not reflect a real academic context, most of the listening tasks created for *Quantum LEAP* correspond to authentic situations in academic life. Through the listening activities in our online environment, students are exposed to authentic input, for example, lectures, documentaries of academic interest, interviews, and films, meant to be listened to for a real purpose. The listening section of the module on *Internet Piracy* is an example of how skills are integrated and how students approach listening activities for a real purpose related to academic life. In this module, students have to watch a video about the relationship between piracy and plagiarism and do a set of listening comprehension exercises which, in turn, provide them with input for a speaking activity on academic plagiarism.

The use of authentic audio and video materials allows students to listen to different English dialects as well as to non-native varieties of English – that is, global English in use around the world, which in fact constitutes the largest English-speaking community. This aspect is particularly important in the context of EHEA, as European mobility programs strongly encourage university students to participate in academic life using global English. In fact, the module on *Globalization and the*

English-Speaking World deals entirely with these issues. The listening activities include audio and video materials that reflect the importance of global English in university life and they also provide students with a variety of socio-cultural issues, encourage them to develop and enhance (inter)cultural awareness, and allow them to explore attitudes towards language in general.

In *Quantum LEAP*, authentic audio and video materials are used as input in listening tasks to encourage students' involvement in different communicative situations. Thus, listening tasks are designed to be purposeful and meaningful for students, aiming at meeting their interests and encouraging them to make the most of the listening practice. In this sense, the input received in the listening task may be designed to encourage some oral response, thus integrating listening and speaking skills. The integration of skills is enhanced by the potential of a web-based environment where interactive and multimedia teaching materials can be exploited to respond to authentic communicative needs. Listening tasks in *Quantum LEAP* enable students to move through the different kinds of materials and tools easily and readily. For example, they may access the audio and video input and then use a recording tool to save an oral contribution that can be used for different communicative purposes.

As for the types of activities, an online environment offers more possibilities than audio-based listening activities in a coursebook, because of the potential of computers and online environments. The listening tasks in *Quantum LEAP* have audio and video material together with a variety of hypertextual tools, such as text support (transcripts or extra information that can appear as a pop-up window), or glossaries, which the student can have access to any time simply by clicking on an icon. An example of that can be seen in the screenshot below (see Fig. 3), which shows a listening activity in the module on *Science Fiction or the Limits of Science in Fiction* and contains different pop-up windows that provide the student with background information on the classic science-fiction movie *Blade Runner* (with a transcript of each video excerpt in the activity). In this sense, the use of technology greatly enriches listening activities and, undoubtedly, constitutes a major difference with the use of tapes in traditional face-to-face tuition. Another significant difference is the fact that the teacher relinquishes control over the listening activity in favour of a more active role on the part of the student.

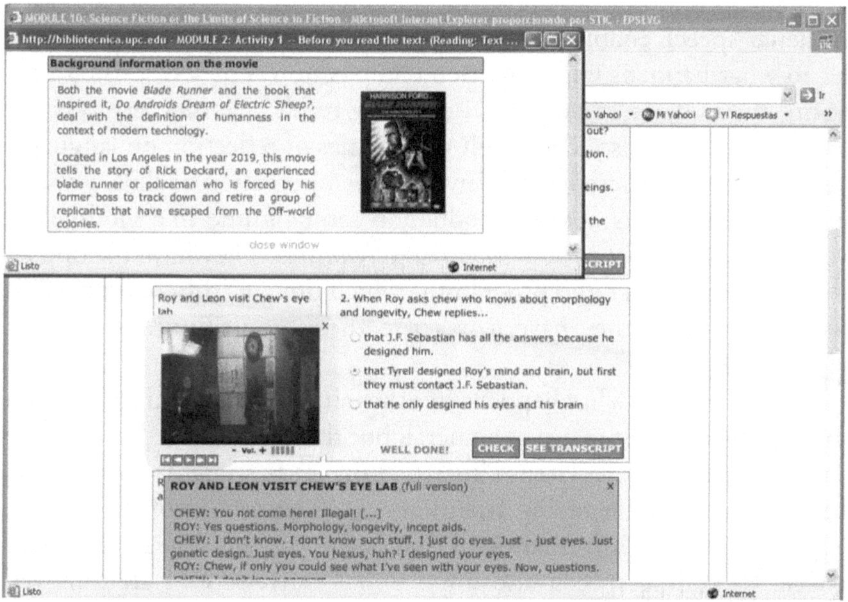

Fig. 3. Listening activity from *Science Fiction or the Limits of Science in Fiction.*

3.1.4 Speaking

Both the writing and speaking sections of *Quantum LEAP* require students' production, focusing on the process and the product, which can be stored and displayed through the electronic portfolio. The notion of process is central to our approach to both skills, which means that attention is paid to all the stages of the process, which was taken into account in the development of the virtual learning environment. In this sense, students are presented with authentic situations that require their contribution. Through hypermedia, input from different sources is combined so as to engage students with real content, including both written and spoken sources, to create the context for a meaningful activity that calls for students' spoken production, either individually or interacting with other students.

The application developed in *Quantum LEAP* to record and save students' speech enables them to pay attention to the process as – similar to what happens with a written composition – they can listen to it again, revise it, or re-record it until they reach a satisfactory version. Such production also lends itself to activities of reflection on language. An example of an activity that involves the integration of skills towards promoting students' spoken production can be found in a module devoted to *GMOs: Genetically-Modified Organisms*. They have the opportunity to listen to a radio programme which presents different opinions on the topic and they have to react to them, contributing their own views.

As opposed to what happens in other situations, speaking activities in *Quantum LEAP* are not ephemeral, but they are recorded and can be shared or accessed to later. This situation leads students to aim at a better product while paying attention to different stages of the process, such as organizing information or finding appropriate and accurate language. Recording speech also implies that conversations are removed from their immediate context (vs. face-to-face interaction). The fact that teachers or other learners can have access to the recorded speech implies that students need to take special care to make it intelligible, since listeners cannot interact with the speaker nor can they use context or gestual clues to derive meaning. On the other hand, the student who produces a spoken contribution is faced with the challenge of preparing an oral text that goes beyond the most immediate context and can be used by other students, for example to engage in real listening activities based on students' production.

Both the listening and speaking sections include integrated listening and speaking activities, although the difference is found in the objectives for each section, which are to promote listening or speaking skills, respectively. In particular, within speaking skills, emphasis is placed on questions of genre, taking into account the profile of EAP students. Therefore, in some of the activities, students are guided in preparing an oral presentation, giving arguments orally, or reporting what others have said, for example. Related to these objectives, speaking activities aim at a balance between fluency and accuracy. On the one hand, the activities try to encourage students to communicate meaning while, on the other, they provide guidance on how to prepare oral texts in EAP, encourage attention to form, and promote reflection on students' performance. In particular, with regard to the relationship between attention to language form and the development of speaking skills, this project includes a tutorial focusing on pronunciation, which is particularly aimed at the needs of our students, native speakers of Catalan and Spanish. This interactive multimedia tutorial, which is included as a self-contained complementary resource, is linked to the pronunciation activities in the modules of *Quantum LEAP*, so that students can decide to work systematically on certain aspects of pronunciation in English both at the segmental and suprasegmental levels. It is one of the distinctive feature of this project, as opposed to other online learning environments and multimedia packages which include resources dealing with grammar and vocabulary and neglect a systematic approach to spoken English.

Students' spoken production can be recorded, stored and transmitted to others. This potential of ICT opens up endless possibilities not only for subsequent reflection on students' oral production, as mentioned before, but more important, for instilling in them a sense of authorship, since they can become authors of valuable contributions that can be used by others. To encourage this attitude, when selecting the speaking models presented in *Quantum LEAP*, we ensured that different accents and varieties of English were included, and given the spread of English as an international language, that both native and non-native varieties were taken into account and considered as valuable models. This approach is particularly relevant to our students, since they should aim at proficient non-native models, to develop the skills to communicate orally in an effective manner.

3.2 Tools for promoting autonomy

As mentioned above, this learning environment has been designed to support language courses – both classroom-based and in distance mode – and to be used by students in a self-access situation. This premise has guided the use of technology in materials development, as we were faced with the challenge of creating highly motivating tools for students to work independently, if so they wish, to communicate written and spoken messages in a meaningful context, and to evaluate their own production and progress. In this context, we viewed the incorporation of ICT as a resource to promote learner autonomy – not, of course, considering autonomy as students working alone with the computer, but as a set of skills and attitudes required to become more effective learners.

Therefore, one of the key notions in our project is that of learner autonomy, and especially its relationship with ICT. Such a relationship is not new and, throughout the history of CALL, we have witnessed a move from the students' use of highly-controlled materials under the guidance of the computer towards promoting a greater degree of learner control over learning processes through the choice of materials and different learning routes (Warschauer and Healey, 1998; Kern and Warschauer, 2000). The evolution of the application of ICT in language learning has gone hand in hand with that of learning paradigms, with the notion of autonomy occupying a prominent position (Kenning, 1996; Shetzer and Warschauer, 2000; Benson, 2001; White, 2003). This relationship to autonomy has become more apparent with the growing potential of the Internet, which opens up new possibilities for interaction, both with authentic materials and resources such as a "virtual self-access centre" (Little, 1997) and with fellow learners, teachers, and other internet users.

This broad view of the potential of ICT in language learning, especially multimedia and web-based resources, has been taken into account in the development of *Quantum LEAP*. At this point, and before moving on to the specific uses of technology to promote autonomy, we should outline our notion of learner autonomy. It is based on key concepts such as responsibility, control, learner training, collaboration and critical reflection, which are recurrent in works on autonomy, whether associated with classroom-based environments or distance education (Holec, 1981; Dickinson, 1987; Little, 1991; Benson, 2001; White, 2003). Learner autonomy is considered as a skill, defined by Holec (1981, p. 3) as "the ability to take charge of one's own learning". Little (1991, p. 4) also provides a similar definition, considering autonomy as "a capacity – for detachment, critical reflection, decision-making, and independent action", and he adds a psychological dimension to the concept of autonomy, which entails that "the learner will develop a particular kind of psychological relation to the process and content of his learning". A further notion in our view of autonomy is that of "collaborative autonomy" in an online environment, which refers to encouraging students to work together in a virtual self-access centre (Ding, 2005).

The notion of autonomy as both a skill and an attitude is important in this project and has therefore been taken into account in the development of the learning environment. Based on the broad notions of "choice" and "responsibility", which underlie autonomy (van Lier, 1996), *Quantum LEAP* was designed to enable learners to make informed decisions on the areas and activities that they wish to focus on, according to their level, needs and interests. A series of tools are also included to help students manage the process, so that they can take actions such as setting learning objectives, evaluating their progress, or finding information about language, for example. Each of the modules contains a "study guide", with information on the objectives, contents, and structure of the module, for students to choose the activities that they want to focus on. Students also have access to a "personal log", a space where they can keep track of their progress, and an electronic portfolio, where they can store their written and oral production. As complementary tools, students also have access to language resources online, such as grammars and dictionaries ("online resources"), and a pronunciation tutorial especially designed for *Quantum LEAP*. The hypertextual structure of the interface has also been designed to facilitate navigation between the different sections and activities of the modules as well as between modules, with cross-referenced activities across modules. The screenshot below (see Fig. 4) shows the different sections and tools of the interface.

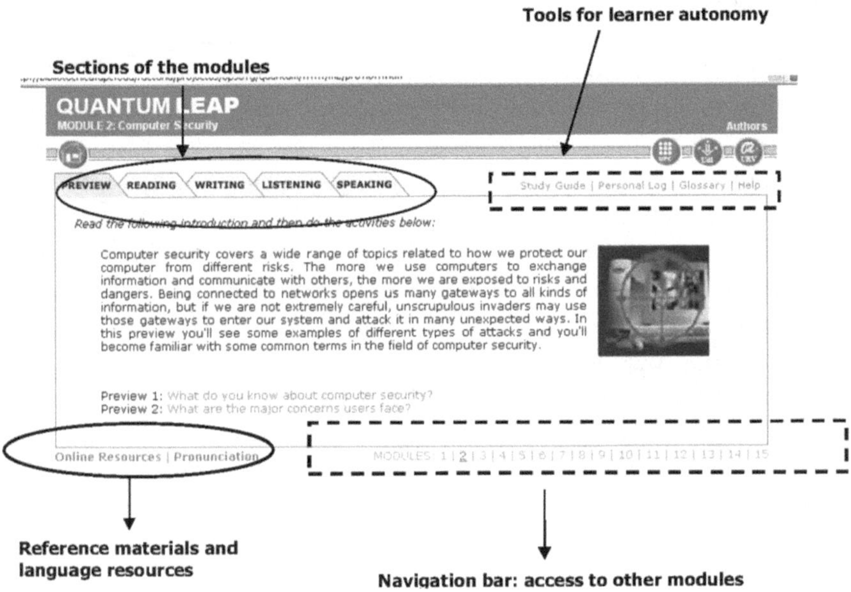

Fig. 4. Structure and organization of the interface of *Quantum LEAP*.

According to the concept of autonomy defined in this section, *Quantum LEAP* tries to help students develop and display autonomous behaviour, with a series of tools that not only enable them to make decisions and keep track of their progress, but also provide them with a record of the activities that they have done and the skills they are developing. In this sense, the tools described above, such as the "study guide", "personal log", and electronic portfolio are adapted to the levels and descriptors of the CEF. The aim is to make students' outcomes transparent to other institutions or authorities at national and international levels, especially considering the prominence of mobility programs and their relevance to university students in the new framework of the EHEA.

In this section, we have dealt with the notion of autonomy that lies at the core of the development of this project. However, as mentioned above, autonomy does not mean working on self-access resources, but it refers to skills and attitudes for students to develop whether they work on *Quantum LEAP* as part of a course or independently. In the development of the learning environment we have taken into account its twofold purpose and thus versatility was one of our main guiding principles, envisaging certain roles for teachers and students. The modules can be used as course materials and serve as a springboard for class activities, whether in online or classroom-based courses. Using an online environment such as *Quantum LEAP* implies a shift in teacher and learner roles. On the one hand, learners have a greater degree of control over the material as they can choose their learning path, control equipment (e.g. listening) or work at their own pace. They also have access to the materials (with self-correction if they are closed) and to information (for example, guidelines for writing an essay or giving an oral presentation). This implementation means that the teacher is no longer the sole provider of information, but rather acts as a guide and mentor, and that class sessions can be devoted to open-ended activities and discussion on students' production.

4. Guidelines for developing online materials and courses for EAP

From our experience on the development of the project *Quantum LEAP*, whose rationale has been presented in this article, we can derive some guidelines to be considered by the developers of online materials and courses for EAP students. In this context, the following criteria can contribute to creating motivating online materials:

- *Meaningful tasks.* Students should be encouraged to perform a meaningful and purposeful task related to their academic needs (like reading a report, taking notes or participating in a debate).
- *Academic orientation.* The thematic contents of the materials should arouse in students a genuine academic interest and should be based on authentic and varied input from different sources, by combining different media.
- *Engagement with topics and tasks.* The topics used in the materials and tasks should lend themselves to engagement in critical thinking, discussion, and the exchange of ideas and opinions.
- *Multi-faceted role of the Internet.* The Internet is central in this type of project, as it becomes not only the medium for the presentation of materials and communication among users, but it is also a source of input and a learning objective in itself. The Internet provides authentic multimedia materials and resources for learning and, at the same time, it becomes a learning objective in itself. Students are encouraged to develop the internet skills that are part of new literacies, which are closely related to English language teaching and are integrated with language and communication skills (Shetzer and Warschauer, 2000).
- *Genres.* The notion of genre is key to EAP students. The materials deal with genres relevant to university students and include activities focusing on the distinctive characteristics of each (different types of articles, lectures, academic essays, etc.).
- *Exploiting technological resources to promote oral and written production.* Related to the question of genres, one of the priorities in this project has been to provide students with guidance to enable them to produce genres, both oral and written, that are relevant to their needs. Technology can be used to help students produce texts, not only written, but also oral and "cybergenres" (Shepherd and Watters, 1998), which are then recorded and can be shared and used for reflection. A variety of genres are explored such as oral presentations, seminar discussions, electronic and paper correspondence, reports, or academic essays.

- *Process-product.* The materials and tasks do not only focus on the resulting product but pay special attention to the process, with emphasis on the different stages and sub-processes involved in it. A related notion is that of collaborative work.
- *Hypertextual structure for different learning routes.* Proposing varied and flexible activities and making use of the hypertextual structure of the Web allow different learning routes for students through the materials and within individual activities, which they can adapt to their own needs and levels of proficiency, in keeping with the principles of a constructivist view of learning.
- *Focus on form.* In the context of activities oriented towards communication, attention is paid to questions of form and genre that are relevant to EAP. Focus on form is carried out in a contextualised manner to aid in the comprehension or production of messages.

5. Project innovation and future developments

Quantum LEAP is the result of an inter-university project whose main distinguishing feature is that it offers an open learning environment which can be accessed either by students working independently or by groups of users (e.g. a class) who wish to use it as part of a course. Earlier in this chapter, it was mentioned that this project can be situated halfway between closed multimedia materials and open-ended virtual environments, in which participants can communicate and exchange contents. It is an ambitious project that contains multiple resources, emphasizes written and spoken production, and offers a systematic approach to pronunciation.

The project is currently under technical development. At this stage, after designing the virtual environment as well as the materials and tasks, we are working on the integration of the multimedia materials into the system. As the online environment develops, we are piloting the materials with students, both in classroom-based sessions and as self-access situations. Our future work will be based on students' reactions, focusing specifically on the results of *Quantum LEAP* as a learning tool. On the technical side, we are also evaluating the design of the interface, paying attention to aspects of ergonomy and usability.

References

Arnó, E., Soler, A., & Rueda, C. (2006). Information technology in languages for specific purposes: prospects on a brave new world. In E. Arnó, A. Soler & C. Rueda (Eds.), *Information technology in languages for specific purposes. Issues and prospects.* New York: Springer, 247–261.

Benson, P. (2001). *Teaching and researching autonomy in language learning.* Harlow, Essex: Longman.

Council of Europe. (2001). *Common European framework of reference for languages.* Cambridge: Cambridge University Press. Retrieved May 5, 2007, from http://www.coe.int/t/dg4/linguistic/CADRE_EN.asp.

Derewianka, B. (2003). Developing electronic materials for language teaching. In B. Tomlinson (Ed.), *Developing materials for language teaching.* London: Continuum, 199–220.

Dickinson, L. (1987). *Self-instruction in language learning.* Cambridge: Cambridge University Press.

Ding, A. (2005). Theoretical and practical issues in the collaborative learner autonomy in a virtual self-access centre. In B. Holmberg, M. Shelley & C. White (Eds.), *Distance education and languages.* Clevedon, UK: Multilingual Matters, 40–54.

Doughty, C., & Williams, J. (1998). *Focus on form in classroom second language acquisition.* Cambridge: Cambridge University Press.

Felix, U. (2002). The Web as a vehicle for constructivist approaches in language teaching. *ReCALL, 14* (1), 2–15.

Flowerdew, J., & Peacock, M. (Eds.). (2001). *Research perspectives on English for academic purposes.* Cambridge: Cambridge University Press.

Hyland, K. (2003). *Second language writing.* New York: Cambridge University Press.

Holec, H. (1981). *Autonomy in foreign language learning.* Oxford: Pergamon.

Holmberg, B., Shelley, M., & White, C. (Eds.). (2005). *Distance education and languages.* Clevedon, UK: Multilingual Matters.

Jordan, R.R. (1997). *English for academic purposes*. Cambridge: Cambridge University Press.

Kenning, M.M. (1996). IT and autonomy. In E. Broady & M.M. Kenning (Eds.), *Promoting learner autonomy in university language teaching*. London: Association for French Language Studies/CILT, 121–38.

Kern, R., & Warschauer, M. (2000). Theory and practice of network-based language teaching. In M. Warschauer & R. Kern (Eds.), *Network-based language teaching: concepts and practice*. Cambridge: Cambridge University Press, 1–19.

Kern, R., Ware, P., & Warschauer, M. (2004). Crossing frontiers: New directions in online pedagogy and research. *Annual Review of Applied Linguistics, 24*, 243–260.

Kramsch, C. (1993). *Context and culture in language teaching*. Oxford: Oxford University Press.

Little, D. (1991). *Learner autonomy. 1: Definitions, issues and problems*. Dublin: Authentik.

Little, D. (1997). Responding authentically to authentic texts: A problem for self-access language learning? In P. Benson & P. Voller (Eds.), *Autonomy and independence in language learning*. London: Longman, 225–236.

Luzón, M. J., & González, M.I. (2006). Using the Internet to promote autonomous learning in ESP. In E. Arnó, A. Soler & C. Rueda (Eds.), *Information technology in languages for specific purposes. Issues and prospects*. New York: Springer, 177–190.

Monereo, C. (Ed.). (2005). *Internet y competencias básicas*. Barcelona: Graó.

Palfreymann, D. (2007). Online media: New dimensions for language awareness. *Language Awareness, 16* (1), 1–6.

Pulverness, A. (2003). Materials for cultural awareness. In B. Tomlinson (Ed.), *Developing materials for language teaching*. London: Continuum, 426–438.

Shepherd, M., & Watters, C.R. (1998). The evolution of cybergenres. *Proceedings of the thirty-first annual Hawaii international conference on system sciences (HICSS' 98)* (Vol. II, pp. 97–109). Hawaii.

Shetzer, H., & Warschauer, M. (2000). An electronic literacy approach to network-based language teaching. In M. Warschauer & R. Kern (Eds.), *Network-based language teaching: concepts and practice*. Cambridge: Cambridge University Press, 171–185.

Soler, A., Rueda, C., & Arnó, E. (2006). A hypermedia project for EAP students: interactive materials in a virtual learning environment. *Proceedings of the 5th international AELFE conference*. Zaragoza, 572–581.

van Lier, L. (1996). *Interaction in the language curriculum: Awareness, autonomy, and authenticity*. London: Longman.

Warschauer, M., & Healey, D. (1998). Computers and language learning: An overview. *Language Teaching, 31*, 57–71.

Warschauer, M., Shetzer, H., & Meloni, C. (2000). *Internet for English teaching*. Alexandria, VA: TESOL Inc.

Waters, A., & Waters, M. (2001). Designing tasks for developing study competence and study skills in English. In J. Flowerdew & M. Peacock (Eds.), *Research perspectives on English for academic purposes.* Cambridge: Cambridge University Press, 375–389.

White, C. (2003). *Language learning in distance education.* Cambridge: Cambridge University Press.

ANA GIMENO SANZ

Online Courseware Design and Delivery: The *Ingenio* Authoring System

1. Introduction

Teaching on-line is a rapidly expanding 21st century phenomenon in language teaching, and more so as far as teaching English is concerned. Just as an example, when the exact string "teaching English online" is typed in the *Google* search engine a total of 25400 occurrences are called up, whereas all other major European languages call up only a few screens of results. The occurrences include sites addressing learners – listing courses, materials, resources, etc., as well as tutors and instructors or researchers in the field. In addition, typing in "learning English online" calls up a further 35700 results, most of which either advertise commercially available online courses or offer free ready-made exercises. If we restrict the search even further and include + beginner level / elementary level / intermediate level / advanced level, we find in both strings that the higher the language level being targeted, the more results appear in increased progression. This may imply that lower levels of proficiency such as beginners and elementary learners prefer face-to-face tuition and classroom contact, whereas intermediate and advanced learners are more willing to explore autonomous learning scenarios; a fact that seems only natural considering that learners who have an intermediate or advanced level of proficiency can, to a larger extent, become independent learners due to an existing knowledge base and subsequent understanding of the target language. This suggests that the Internet is slowly becoming an integral part of our English language teaching practice, especially at levels targeting higher intermediate to advanced learners, that there is an audience for these courses and that learners are increasingly in need of materials and learning scenarios outside the limits of more traditional teaching. However, it does not come as a surprise that when we search for teaching or learning professional or academic English online, there are no results whatsoever. Although there is a large community of language learners who seek to learn languages for specific or academic purposes, there is a very small community of language teachers who are willing to embark in creating tailor-made materials for their learners' specific professional needs; and, understandably so, if we take into account, even today, the amount of time, will and effort that goes into designing interactive multimedia materials for the Web.

The wish to change this led us to design the *InGenio* online authoring shell, an entirely web-based multilingual tool that enables language teachers from around the world to design and publish language learning courseware very easily without having to acquire additional computer programming skills. The tool was developed within *Proyecto InGenio*[1], which produced three basic outcomes in addition to the language independent, on-line multimedia authoring shell; i) an on-line learning environment offering the courseware designed and created within the *InGenio* authoring tool; ii) a student assessment and on-line tutoring interface; and iii) a translation tool to adapt the materials into different support languages (L1s). These four components are currently being integrated into the *InGenio* Content Management System (CMS), an interface specifically devoted to managing, facilitating use of and sharing web content designed and published with our system.

After designing the authoring shell, we then embarked on designing an intermediate level online English course intended for learners of English for engineering purposes as a prototype to illustrate some of the

1 *Proyecto InGenio* was developed by the CAMILLE R&D Group and entirely funded by the Universidad Politécnica de Valencia (Spain). For further information please refer to the following site http://camilleweb.upv.es/camille.

things that could be done with the tool. The course is known as *Intermediate Online English.* The examples given below will all refer to this courseware.

2. Approaches and methodology – independent & autonomous learning

When combining the principles underlying teaching languages for professional or academic purposes and e-language learning, one comes to the conclusion that the learning process must foster a number of strategies to ensure deep learning[2] through critical thinking and analysis of new information and ideas, linking these to already known concepts, and leading to the understanding and long-term retention of (newly acquired) knowledge. In addition, the use of Information and Communications Technologies (ICT) in the language curriculum has, to some extent, been responsible for the shift from focusing on the teacher to focusing on the learner when designing web-enhanced materials, and has led courseware designers to adopt a constructivist approach to learning, whereby the student is encouraged to construct knowledge actively and the teacher becomes a guide to support learners through the process of learning. In so doing, students must be equipped with all the necessary tools to become independent learners and take responsibility for their own learning. As pointed out by Blin (2005, p. 33),

> Independent language learning environments present language learning opportunities that do not require the constant intervention of a teacher or that can be pursued outside the framework of an educational institution.

2 *Deep learning* as opposed to *surface learning.* Weigel, V. B. (2002). *Deep learning for a digital age: Technology's untapped potential to enrich higher education*. San Francisco: Jossey-Bass.

Thus, online learning resources such as the ones which can be developed using the *InGenio* platform should ultimately encourage "active learning", that is, a context where the learner is encouraged to write, speak, actively participate, interact with fellow learners, etc. in a resourceful and stimulating learning environment, yet not necessarily under the constant supervision of a teacher. This scenario naturally implies making use of currently available technologies such as video and audio conferencing tools, instant messaging tools, blogs[3], wikis[4], etc. The very nature of these tools provide learners with a fair amount of independence which nevertheless also requires guidance by a qualified instructor to help the learner orient his or her activity toward the learning process itself and not deviate attention towards other possible distracting scenarios. Learner autonomy, understood as the capacity to self-manage learning, is also one of the key concepts which have rapidly evolved due to the integration of Computer Assisted Language Learning (CALL) into the language curriculum. As Littlewood (1997, p. 83) points out, "The autonomous learner takes responsibility for his or her own learning, has developed useful and effective learning strategies and is able to work independently". In CALL materials' design, most authors are aware of the fact that a variety of teaching strategies have to be implemented in the courseware in order to facilitate and encourage learners to take up the endeavour of second language acquisition. To this end, the *InGenio* authoring tool has been designed to include, as well as a considerable number of exercise templates, reference materials such as grammar notes, cultural information, multilingual sound-enhanced dictionaries and glossaries, etc. in order to provide learners with all the necessary resources that contribute toward enriching comprehension

3 Blog, a term that originates from the combination of "web" and "log", is a website where entries are made and normally displayed in reverse chronological order. Visitors may add comments to these entries.

4 A wiki is a website that allows the visitors themselves to add, remove and otherwise edit and change some available content easily, sometimes without the need for registration; wikis are especially useful for collaborative writing projects.

and understanding of the target language. Another important factor to bear in mind is the need for the inclusion of meaningful corrective feedback on which the learner can rely to support their progress.

In terms of methodology, *InGenio* can be adopted to suit a large number of teaching methodologies, ranging from structural methods to a more communicative approach to language learning. The exercise templates are particularly suitable for designing courses that attempt to acknowledge the fact that a true linguistic competence implies being able to use the language that is appropriate to a given social and cultural context in order to achieve a specific communicative goal. To do this, learners need knowledge of the linguistic forms, meanings and functions for a given context. To achieve this end *InGenio* provides a variety of goal-oriented learning strategies in a media rich electronic environment that supports the study of the target language. The notion of supporting the study of the language is crucial here. Our objective was not so much the creation of software to "teach" the language, but the construction of learning resources in the shape of an environment that would provide the student with all the tools and information, short of a live teacher, that they might need to undertake a language course.

Since "there are strong arguments to support the notion that students will need higher levels of explicit and implicit assistance in computerised than in face-to-face environments" (Trinder, 2006, p. 97), online courseware must replace the absence of face-to-face interaction with techniques and strategies which give the student appropriate support. In order to illustrate this more thoroughly, the following section deals with an overview of the *InGenio* authoring system[5]. As we can see

5 Versions of the description of the *InGenio* authoring system that follows have been previously published in Gimeno (2006) and in "How can CLIL benefit from the integration of Information and Communications Technologies?", shortly to be published in a special issue dedicated to Content and Language Integrated Learning (CLIL), edited by Do Coyle & Hugo Baetens-Beardsmore, of the *International Journal of Bilingual Education and Bilingualism.* Clevedon: Multilingual Matters.

in Figure 1, the system features, including registration of users (authors, students, tutors and translators), as well as the authoring shell, can be accessed by clicking on the main menu items on the left.

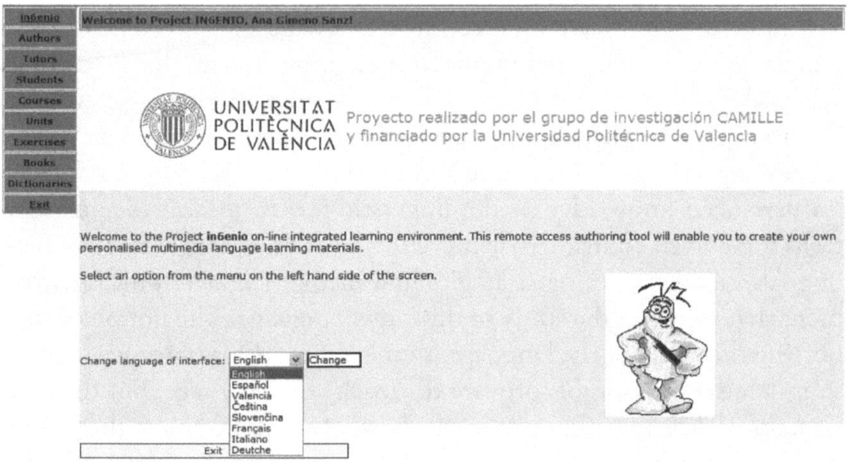

Figure 1. The *InGenio* authoring shell front page.

3. Exercise templates

In order to implement activities that engage learners in the construction of knowledge, the authoring tool comprises two templates that are suitable for fact-finding and for retrieving relevant data from a particular source of information, whether it be audio, video, text or a combination of these. Activities such as note-taking, which can play an important role in improving the learner's long-term retention of newly acquired knowledge (Perry, 2007), completing information gaps and diagrams, etc. can be designed with the following templates.

a) *Presentation of information.* This template permits the inclusion of any text type, in addition to images and audio. These templates have been devised to introduce the lesson contents, task or problem by means of an introductory text, illustration(s) and/or sound file(s). They are the simplest of the templates but are particularly appropriate, for example, to introduce the text preceding a reading comprehension exercise or to give a set of instructions. Students can be led to find facts from the information provided. Because lengthy reading from a screen is not advisable (Dillon, 2004), texts should be presented in reasonable chunks without altering their semantic structure and accompanied by exercises specifically designed to ensure understanding of text content.

b) *Video sequence and script.* This template enables the insertion of video sequences in any of the most common formats at three transfer rates[6] in order to accommodate different bandwidths. Additionally, the video script can be included although the default mode does not automatically unveil the script, but instead, has to be called up. This template is particularly suitable for introducing the video sequence preceding a listening comprehension exercise to assess learner understanding. Presenting descriptions, processes, procedures, etc. audio-visually has a high impact on input retention. In terms of English for Academic and Professional Purposes (EAPP), where the language syllabus would normally incorporate topics dealing with the given professional subject matter, this template would allow instructors to introduce a new topic from the syllabus and accompany it with follow-up exercises whilst simultaneously designing exercises focussing on the language content of the video sequence.

c) Tasks such as ordering and sorting information can also be transferred onto the computer screen be designing exercises for students to classify and categorise elements according to specified criteria. Rearranging information is a useful task when requiring learners to sort ideas and concepts that are depicted in a preceding text or audio-visual.

6 A choice of 56, 256 or 512 kbps is available.

For example, these exercises can be useful to verify listening comprehension after listening to an audio sequence presenting source information. In terms of functionality, the *reordering* template allows content providers to create exercises where images or text have to be reordered either vertically or horizontally on the screen. The text to be reordered can be an individual word or an edited fragment (e.g. parts of a letter). It includes the option of adding a sound file as input to aid in completing the exercise.

d) Tasks dealing with comparisons such as matching, finding similarities and differences can be appropriate to enhance associations of ideas and concepts. To this end, the *matching* template allows courseware designers to create exercises based on assembling items appropriately. Associations can be made by matching textual input, images or sound to a given text. An introductory video clip or audio file can be optionally included, as well as visual support. The options can be randomised, allowing up to 25 options per question. The options appear in a pull-down menu alongside the exercise input. Matching exercises are commonly used for recognition of relationships and for making associations of various nature, e.g. terms and definitions, symbols and names, questions with answers, cause with effect, parts with functions, procedures with operations, principles with situations in which they apply, etc. They can therefore have countless functions and measure a great variety of learning outcomes.

Problem solving is no doubt one of the key activities in a learner-centred approach to task design. Problem solving involves analysing real or hypothetical situations, reasoning and decision-making. The outcome of these tasks is the solution to the problem, which can subsequently be evaluated and assessed. These tasks imply allowing learners to write open input during their course of study. The two following templates have been designed with this premise in mind.

e) *Open input without sound.* This template has been designed to create activities where learners are requested to write their own input. These can take the form of rewriting, information transfer, giving short answers, etc. Open questions that require students to provide short answers can be used to assess recollection of data (as opposed to recognition) thus providing an opportunity for higher-level questions. These should encourage students to analyse data and subsequently reason their answers. In this template learners are requested to write their answers in a blank box provided, thus enabling student input to be transferred to the *InGenio* server where it can be accessed by a tutor for assessment and for provision of appropriate feedback. Images can also be added as visual aids.

f) *Open input with sound.* This template resembles the previous one; however it includes the possibility of adding an audio file. Learners can follow oral instructions to carry out written tasks and transfer their input to the *InGenio* server for a tutor to correct and provide feedback.

Monitoring comprehension is crucial to assess learning outcomes. Providing relevant information and designing tasks to support the acquisition of new knowledge in a specific discipline is generally followed by a final stage, which is to assess our learners' intake and monitor learning. The following four templates have been designed to measure comprehension in two different ways, by selecting an appropriate answer from a range of options or by completing an information gap with relevant data. Multiple-choice questions are useful to measure many kinds of subject matter and learning outcomes, as well as providing objective scoring. They can be used to check memory for facts, to check recognition, etc., as well as providing diagnostic information when learners are additionally requested to support their answers.

g) *Multiple-choice questions (single selection with pull-down menu).* This template combines text, audio and image. It can take a variety of forms such as listening to an introductory audio sequence or reading a question and then clicking on the appropriate option. This exercise allows only one correct answer. It is particularly suitable for listening or reading comprehension activities such as True/False questions, which measure the ability to identify whether statements of facts, principles, generalizations, relationships, or evaluative statements are correct. They can be factual or involve reasoning if learners are additionally requested to support their answers.

h) *Multiple-choice questions (single selection menu).* This multiple-choice template allows courseware designers to include a video sequence or a sound file and an image to support exercise completion. This variety permits only one correct answer. Hints associated to each of the options (in the form of a "tool-tip") can be displayed if required. As well as the exercise text input, additional explanatory notes can be added below the options. These can be randomised so that they appear in a different order each time the exercise is accessed.

i) *Multiple-choice questions (multiple selection).* This multiple-choice template allows for several possible answers, as well as the possibility of including a video or an audio clip as initial input. It also permits the inclusion of images, both as support material and as selection items (options). It can have up to 25 options to choose from and each of these can have a hint associated to it. The options can be randomised so that they appear in a different order each time the exercise is accessed.

j) *Gap-filling exercises.* This template also allows the inclusion of an image or an audio file as additional input. Each gap can have up to a maximum of three correct answers, as well as a hint to aid the learner in its completion. We can also attach a help facility to each gap – which appears as a "tool-tip" –, in addition to specific positive and negative feedback. The learner can choose to see the correct answer partially, after having filled each gap, or completely, after having completed the entire exercise.

Additionally, in order to reinforce specific vocabulary relating to the target subject matter, *InGenio* provides a number of templates designed to aid vocabulary acquisition of the foreign language, as well as being a means of rooting key concepts that are relevant to the subject.

k) *Vocabulary building.* This template allows authors to write lists of words and optionally to include text, pictures and audio files to either provide a definition, translation, illustration and/or pronunciation of a given word or expression. Students tend to find this type of exercise challenging and very rewarding when satisfactory results are achieved.

l) *Clickable image (hot spots, single selection).* This template allows authors to create observation (passive) exercises that are specially suited to vocabulary practice. In student mode, an image is displayed (a photo, picture or illustration) and a number of "hot spots" can be selected which will activate a response by the computer when clicked on. This response can be audio, text or both. Up to 10 "hot spots" can be designated.

m) *Clickable images (multiple selection).* This template allows content providers to create exploration (active) exercises resembling the previous one but differing in that the audio or visual input triggers a response from the learner and appropriate feedback is provided immediately afterwards. In this model the learner is requested to make a choice out of a number of visual options. Both this and the previous template allow authors to include notes or additional activities below the pictures.

n) *Word search puzzles.* The authoring tool comprises two templates to create word games aiming to combine entertainment and learning. The first one enables materials writers to create word search puzzles. The number of words to include in the grid and the level of difficulty depends entirely on the author. The template offers the choice of providing or hiding the list of words that have to be found. These puzzles may prove very useful for vocabulary revision at the end of a practice unit. Hints to aid in completing the game and feedback can also be included in this typology.

o) *Hang-man exercises.* The second word game template allows content providers to create hang-man exercises, which can work at letter, word or sentence level. The number of attempts is limited to 6, which are the number of elements comprising the hanged-man. This typology is also useful for vocabulary practice and is suitable when seeking distraction from other activities that require far more student concentration.

4. General features of the system

Time limits can be given to all the exercises and the number of attempts that a student is allowed to complete an exercise can also be restricted. These options have been programmed to enable authors to create a variety of assessment tests.

The images, audio or video files embedded in the exercises can be called up directly from within the authoring shell to enable content providers to be aware at all times of all the multimedia components that integrate a sole activity. Images, furthermore, are automatically resized to fit their location within the learner-template, thus avoiding authors from having to edit images unnecessarily. When designing an activity the content provider may at all times see a preview of the exercise in student mode. This is possible because every time the materials are updated the information is automatically uploaded onto the *InGenio* server[7].

One of the features that can be specified in all the templates where the learner is requested to write is whether we wish student input to be case sensitive or not. This option becomes especially useful when designing exercises that focus more on meaning than on form and where it may be relatively irrelevant whether punctuation is respected.

Although voice recording has not been programmed into the system, it is nevertheless possible to design exercises where the learner is requested to record his or her own utterances by accessing the Windows Media Player, which can be called up and minimised when not in use. Evaluation of oral production will be subject to learner comparison with a pre-recorded model or by tutor intervention. Future developments include incorporating voice recognition software into the *InGenio* system.

In any of the exercise or reference materials templates links to other websites can be included. This is particularly suitable when designing

7 The *InGenio* server is hosted by the Universidad Politécnica de Valencia's Information and Communications Office.

exercises where the learner is requested to access another existing web page, for instance to read or listen to a passage, or even watch a video sequence, and then complete our own exercise. This obviously avoids problems with copyright clearance issues.

5. Provision of reference materials

Provision of appropriate reference materials for the language level and purpose of the course being designed is, needless to say, of vital importance in autonomous language learning. Designers must ensure that the target language is not deprived of any element that may support the learner's acquisition process. Thus, *InGenio* provides a number of templates to enable content providers to create reference materials that can be associated individually to exercises or called up as independent tools during the student's course of study.

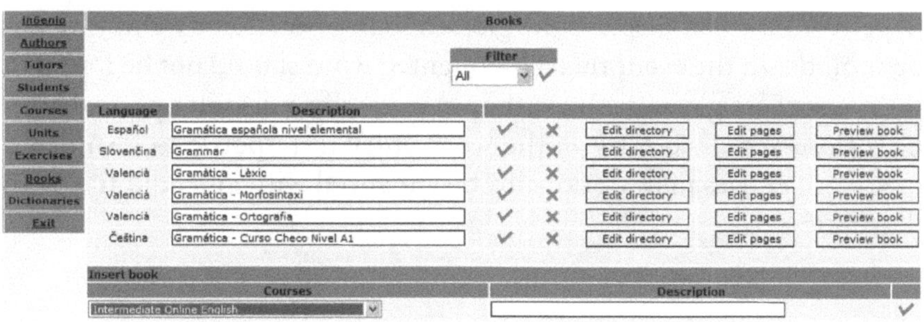

Figure 2. *IN6ENIO* reference materials editor.

As we can see in Figure 2, new reference materials can be immediately added by indicating the language, giving it a reference number and a description. The new "book" will be created and immediately entered into the list of already existing reference sources. This screen also enables us to edit the contents directory and preview any of the "books" by clicking on the appropriate items.

The actual "pages" within any of the books can be created, modified, edited or deleted with great ease. The contents of a given page are inserted using hypertext mark-up language (HTML) with an external web editor,[8] thus allowing authors to edit the text according to their preferences. The source code simply has to be copied and pasted into the appropriate field. This screen also automatically previews the contents of the page so that authors can immediately verify them. These newly created pages can additionally be linked to existing exercises or included as an introductory section to the exercises within a learning unit.

The *InGenio* authoring tool also enables authors to create monolingual or multilingual glossaries and dictionaries. Each of the exercise templates includes an option whereby any of the words can become a hypertext link that displays the glossed item or dictionary entry in student mode. In the event that a highlighted word should not be found in the courseware glossary, the author may specify a default online dictionary from which to retrieve the word entry in response to a student's query. All entries may, optionally, be enhanced with an audio file of an illustration.

8 Macromedia Dreamweaver and Microsoft FrontPage are two of the most commonly used web editors.

6. Student assessment

Students can, at all times, check correct/incorrect answers, call up and see correct answers or request evaluation. Until the student actually requests evaluation, an exercise may be refreshed and any number of attempts made, unless the exercise has been marked as being a test, in which case the "refresh screen" option will have been disabled.

Progress reports can be called up at any point during the learning process since a link to the assessment function is permanently available on the screen. The data is automatically transferred to the server while the materials are in use, therefore allowing students to monitor their progress during the course of their work. The results are presented in percentages, registering date and time, number of completed exercises, scores, etc., as shown in Figure 3.

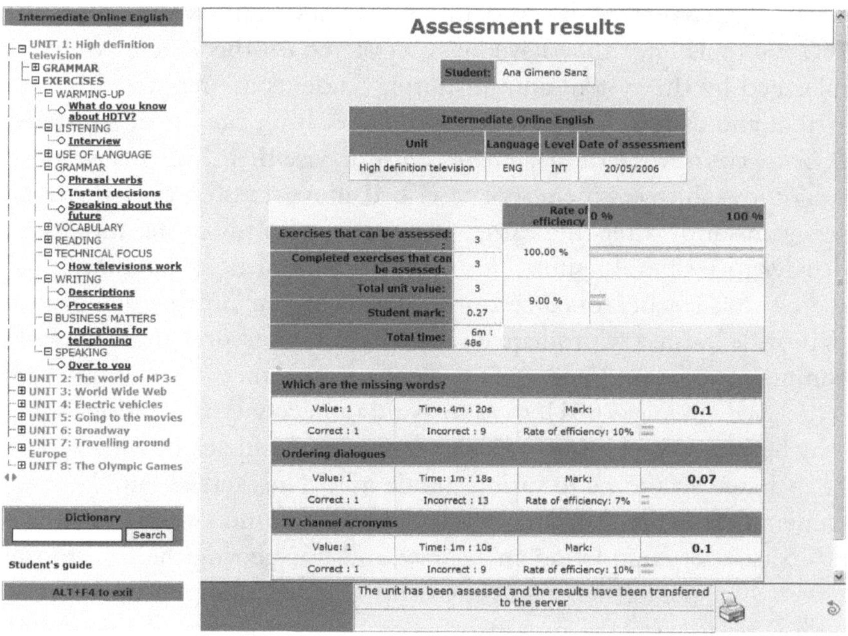

Figure 3. *InGenio* student assessment report.

Since the system automatically registers and tracks student performance, tutors using the course materials with registered users may access progress reports, as well as the student's written production deriving from open input activities in order for them to correct and mark these, and provide appropriate feedback. These marks will automatically be averaged by the system in order to give students a final mark or score. When specified in a template, learners may also upload any type of file (spreadsheets, audio, etc.) onto the server for their tutors to evaluate and assess together with any other course work.

7. Feedback and tutor interface

Users (materials writers, students, tutors and translators) access the *InGenio* tools once they have been registered on the system, which is managed by the system administrator. Students are registered on the system and assigned a tutor, if appropriate, from the list of registered *InGenio* courseware tutors. These can supervise their students' work in real time as the assessment tool described above transfers the data to the server instantly after the learner is satisfied with his or her input and decides to seek evaluation. This action is equivalent to handing in an exercise to a teacher for correction and marking. In our view, it is crucial to provide learners with adequate assessment tools (scores, individualised comments, etc.) and appropriate feedback, whether this is immediate or delayed (Pujolà, 2001), so as to avoid unnecessary frustration which may be caused by feelings of lack of support. Feedback in *InGenio* can be included according to various modalities. The exercise templates include a default feedback mode that provides learners with immediate feedback after completing an exercise and transferring the data to the server. This default feedback opens up as a separate pop-up window with a random comment and/or recommendation from a list of possible comments/recommendations that have been programmed into the system following a number of parameters describing learner performance. Scores themselves are also given, in addition to an indication of the time that has been spent on a given exercise.

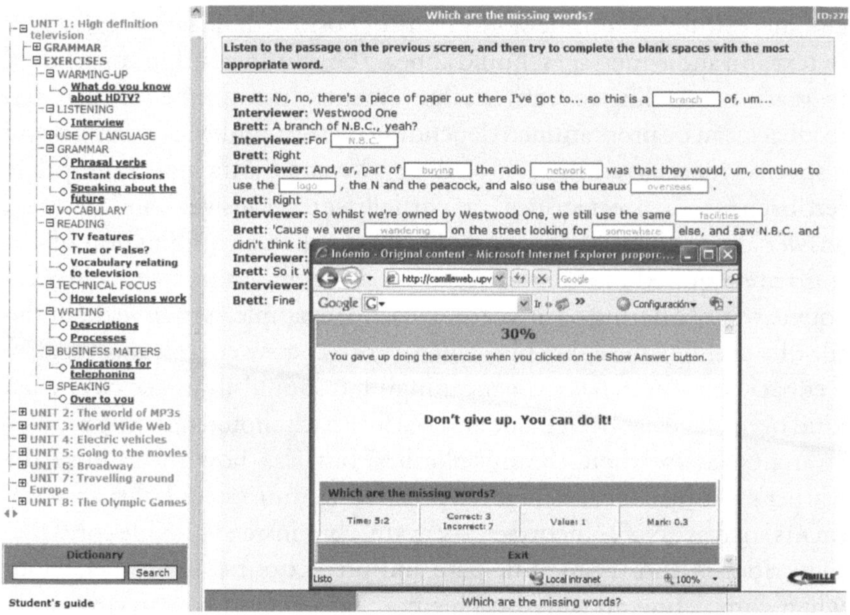

Figure 4. Default immediate feedback.

The default feedback can be altered by the materials writer at any time by supplying specific feedback for a particular exercise, although individualised corrective feedback may only be provided by the tutor when supervising the learner's input through the *InGenio* tutor interface. In a gap-filling exercise, for instance, both positive and negative feedback can be provided for each blank space to be completed by the learner – as well as a hint and contextual help to aid comprehension and exercise completion –, in addition to overall feedback after completing the entire exercise. Since one of the advantages of multimedia technology is the computer's immediate response to a mere touch of a key or mouse click, this is very useful when dealing with positive or negative feedback in reaction to the learner's performance in completing an activity or exercise. Learners, we have observed, tend to find it encouraging to read and / or hear immediate positive feedback when they have completed an exercise successfully. A considerable variety of positive or negative text, audio or text and audio messages should appear / be heard at random and should be graded according to learner achievements. In a number of exercises, feedback can be programmed depending on the number of attempts and a specific score given to each of these. We should include appropriate feedback for a "correct answer", a "partially correct answer", an "incorrect answer", or even exercise-specific feedback when a combination of options are required in order to complete an exercise successfully. An adequate way of offering positive feedback, for example, is to have the audio file of a particular exercise play when a correct answer is given. Negative feedback, of course, has to be meaningful. It should always be clear what kind of mistake has been made and the feedback should not only provide awareness as to where the mistake lies, but also how to improve the learner's performance. Wherever possible we must avoid abrupt statements such as "No", "Incorrect, try again", but instead provide constructive criticism and try to anticipate and predict our learners' behaviour when completing an activity. This may be achieved by carrying out – prior to the design stage – an error analysis based, for example, on L1 interference. (Gimeno, 2002)

The *InGenio* tutor interface (see Figure 5 below) comprises two viewing modes. One that includes the list of registered learners and general information such as the course a learner is registered on, average mark achieved, percentage of course completed, etc., and a more detailed one that provides information indicating specific performance on each exercise that has been evaluated. When a learner transfers an open input text, the programme gives the student an overall provisional grade until the tutor has personally assessed that exercise, scored it and, optionally, provided specific individualised feedback, which the learner subsequently has access to. Current system developments include the possibility of learners being able to upload files.

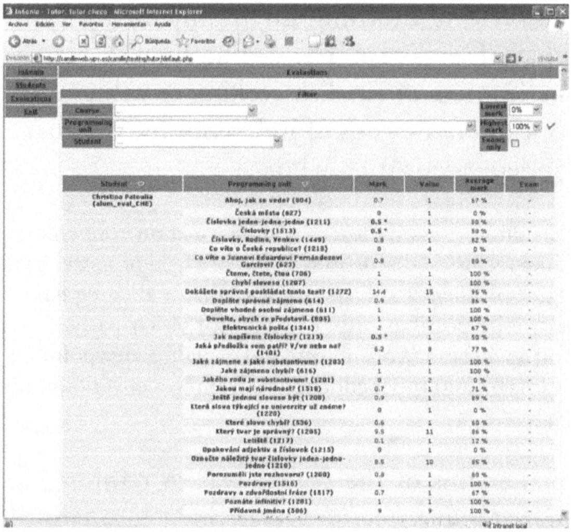

Figure 5. *InGenio* tutor mode.

Tutors who are registered on the *InGenio* system are thus advised to make use of the various feedback utilities included in the system in order to provide learners with corrective feedback that is relevant for the learning process, as well as inspiring and motivating for students.

8. *Intermediate Online English*

Intermediate Online English, as mentioned above, was designed as a prototype to illustrate what could be done and how the *InGenio* authoring tool worked. It has since been updated and is currently being used as the basis for a course delivered at the Universidad Politécnica de Valencia (UPV) called "Computer Assisted English"[9]. The online course is em-

9 This is an elective subject worth 4.5 credits (45 hours of student workload) open to all UPV students.

bedded into the *InGenio* Learning Environment (LE), to which registered students have free access. The online English course is intended for intermediate learners of English seeking to achieve level B2 of the Common European Framework of Reference for Languages (CEFRL), i.e. that of an independent user, who

> [...] can understand the main ideas of complex text on both concrete and abstract topics, including technical discussions in his/her field of specialisation. Can interact with a degree of fluency and spontaneity that makes regular interaction with native speakers quite possible without strain for either party. Can produce clear, detailed text on a wide range of subjects and explain a viewpoint on a topical issue giving the advantages and Independent disadvantages of various options. (CEFRL, p. 24)

Because one of the aims of the course was to reinforce technical English, *Intermediate Online English* was divided into two distinct parts; one, devoted to semi-technical issues such as digital devices, ICT, electric vehicles, the WWW, etc., which could be of general interest to our students, and another, focussing on more general topics such as leisure activities, the Olympic games, theatre-going, film festivals, etc. The aim of this division was to balance the intake of formal versus informal language and structures. The courseware aims to provide the conditions in which learners can develop communicative competences in their own way and in their own time. This, we think, is achieved, among other ways, by presenting a default route to follow, offering diversity of activities and developing a progression from receptive to productive skills. Various strategies have been included that are designed to encourage problem solving and resolution of specific tasks, aiming at developing the learners' ability to apply and adapt their knowledge of the target language to specific communicative scenarios. The problems and the tasks, therefore, have been designed to encourage learners to use the target language for a communicative purpose in order to achieve an outcome.

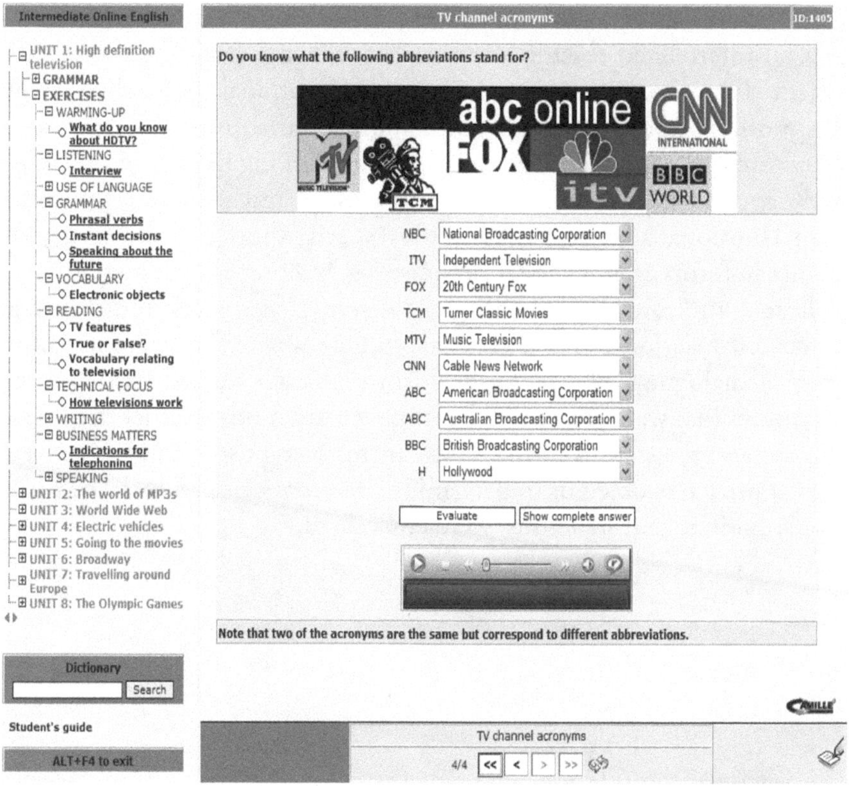

Figure 6. Sample exercise from *Intermediate Online English.*

In *Intermediate Online English,* all eight units are preceded by a grammar section, aimed at revising grammatical notions that are relevant to the course contents, and are divided into the following ten sub-headings: listening, use of language, grammar, vocabulary, reading, technical focus, writing, business matters and speaking, which include a varied number of exercises relating to the section's prime focus. The course itself comprises over 300 exercises and activities designed to expose learners to the intricacies of the target language and generate a sound basis for consolidation and acquisition.

Within this general course outline, the courseware also combines several interrelated teaching approaches; ranging from the more LSP-oriented[10] approaches such as the functional/notional approach, through the more traditional language form approach that primarily focuses on structures, to a more contextual approach. Among the approaches that were applied to determine the course design and structure, the functional/notional approach allowed us to specify the desired learning outcomes in terms of language functions (e.g. making a request, advising a colleague on how to proceed), general as well as specific notions (e.g. duration, location), and rhetorical skills (e.g. extracting information from a dialogue). The language form approach helped to shape the structures that were present in the language functions in order to achieve learner awareness as to the linguistic forms being used, and the contextual approach enabled us to determine the situations in which the functions, notions and structures were embedded.

9. Conclusions

To conclude, the *InGenio* authoring system is a robust and flexible tool that enables language teachers from around the world to collaborate in creating innovative online language learning courseware and to share what others have previously designed. The *InGenio* system comprises 4 integrated modes, i.e. a) author mode, to design and publish online materials; b) learner mode, which gives access to the courses embedded in the *InGenio* Learning Environment; c) tutor mode, to assess students' progress, and d) translator mode, which enables interested parties to adapt the courses to any number of support languages. The system has been designed to foster independent learning and ensures that

10 Languages for Specific Purposes (LSP).

the most recent Internet-based developments can be integrated into the online courses and, due to its versatility, can be constantly updated as the need may arise.

References

Council of Europe (2001). *Common European Framework of Reference for Languages* (CEFRL). Cambridge: Cambridge University Press.

Saskatchewan Education, Canada. *Understanding the Common Essential Learnings. A Handbook for Teachers.* Retrieved June 9th, 2007, from http://www.sasked.gov.sk.ca/docs/policy/cels/el7.html.

Blin, F. (2005). *CALL and the development of learner autonomy – an activity theoretical study.* Unpublished doctoral thesis, Institute of Educational Technology, The Open University, UK. Retrieved June 10th, 2007, from http://webpages.dcu.ie/~blinf/BlinThesis.pdf.

Dillon, A. (2004). *Designing Usable Electronic Text.* 2nd Ed. Bristol, PA: CRC Press.

Gimeno, A. (2002). *CALL Software Design and Implementation: the template approach.* Valencia: Servicio de Publicaciones de la Universidad Politécnica de Valencia.

Gimeno, A. (2006). The *InGenio* online CALL authoring shell. *The EUROCALL Review,* No. 7. Limerick: European Association for Computer Assisted Language Learning. Retrieved June 10th, 2007, from http://www.eurocall-languages.org/news/newsletter/7/index.html#projects.

Littlewood, W. (1997). Self-access: why do we want it and what can it do? *Autonomy and independence in language learning,* Essex: Longman – Applied Linguistic and Language Study, 79–91.

Perry, D. (2007). *Constructing Meaning and Knowledge Acquisition from Expository Texts through Self-Regulated Reading Activities in a Second Language.* Unpublished doctoral thesis, Facultad de Filología, Traducción y Comunicación, Universidad de Valencia.

Pujolà, J. T. (2001). Did CALL Feedback Feed Back? *ReCALL,* 13 (1): 79–98.

Trinder, R. (2006). *Language Learning with Computers: The Student's Perspective.* Frankfurt: Peter Lang.

Mª LUISA CARRIÓ PASTOR

Enhancing Learner-Teacher Collaboration through the Use of Online Activities

Introduction

Collaborative language learning and teaching is an approach that is being used more and more by teachers of technical English. The collaboration that is implied in this study is twofold: on the one hand, we focus on learning, i.e., students collaborate in the update of activities and in the design of specific material appropriate to their needs through periodic evaluations; on the other hand, we focus on teaching, i.e., teachers from different areas of knowledge collaborate in developing tasks that reinforce the language skills and specific vocabulary of the students following a technical degree. Collaborative learning and teaching entails students working together to achieve common learning goals; teachers and students working together to design, select and evaluate the material to be used in the classroom, as well as language teachers and content teachers working together to link content and method (Nunan, 1992).

The novelty of our proposal is the incorporation of the benefits of the Internet and other on-line materials which thereby avoid the inconveniences of software material and the blending of teaching content and language using a collaborative approach. Students and teachers become a compact group that engages in dialogue and negotiates in a non-passive class (González Fernández, 2006, p. 3) that blends content and language integrated learning (CLIL) and computer-supported collaborative learning (CSCL). Some researchers have stated the need of collaborative learning to teach a second language (Nunan, 1992; Burns,

1999; McCafferty, Jacobs and DaSilva Iddings, 2006; Carrió Pastor, 2006) while others have put forward the need to teach a second language integrated in a specific content (Kramsch, 1993; Collentine & Freed, 2004; Butkiene & Vilkanciene, 2005; Darn, 2006) although these approaches have not been combined till now. We consider that technology, collaborative learning and the content and language integrated learning process can be combined in order to obtain communicative, active and professionally-oriented materials for specific contexts.

The objective of this research is to demonstrate that the use of CSCL and CLIL in the design of specific materials improves learners' attitude toward second language acquisition and also that the on-line material created with the collaboration of content teachers, language teachers and students provides learners with stimulating and challenging learning material.

Computer-supported collaborative learning (CSCL) and content and language integrated learning (CLIL)

Collaborative language learning and teaching is an approach based on cognitivism. It enhances maturity, experience and social communication in an academic environment while rejecting passivity, repetition and individuality. It derives from a sociocultural perspective and emphasizes the relationship between social context and language, creating a sense of community to induce learning. Students develop their own learning strategies and select their own objectives and at the same time, they are responsible for what they learn and how they learn a topic (Gros, 1997, p. 99). Additionally, it is being used more and more by domain-specific English teachers (Cortese and Riley, 2002) and content teachers since collaborative teaching allows them to take advantage of individual strengths in planning for instruction and in better pacing and sequencing of increments of instruction. Students learn a second language while using content subject materials in a social process in which they look for topics of shared understanding.

The use of the collaborative approach to learn a second language can be focused on the learner or on the teacher. Collaboration encourages learners to learn better; to increase their awareness about language and consequently to develop metacommunicative as well as communicative skills (Nunan, 1992, p. 3). Teachers take advantage of individual strengths in designing materials; they teach for their colleagues as well as for their learners; the perceptions of an individual teacher are verified by the rest of the group involved in collaborative teaching and finally, collaborative teaching builds program continuity over time (Nunan, 1992, p. 6).

In order to obtain real collaborative learning and teaching, we need to do several things; first, to study the capacities, deficiencies and possibilities of the members of the group; second, to establish similar goals in the individual contributions to the activities; third, to elaborate a specific plan and an evaluation system; fourth, to coordinate the individual tasks and the teamwork of the group; fifth, to ensure that all the opinions and criteria of all the members of the team be considered equally, thus avoiding domination by any one person or group. Finally, we should take into account all the opinions of the members of the group in obtaining the final proposal (Burns, 1999, p. 217; Calzadilla, 2001, p. 5).

All the members of the group act as leaders of the tasks they are performing. Each member explains the task he/she proposes to the rest of the group and this is why communication is essential in collaborative learning. The proposals should be explained in direct and concise language and the success of the activities depends on the sincerity of the evaluation performed by the rest of the group (Carrió Pastor, 2006, p. 11).

Each participant assumes his or her role in the group, both as carrier of the knowledge he/she is going to transmit and as evaluator of the activities proposed. The team that elaborates the activities needs the involvement of all the participants: the language teacher assesses second language learning approaches and strategies; the content teacher provides the specific topics and outline of exercises, and the student selects the most appropriate activities for his/her needs. Interdependency and mutual respect between the components of the collaborative activity is essential to obtain a coherent proposal.

Bailey, Dale & Squire (1992) identify two different patterns of the teacher's role in collaborative activities. In the first pattern, teachers from different areas of knowledge collaborate in order to offer learning tools to students; in the second, students work collaboratively in the classroom to carry out the tasks proposed by the teacher. In both, the roles of the teachers and students are different. In the first one, the teacher leads the teaching activity, facilitating the interdisciplinary tasks for the 'passive' students. In the second, the teacher's role is less active, helping the students but not interfering in the learning process which is piloted by them. We propose a third pattern which combines these two, teachers and students teach and learn from each other in an equitable way. They collaborate in the design and evaluation of the learning-teaching process, therefore designing materials that are tailored to the needs of the students.

Nonetheless, sometimes situations of shared responsibility can result in no one taking full responsibility. It is important to be very clear about who must accomplish which tasks. In order to decide teacher and student's roles in the whole collaborative process, we can choose between the strategies provided by Tudge (1994): the interaction between students with different levels where teachers are the coordinators; the tuition by students with more knowledge of the subject to those students with a lower level where teachers are the evaluators of the activity or students working as a whole group where teachers are the mediators of the tasks, acting as leaders of the group. Each group needs a specific strategy and the teachers involved should specify the best one in order to avoid misunderstandings. Collaboration implies interaction between the different members of the group and the different proposals should act as webs of knowledge that combine to offer a compact result (Strijbos, Martens and Jochems, 2004, p. 403).

Both information and knowledge should be shared by all the members of the group as collaborative learning and teaching is focused on communication. Collaborative learning and teaching has become a reality even in very remote locations with the help of computers and internet. Computers act as mediators in the technology and communication era (Baeza et al., 1999, p. 3). Collaborative learning and teaching benefits from technology as (Calzadilla, 2001, p. 8):

a. It stimulates interpersonal communication through virtual learning.
b. It facilitates collaborative learning through chats, files, etc.
c. All the members of the team can follow the progress of the activities any time as they can be connected to all the participants.
d. The information is accessible to all the members of the team through a data base.
e. The administration and management of the students involved is easier.
f. On-line activities are possible and then virtual teaching is accessible to students in remote locations.
g. Previous experiences are accessible in order to observe the progress or evolution of activities.
h. Each participant can choose his/her own pace and group, depending on his/her background.

Collaborative learning and teaching implies interactive learning and technology facilitates communication and makes the learning process more effective (Freeman, 1992; Sturman, 1992; Zañartu Correa, 2000; Slaouti, 2002; Martínez Carreras et al., 2004; Chen, 2005; Liaw, 2006). Computer-supported collaborative learning (CSCL) generates a positive interdependency, promotes verbal exchange, values individual contributions, stimulates personal and group skills and finally, involves the self-evaluation of the group and the attainment of the objectives previously established. CSCL implies that materials can be designed through a combination of collaboration and technique. Several researchers (Barros, Vélez & Verdejo, 2004; Osuna Gómez et al., 2004; Adell, 2004; Martínez

Carreras et al., 2004; Chen, 2005 and McCafferty, Jacobs & DaSilva Iddings, 2006; Carrió & Gimeno, 2007) have shown that CSCL is a successful reality.

Computer-supported collaborative materials can be used in different contexts and for different purposes, but they are specifically relevant for interdisciplinary subjects, i.e. the learning of domain-specific languages. The content and language integrated learning (CLIL) approach integrates second language acquisition and content subjects learning. As Marsh, Maljers & Hartiala (2001, p. 17) describe it "CLIL is an educational approach in which non-language subjects are taught through a foreign, second or other additional language." As knowledge of the language becomes the means of learning content, the student is highly motivated and language acquisition becomes stimulating.

There are some principles underlying CLIL (Darn, 2006, p. 2) that should be noted in order to design collaborative materials: language is used to learn and communicate (receptive and productive skills); a CLIL lesson should combine content, communication, cognition (develop thinking skills) and culture; language is functional and is adapted to the subject; language is approached lexically, grammar is not important and finally, learners needs should be taken into account in task types.

A CLIL framework for a lesson should be prearranged considering the reading comprehension of texts and activities related to the organisation of knowledge and processing of texts. The teachers who design the domain-specific materials cannot explain the language structures or correct the language errors as it is not their task, and fluency is more important than accuracy. The content teacher should combine the CLIL activities with some language classes as language assessment is essential in order to reinforce students' language skills. The subject teacher should be able to exploit opportunities for developing language skills and improve the content but also the language knowledge of the students (Carrió Pastor, 2007).

CLIL and CSCL can be combined in order to teach specific topics using a more dynamic and flexible approach that allows students to improve a second language. As Soetaert & Bonamie (2006, p. 5) state

"The computer-as-a-tool agrees with the fact that today a number of educators are seeking ways to teach in more content-based approaches." The combination of both approaches enables the collaboration of teachers and learners to increase students' confidence in content and language subjects as well as self-esteem.

The use of CSCL and CLIL in the design of domain-specific material improves second language awareness and social interaction skills. Students are involved in the process of the preparation and updating of material, as a consequence, their attitude is more positive towards the subjects involved. There are different benefits achieved from material design using the CSCL and CLIL approaches with respect to the improvement in the learners' attitudes: collaboration affords the opportunity to overtly discuss and reflect upon a wide range of learning activities, it creates discussion between teacher and learner and helps students to feel they are responsible for their own learning instead of always depending on teacher feedback. The working partnership between the content teacher and the language teacher demands a high level of individual accountability between them. The material has to be professionally prepared and has to demonstrate professional competence, thus teachers grow professionally in the process as they are evaluated by their partners.

The process of material design

The project discussed in this paper was carried out at the Applied Linguistics Department of the Polytechnic University of Valencia in order to offer domain-specific English materials to students of Industrial Engineering. A group of team teachers, content teachers and students set up several units which combined second language learning and topics from the content subjects of the degree. All the tasks were based on the specific-content websites and the activities were available online to our students through a private website of the university. The activities were supervised in tutorials by English teachers and content teachers, who were also responsible for providing feedback on the tasks in order to adapt them to the needs of the students.

The project involved two parts: the first part focused on the selection of previously analysed websites and the design of activities with the collaboration of a group of students and a group of technical content teachers, both coordinated by English teachers. Students chose ten topics from the content subjects and those were approved by content teachers and language teachers. Then, students were divided in five groups and each one had to select three websites for each two of the chosen topics. Students were given suggestions as to how to divide the work but were free to choose the method they found most effective. Content teachers and language teachers decided that websites had to be chosen taking into account the following criteria:

a. Reliability and renewal of the contents of the website.
b. Identification of the creator of the website and/or its contents.
c. The stability of the website (e.g. is it institutional, corporative or individual?).
d. Specific sections of the website and its overall coherence.
e. Technical facilities for navigation through the different sections.
f. Simple instructions to follow in parts of the website.
g. Lexicon adapted for the practice of a second language.
h. Interaction between the website and its user.
i. Degree of understanding of the contents (organization).
j. Game sections on the website.

Students ranked the websites from 1 to 10 depending on the fulfilment of the criteria. The three most appropriate websites for each topic were chosen. Content teachers and language teachers supervised the adequacy of the selected websites to the second language level and the specific needs of the students. The websites were grouped in different units in order to perform different topics related to technical matters and, in this way the vocabulary included in the content subjects of the Industrial Engineering degree could be practised and reinforced.

Once the websites were selected, each activity of the units was designed by content teachers and language teachers taking into consideration the principles of CSCL and CLIL approaches. The reading material was chosen from the websites by the students who worked together collaboratively and were coordinated by language teachers. Content teachers designed the vocabulary and content questions and also the writing exercises appropriate to the content level of the university students. Language teachers designed activities based on the grammatical structures which appeared in the selected texts, set up communicative and group activities and the listening and oral tasks. All the units followed the same sections although their exercises varied depending on the approach followed by the content teacher or the language teacher. The exercises were topic centred although they were mostly approached from a linguistic point of view. The detailed parts of each unit with examples can be observed in the following section of this paper. Then, the exercises were done by one group of forty students in the first semester and another of thirty students in the second semester of the academic year. The students worked in a group of five (they could select their own group members) and intergroup collaboration was encouraged. The tools they use to communicate with their partners in the language laboratories were e-mail and chats.

The second part of the project combined the evaluation of the materials using the feedback from our students and the incorporation of any changes suggested by updating the on-line materials. The evaluation process followed different steps: teacher evaluation; peer evaluation and self-evaluation.

Teacher evaluation was carried out reviewing the written exercises for the units. Team teachers and content teachers focused on whether students followed the guidelines given and on comprehensibility. Also, students were observed during their interactions and L1 (Spanish) use was disallowed during the class. Teacher comments were directed to the group rather than to particular individuals as all group members were responsible for the final evaluation of the exercises. The groups of students completed the exercises of the units and the content teacher and the language teacher compared the different answers and the adequacy of the questions to the content and language level of the groups in order to evaluate the materials. Students received a group grade that reflected attendance, participation and content and language acquisition in order to enhance collaboration.

Peer evaluation was performed anonymously and was focused on the exercises that involved oral presentations or discussion tasks. Students had to grade in an individual form their satisfaction regarding the language and subject-matter acquisition of their partners and the collaborative work of the group.

Self-evaluation was fulfilled by the content teachers, the language teachers and the group of students involved in the project (selection of topics, websites and exercises). All the materials designed were divided between all the members of the group (content teachers, language teachers and students) and each one had to write a report for one unit of the selected topics. The self-evaluation of the materials was performed with a form which included items asking about the content of the exercises; the collaborative activities; the second language acquisition tasks and if the activities embodied aspects that could be difficult for students (see Appendix 1). Students' self-evaluation was supervised by both content teachers and language teachers.

The tasks, which resulted from the enhancement of learner and teacher collaboration, were a combination of the computer-supported collaborative learning and the content and language integrated learning approaches to obtain specific material, but with the novel introduction of using websites and the collaboration between teachers and students as a team that kept and updated the activities.

As a result of the evaluation process, the activities were updated regularly at the beginning and at the end of each semester in order to adapt the exercises proposed to the needs of the students. At the end of the academic year the content teachers and language teachers collaborated in order to incorporate the changes proposed by them and by the students. All suggestions and comments were discussed in a brainstorming activity and the changes to be incorporated into the on-line proposal for the forthcoming academic year were agreed to by the whole team.

CSCL and CLIL tasks in practice

The course is online and, as aforementioned, the activities are specially designed following a collaborative process to integrate domain-specific language and technical content learning. The tasks are included in ten content-based units which are composed of the following parts: first, an introduction to the specific topic; second, the objectives and content outcomes expected in the unit; third, the exercises based on reading comprehension, scanning texts, summarising ideas, looking for information in other webs, vocabulary, problem solving, definitions, group activities, oral presentations and collaborative and communicative tasks; fourth, a follow-up section, with links to topic related websites and finally, a dictionary with definitions of the specific words included in the Web.

The specific topic of each unit is introduced with general concepts at the beginning of the unit (introduction section). Then, the student is made aware of the purpose of the content and collaborative learning (objectives section), and finally, the web based exercises focus on the specific understanding and vocabulary of the website through collaborative activities. Furthermore, students can learn additional terms (follow up section) and can understand better the unit through the key words (dictionary section).

The units contain topics from the content subjects of the Industrial Engineering degree and are ranked from less to more specific, so students can acquire knowledge of terms and contents at the same time. We have integrated content and language learning in each unit, using technology as a tool to improve knowledge and collaboration between teachers and students. At the same time the students are learning domain-specific English, the topics the content teacher includes in the syllabus and computing skills. Most of the activities were centred on the practice of reading and writing skills, however we also included some activities that allowed them to practise speaking and listening, as collaborative activities are mainly stimulated through oral tasks. Listening activities were difficult to find in the Internet as videos or recordings sometimes do not work properly or they need special software to obtain high quality sound reproduction. As a consequence, we only included those recordings that stimulate the understanding of a second language and discarded those listening activities that were difficult to understand or used incorrect terms.

Some examples of the activities designed which use the CLIL and CSCL approaches are (Carrió, Gimeno, Perry & Seiz, 2006):

– Example of the 'Introduction section':

(From http://www.munters.com/home.nsf/FS1?ReadForm&content=/products.nsf/ByKey/ABRL-54YFZR)

1. INTRODUCTION

In spite of being a commercial website (created by *Munster Company),* the major part of the contents are related to the explanation of different concepts connected to corrosion. First, Munters Desiccant Dehumidification Principle is shown. Munters has created a dehumidifier to remove the excess dampness and moisture to reduce indoor humidity and in this website they explain the principle that underlies their system. They explain how the system works using easy concepts and vocabulary. Then, they describe the way corrosion affects materials, how it can be detected, and whether it is due to the negative chemical reactions produced by substances. The majority of these reactions, basically those involving oxygen, are catalysed and accelerated by moisture.

There is a brief account of condensation prevention, moisture regain prevention, product drying and mould & fungus prevention; moreover, they reason the need to use a dehumidifier to control corrosion.

Finally, the authors of the page ask themselves "Where does moisture come from?" which is answered with an animated picture that represents the cycle of humidity. The company highlights the importance of employing a dehumidifier to fight against the humidity that causes corrosion.

– Example of the 'Objectives and outcomes' section:

2. OBJECTIVES AND OUTCOMES
The main objective of this website is to show how to use the devices that fight against corrosion. The vocabulary included in this website is related to moisture, condensation and corrosion, the devices that are affected by these and ways to prevent the effects that humidity can cause. The site also includes a very useful glossary.

The vocabulary and structures of the texts available on this website are used to explain technical devices, but the main objective is that the reader understands the different concepts.

Finally, students obtain an overview of dehumidifiers, condensation prevention, product drying, fungus prevention and moisture. If they are interested in going deeper into this subject, they can click on the related websites offered in the follow up section of this practical.

– Example of the 'Web exercises' section:

(From the website: www.energyquest.ca.gov/education)

Task 2.1. Introductory task
Define the terms energy and fossil fuels and their importance nowadays. Also, explain and give examples of the alternative fuel vehicles you can find in this website. Send an e-mail with this document to another student in the class and receive his/hers. Underline any errors you can find in his/her writing, then sit together and try to improve them.

– Example of an oral presentation exercise:

Task 2.6. Oral-web activities

a. Work in pairs. Both of you need to look at the section called *Art Gallery*. Taking turns, one of you describes one picture to the other, who has to spot which picture his or her partner is describing.
b. Go to the section called *Science Projects*, where you can find many experiments and projects you can carry out in practice. Choose one of them and do it. Write down a report or summary of what you did (suggested length: 50 words).

Present the project that you carried out briefly (5 minutes maximum) to your partners. You can previously prepare a Power Point presentation attaching pictures from the *Follow Up* section.

– Example of a group activity:

(From http://www.epa.gov/epahome/students.htm/ http://www.epa.gov/students)

Task 3.6- Writing a company pollution report
Imagine you work for an industrial company. Your boss wants you to report on the types of pollution and waste produced by your company. Considering the characteristics and activities of the company, you should write a short report (it can be a text or an organized list) about the types of pollution and waste relevant to your company. To make your report complete, please include a brief overview of the company (name and activity) at the beginning, and comments (or recommendations) about how to prevent pollution in your company at the end. Be concise and realistic!

To find useful information, access http://www.epa.gov/students/waste.htm, then go to "Superfund: Hazardous Substance and Hazardous Waste" (at http://www.epa.gov/superfund/students/clas_act/index. htm), and finally to section "Waste Site Activity" (http://www.epa.gov/superfund/students/wastsite/index. htm). You can also use the information from section 3.5.

– Example of a listening activity:

Task 3.10- Watching a video
Access http://www.epa.gov/students/conserva.htm and then go to "Ozone Depletion" at http://www.epa. gov/ozone/science. Then enter "Forecast Earth" (http://www.epa.gov/ozone/science/movies/index.html), where you can play videos on environmental issues, and see a full written transcript. Watch one video and write a glossary of key words (include the pronunciation and definition or translation of the words). Now you can practise the pronunciation of the words in your glossary.
Only if you have time, summarize the video very briefly.

– Example of the 'Follow-up' and 'Glossary' sections:

4. FOLLOW-UP
By clicking on the following links you can visit more useful websites.
- http://www.enviro-aircontrol.com/whatis_frames.htm What is dehumidification?
- http://www.nrel.gov/desiccantcool/ Advanced Desiccant Cooling & Dehumidification Program.
- http://www.eren.doe.gov/femp/prodtech/desiccant.html Desiccant dehumidification technology.
- http://www.energy.wsu.edu/cfdocs/tg/10.htm The purpose of this Guide is to make available introductory information about desiccant technologies considered for application in Federal facilities.

- http://www.pnl.gov/fta/8_tdd.htm This Technology Alert report provides information and procedures that a Federal energy manager needs in evaluating the cost-effectiveness of a desiccant system.
- http://www.bryair.com/pdf/articles/deh/deh_paper.pdf Dehumidification report.
- http://www.dhtechno.com/DHTech_temporaryControl.html A dehumidification company website.

5. GLOSSARY

FACILITY:	a place planned or constructed for a specific activity.
TO TEST:	a means of measuring the quality or presence of something.
RUST:	the orange-red coating that forms on metal surfaces because of oxidation of the iron in their contents, by exposure to air and water.
MOISTURE:	a small amount of diffused or condensed liquid, esp. water, felt as vapour in the air or as dampness on surfaces. Humidity.
SUBTLE:	difficult to detect or define; elusive or ambiguous.
TO ACCELERATE:	to cause (a particular activity or process) to happen faster.
TO COOL:	to become cool or less warm.
RESIN:	a sticky organic substance secreted by fir trees and certain other plants and used mainly to make plastics, medicines, and varnishes.
TO STORE:	to accumulate and keep for future use.
YEAST:	any of the minute cells or froth of certain fungi used to ferment alcohol, make dough rise, or manufacture certain medicines.
FUNGUS:	any organism, including mushrooms, yeasts, moulds, rusts, and others, characterized by lack of chlorophyll and by subsistence on organic matter.

Language teachers use these exercises as practical activities to teach a second language, but they are also used by content teachers. These activities are done weekly in two-hour sessions. Students do the activities in groups of five and the answers are discussed in class or sent to the teacher in electronic format (e-mail; forum of the subject, etc.). The activities are online; therefore they are accessible to students who cannot attend the weekly classes. These units are a complement to traditional classes which are focused on learning a second language or a content subject with a textbook as teaching material.

Students should go to tutorials to evaluate the tasks and consequently, the content teacher or the language teacher can change the activities that are not appropriate for the objectives of the subject. This creates an atmosphere of equality and democracy in that teachers evaluate students and students evaluate teachers, which is consonant with collaborative learning.

The results of the evaluation process followed were positive. With reference to teacher evaluation, all the students concluded the semesters with high marks both from content teachers and from language teachers. With respect to peer evaluation, students evaluated the collaborative activities as highly motivating and some expressed that a peer model provided a more attainable standard of oral English than a native-speaker model. As regards self-evaluation, the collaborative selection, design and evaluation of material was encouraging for the content teacher, who adapted to the needs of the students and also practised a second language; for the language teacher, who could observe how the student awareness of a second language increased steadily; and also for the student, who enjoyed group activity and could study English and content subjects at the same time.

Concluding remarks

The benefits of using the CSCL and CLIL approaches in the elaboration of domain-specific units based on websites are diverse, as evidenced in the evaluations and in the tutorials with the students. First, there was full collaborative work among the content teacher, the language teacher and the students to choose and evaluate materials. There was also collaboration between content teachers and language teachers in the design, evaluation and correction of materials. Second, the activities were considered authentic by the students as the websites selected were designed by companies or government institutions; thus, students identified the activities with their future professions and their attitude towards the learning process was positive. Third, students had to use language for meaningful purposes and they improved their learning of both language and content as was evidenced in the evaluation processes. Fourth, the collaboration of content teachers, language teachers and students was enriching and enabled teachers and students to learn the opinions of all the members about the teaching-learning process, creating a friendly atmosphere in class. Finally, students did most of the work with at least one partner, therefore the activities also stimulated interpersonal and collaborative communication within the groups.

Furthermore, students' attitude towards the subjects is positive as they are involved in the process of material preparation. Students learn better when they are motivated and consider that they are learning an interesting or profitable topic. The collaboration of content teachers in the development of these materials was very important as they guided the language teachers in the topics and in the approach to the activities from the point of view of technical professionals and their communication needs.

It was also observed in this project that online material based on internet stimulated attendance at content and language classes. Students preferred to be guided in their learning process since the activities involved collaborative and content tasks that could be done more effectively with their classmates. The activities based on internet websites incorporated more flexibility and user-friendliness than the software courses that our students could use in the language laboratory. Students scanned texts, looked for the websites they were interested in, felt they used up-to-date materials and could interact with other students in the same classroom. They were involved in the design and evaluation process and, as a consequence, they considered themselves the creators of their own material which was personalised and adapted to their needs.

Internet is an enormous resource for language learning but we do not always take advantage of all the possibilities it has to offer. By adopting a more dynamic and flexible approach to the creation of teaching-learning materials and using recent developments in technology, we have been able to involve our students in the choice of materials, increase their motivation and, improve their learning of subject-matter content and language.

References

Adell, J. (2004). Tendencias en educación en la sociedad de las tecnologías de la información. Retrieved July 20, 2005, from http://nti.uji.es/jordi.

Baeza, P., Cabrera Carrasco, A. M., Castañeda Díaz, M. T., Garrido Miranda J. M., & Ortega Vargas, A. M. (1999). Aprendizaje colaborativo asistido por computador: La esencia interactiva. *Revista Digital de educación y nuevas tecnologías: Contexto educativo*, 2, 1–10.

Bailey, K. M., Dale, T., & Squire, B. (1992). Some reflections on collaborative language teaching. In D. Nunan (Ed.) *Collaborative language learning and teaching.* Cambridge: Cambridge University Press, 162–178.

Barros, B., Vélez, J., & Verdejo, F. (2004). Aplicaciones de la teoría de la actividad en el desarrollo de sistemas colaborativos de enseñanza y aprendizaje. Experiencias y resultados. *Inteligencia artificial*, 24, 67–76.

Burns, A. (1999). *Collaborative Action Research for English Language Teachers.* Cambridge: Cambridge University Press.

Butkiene, J., & Vilkanciene, L. (2005). Integrating content-based tasks into the language classroom. *ESP World*, 2 (4), 1–13.

Calzadilla, M. E. (2001). Aprendizaje colaborativo y tecnologías de la información y comunicación. *Revista Iberoamericana de Educación,* 39, 1–10.

Carrió Pastor, M. L. (2006). Definición y características del aprendizaje colaborativo asistido por ordenador. In M. L. Carrió (Ed.) *Aprendizaje colaborativo asistido por ordenador*. Valencia: Blauverd impressors, 9–35.

Carrió, M. L., Gimeno, A., Perry, D., & Seiz, R. (2006) *Online Activities for Engineering Purposes.* Valencia: Universidad Politécnica de Valencia.

Carrió Pastor, M. L. (2007). Internet as a tool to learn a second language in a technical environment. *European Journal of Engineering Education.* (forthcoming).

Carrió Pastor, M. L., & Gimeno Sanz, A. M. (2007) Content and Language Integrated Learning in a technical higher environment. In D. Marsh & D. Wolff (Eds.) *Diverse Contexts – Converging Goals.* Frankfurt: Peter Lang, 103–114.

Collentine, J., & Freed, B. F. (2004). Learning context and its effects on second language acquisition. *SSLA*, 26, 153–171.

Cortese, G., & Riley P. (Eds.). (2002). *Domain-specific English. Textual practices across communities and classrooms.* Berlin: Peter Lang.

Chen, P.-Ch. (2005). Effective implementing a collaborative task-based syllabus (CTBA) in EFL large-sized business English classes. *ESP World*, 2 (4), 1–10.

Darn, S. (2006). CLIL – A European Overview. Retrieved April 11, 2006 from www.teflturkey.com/iue.

Freeman, D. (1992). Collaboration: constructing shared understandings in a second language classroom. In D. Nunan (Ed.) *Collaborative Language Learning and Teaching.* Cambridge: Cambridge University Press, 56–80.

González Fernández, R. (2006). Las estrategias y técnicas didácticas en el rediseño. Retrieved January 15, 2006, from http://www.sistema.itsm.mx/va/dide/inf-doc/estrategias/colaborativo.html.

Gros, B. (1997). *Diseño y programas educativos. Pautas pedagógicas para la elaboración de software.* Barcelona: Ariel.

Kramsch, C. (1993). *Context and culture in language teaching.* Oxford: Oxford University

Liaw, M. (2006). E-learning and the development of intercultural competence. *Language Learning and Technology*, 10 (3), 49–64.

Marsh D., Maljers A., Hartiala A. (2001). *Profiling European CLIL Classrooms.* Jyvaskyla: University of Jyvaskyla. Retrieved July 15, 2007, from http://www.cec.jyu.fi/kasvatusjaopetus/clil/clilprofiling.

Martínez Carreras, M. A., Gómez Skarmeta A. F., Martínez Gracia, E., & Mora González, M. (2004). COLAB: A collaborative platform for simulations in virtual laboratories. *Inteligencia artificial,* 24, 45–53.

McCafferty, S. G., Jacobs, G. M., & DaSilva Iddings, A. C. (2006). *Cooperative Learning and Second Language Teaching.* Cambridge: Cambridge University Press.

Nunan, D. (Ed.). (1992). *Collaborative language learning and teaching.* Cambridge: Cambridge University Press.

Osuna Gómez, C., Rocha, L., Romero, M., Villa, L., Sheremetov, L., & Niño, O. (2004). Uso del modelo APRI para la evaluación de la intención en entornos de aprendizaje colaborativo. *Inteligencia artificial,* 24, 109–119.

Slaouti, D. (2002). The World Wide Web for academic purposes: old study skills for new? *English for Specific Purposes*, 21, 105–124.

Soetaert, R., & Bonamie, B. (2006). New rules for the language & content game. From CBLT/CALL to CLIL/TILL. Retrieved January 15, 2006 from www.euroclic.net/index.

Strijbos, J., Martens, R. L., & Jochems, W. M. G. (2004). Designing for interaction: Six steps to designing computer-supported group-based learning. *Computers & Education*, 42, 403–424.

Sturman, P. (1992). Team teaching: a case study from Japan. In D. Nunan (Ed.) *Collaborative Language Learning and Teaching.* Cambridge: Cambridge University Press, 141–161.

Tudge, D. (1994). *Vigotsky: la zona de desarrollo próximo y su colaboración en la práctica de aula.* Cambridge: Universidad de Cambridge.

Zañartu Correa, M. L. (2000). Aprendizaje colaborativo: una nueva forma de diálogo interpersonal en red. *Revista digital de educación y nuevas tecnologías. Contexto educativo*, 28, 1–9.

The URLs in this paper were valid at the time of writing the text, October 2007.

Appendix 1

Self-Evaluation Questionnaire

Answer the following questions. Put crosses.

Did you…	yes	mostly	so-so	not really	no
1. understand what to do?					
2. understand the texts?					
3. have enough time?					
4. like the tasks?					
5. manage to guess what new words meant?					
6. consider the topics related to your degree?					
7. collaborate with the teachers of the subjects?					
8. collaborate with your partners?					
9. consider difficult the activities?					

What have you learnt?

____

____

Mª CAMINO BUENO ALASTUEY

Using WebCT in a Course of English for Academic/Specific Purposes: The Case of *English for Agriculture*

Introduction

New technology has meant a great shift in language teaching in the last ten years. It offers opportunities to practise language in real contexts and situations that were previously unavailable to teachers of English in EFL environments. Thanks to the use of the Web, e-mail, chat rooms, newsgroups etc., students can use the language for specific, individualized and realistic purposes inside, and even outside, the classroom with the constant help of a remote tutor who can be contacted by e-mail, chat or video conference. The development of this new technology has contributed enormously to the authenticity of the experience of learning a language in EFL contexts, where previously it lacked such authenticity and, sometimes, even purpose.

Furthermore, this new technology has also been praised for its many advantages regarding the promotion of some of the main factors that have been identified as conducive to language learning such as motivation, exposure to authentic language in context and opportunities for meaningful language use and autonomous learning (Mishan, 2004). Researchers on language learning or CALL generally acknowledge the possibilities of new technology for language learning (Felix, 1998; Warschauer, 2000, 2001). Nevertheless, its integration in the curriculum is so arduous that it has often been used as a mere add-on and, consequently, some authors claim that new technology, especially the resources of the net, must be integrated into the English class "in an organized and comprehensive way in order to, pedagogically speaking, make the most of them" (Felix, 2000). Other researchers add that it is necessary to observe two criteria for the above-mentioned integration, organization (Leloup & Ponterio, 2001) and pedagogic relevancy (Sanz, 2003[1]).

Nowadays, Spanish Universities face the challenge of adapting to both the European Space for Higher Education and the labour market. The former demands student-centred methodologies, in which students' workloads and their learning evolution are considered. Therefore, it becomes necessary to individualise learning to cater for specific needs, styles of learning and different levels of knowledge which demand the acquisition of new tools "such as communication skills, the ability to work co-operatively in teams, problem-solving and critical-thinking skills – sometimes referred to as core or transferable skills" (Condie & Livingstone, 2007, p. 339) and greater emphasis on lifelong learning.

Both to develop student-centred methodologies with a greater emphasis in transferable skills and to promote language learning in places where English is only studied at school, using ICT in class is a must to transform the experience of learning a language into something purposeful and closer to real life tasks. In fact, research "suggests strongly that both the rate of learning and the ultimate attainment level do very much depend on the acquisition context" (Conacher, Taalas & Vogel, 2004, p. 14).

WebCT is a password-protected, course management system for teaching and learning that is being used in many universities all around the world and includes most new technology in the same space, "although most of the individual functions are less powerful than their counterparts available as separate tools" (Jager, 2004, p. 42). It is mainly used for distance learning; however, it can also be used as a supplement to face-to-face teaching. Despite the bulk of research on the use of new technology for language learning, there is an obvious lack of accounts exploring how to use this platform for language learning, and especially in Languages for Specific Purposes.

1 Quoted in Martínez et al., 2004.

In this paper, our aim is to provide such an account by exploring the possibilities of WebCT and the effect different organization, layouts and tools have in students and teachers. First, we will explain WebCT and its advantages for language learning. Then, we will describe the course *English for Agriculture* we offer, together with the tools used, the organization and the way this language course has been taught. Third, we will mention the advantages, disadvantages and attainments from the point of view of the teacher and then the same factors from the point of view of the students. Finally, we will draw some conclusions on how to use WebCT for teaching languages at the tertiary level.

1. WebCT and language learning

WebCT is the virtual platform used at the Public University of Navarre, which was the first Spanish university to introduce a virtual space for every subject taught. It has the enormous advantage that the majority of the tools used for language learning are or can be introduced in the same space.

In the same way as many virtual platforms, WebCT main components are:

- content sections, which can include links to audio and video material from the Web, practice and drill exercises, readings, and solutions;
- e-mail and discussion forums, which promote communication with the teacher and among students;
- assessment sections, which can contain self-evaluation tests, the final exam[2], assignments due dates and folders to collect work done, and even detailed records of students' visits and pages visited;
- a calendar, which can state all the activities to be done in class as well as the homework or assignments with their due date.

2 For an account of such exams, see Bueno, 2004.

The use of these features generates a more favourable context for language learning and contributes to the adaptation of courses to the new demands created by the European Space for Higher Education. Initially, it improves the four main factors conducive to language learning. Exposure to authentic material is possible because the content material is authentic and related to students' specialities. The transmission of information extracted from authentic material in WebCT, the authenticity of the tasks, and the oral exchanges with students of English from other countries offer opportunities for meaningful language use. Autonomous learning is additionally promoted as individual decisions about what to do and when have to be made. Motivation also increases due to the practical use of the foreign language and to the focus on individual needs and wants.

Secondly, WebCT fosters the development of new skills and lifelong learning and the promotion of autonomous learning without the presence of the lecturer. The progress of each student can also be followed more closely and grades depend not only on the final exam but on the work done and effort made, and thus the evaluation of processes becomes possible.

Furthermore, despite the high number of students per class and the variety of proficiency levels – two of the burdens of Spanish University education together with the fact that they share a common language – the use of the virtual platform allows individualised learning as pupils can work at their own pace, in their own tasks, and make decisions about their path of learning. The artificial nature of communication when the mother tongue is common vanishes as individuals are offered the opportunity to speak to students of English in other countries, and in pairs among themselves, using Skype (telephoning software to be used in the computer). Their speaking tasks can be recorded and listened to afterwards. Communication becomes purposeful because, in the first case, it is authentic. Language is used to communicate with people who cannot speak Spanish so the only language for the successful transmission of information is English. In the second case, a task can be fulfilled and part of the purpose of the communication is to be able to monitor and correct language, which is also an authentic task in itself.

Setting up WebCT is not an easy task. As many authors recognise, to maintain and manage a good learning site with good quality materials, links to other pages, updates, and to keep trace of students' work and demands in the form of contributions to the forums or e-mail is very time consuming (Nelson & Oliver, 1999; Rocklin, 2001).

2. WebCT in *English for Agriculture*

2.1. Teaching context

English for Agriculture is a compulsory course for undergraduates of Technical Agricultural Engineering, which is a three-year diploma divided into three specialties. The degree has common core courses, others that are specific for each speciality, and elective ones. English is a common core course in the third year of the degree. The number of students is very high, from 70 to 85, and they are together in a one-hour long class, called theory, and separated in groups of about thirty for another two hours, called practice[3].

The course's number of credits is 4,5 – equivalent to 45 hours of direct tuition – and its main objective is the development up to an upper-intermediate/advanced level of the four skills in the field of Agriculture and Academic English. The proficiency level of the students varies from pre-intermediate to proficiency, with the majority of them in the range of pre-intermediate to intermediate (in all the initial profi-

3 This time distribution will change with the introduction of the European Credit as it promotes new kinds of activities and arrangements such as seminars or collective tutorials. Up to now, credits were associated to direct tuition to all the group and the only possibility of dividing a group of less than a hundred students were practice hours.

ciency tests done in the last five years, nearly 70% of the class had scores at that level). Most of the pupils' contact with English has been very limited for about four or five years and, consequently, their entrance level[4] has dropped significantly.

At Spanish universities, there are three great obstacles to creating the appropriate context to promote language learning. The first is the high number of students per class; the second the different levels of proficiency in English so it is very difficult to create a common syllabus that responds to the needs of all the students (Pierce McMahon, 2004; Fortanet, Palmer, & Ruiz, 2005); thirdly, they all have the same mother tongue and communication is always more effective in their mother tongue so "students are not motivated to communicate, as the situation in the language classroom seems too artificial' (Conacher et al., 2004).

2.2. Course Development

In the context described above and knowing the possibilities offered by WebCT, we decided to use it in our classes and we started in the year 2003/2004). Then, changes were introduced in the following two years – second and third stage of the project – following some of the recommendations from end of course evaluation questionnaires.

Apart from the development of the four skills of reading, writing, listening and speaking, five further objectives were pursued trying to foster the new skills demanded from students by the labour market:

- the individualisation of learning through free choice of tasks depending on personal needs;
- the promotion of learning to learn through the search, selection and transmission of information;
- the improvement of computer skills through the use of the majority of the tools new technologies offer;

4 The level required for university entrance is higher-intermediate.

- the development of speaking skills through real oral use and practice;
- the advancement and support of autonomy, which is completely necessary for lifelong learning.

With all these objectives in mind, the sites – one for each speciality – were set in three stages over the period of three academic years.

Academic year 2003/2004

In the first stage of the project, our main page had four folders visible (see Fig. 1):

- the "calendar" stated the tasks and activities of each day,
- the "programme" introduced some content,
- the "e-mail" allowed communication,
- the "forum", which was not used.

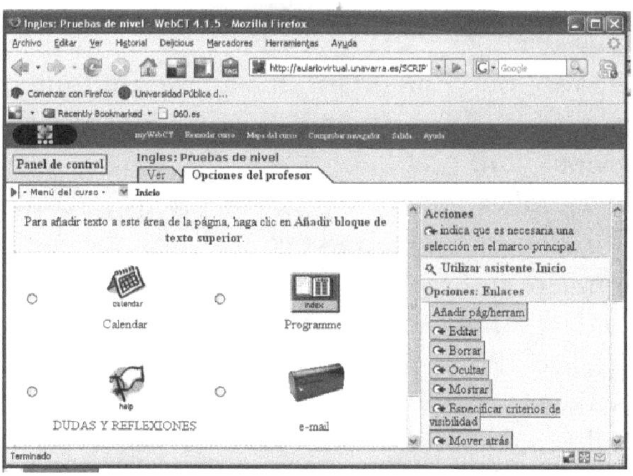

Fig. 1. Main page. Year 2003/2004.

There was a fifth folder – hidden – called "Evaluation", which included the final test and an end of course questionnaire.

The folder "Programme" was divided into two folders:

- "Introduction", which contained the objectives of the course, the syllabus, a daily planning and a grammar review;
- "Modules", which held six folders called "Units", which, in turn, had a grammar and a listening section. In the former, theoretical explanation pages and exercises were placed and, in the latter, two sound files – one based on a lecture and another on one aspect of academic life, such as following instructions for an exam, introduction to a library etc. – and exercises related to them.

The face-to-face classes were designed to include specific readings with comprehension questions and vocabulary expansion exercises, some speaking activities related to the grammar points dealt with in the units, and some pronunciation exercises.

Academic year 2004/2005

The following year, three important changes were introduced following the recommendations from an end of course questionnaire administered the previous year.

The first modification took place in the main page because the "Evaluation" folder was visible and two self-tests, the end of year evaluation questionnaire and the final exam – hidden – were included in it.

The second important adjustment was made in "Programme". Three new folders, called "Pronunciation", "Project" and "Vocabulary", were added to the already existing "Introduction" and "Modules". They included the following:

- "Pronunciation" containing material related to aspects of pronunciation and practice exercises, which were the phonetic transcriptions of some words related to their speciality that had to be correctly spelt[5].

5 All the words to be correctly spelt from the phonetic transcriptions were selected from Pan Sanchez, 1998, pp. 275–335.

- "Project" contained instructions to do a project and an oral presentation.
- "Vocabulary" included six subfolders called "Vocabulary 1", "Vocabulary 2" etc, and consisted of a selection of words from the readings.

The third significant improvement was the inclusion of new folders inside "Units" in "Modules". The previous year, only "Grammar" and "Listening" parts had been available and, in this phase of the project, three new sections were created inside each unit. "Reading" comprised links to authentic texts from the Web related to each speciality – two common and four different ones. "Speaking" contained activities or tasks to be done in pairs or in an exchange with Turkish students. And lastly, "Solutions" consisted of the solutions to the exercises. The former folders remained the same except for some pages of English grammar in Spanish that were added to "Grammar".

Academic year 2005/2006

In the last stage of this study, four new modifications were introduced.

The first change was the expansion of the main page (see Fig. 2) due to two factors: the relocation of the folders "Project" and "Course evaluation questionnaire" in it, and the creation of two new folders. The first, called "Assignments", included a list of all the assignments and their due date and a folder to post them directly. The second, called "Presentations", held instructions to do effective presentations, the evaluation criteria for the Power Point Presentations of the last day of class, and recordings of those presentations, their exchanges with some Turkish students and speaking tasks and activities done in class.

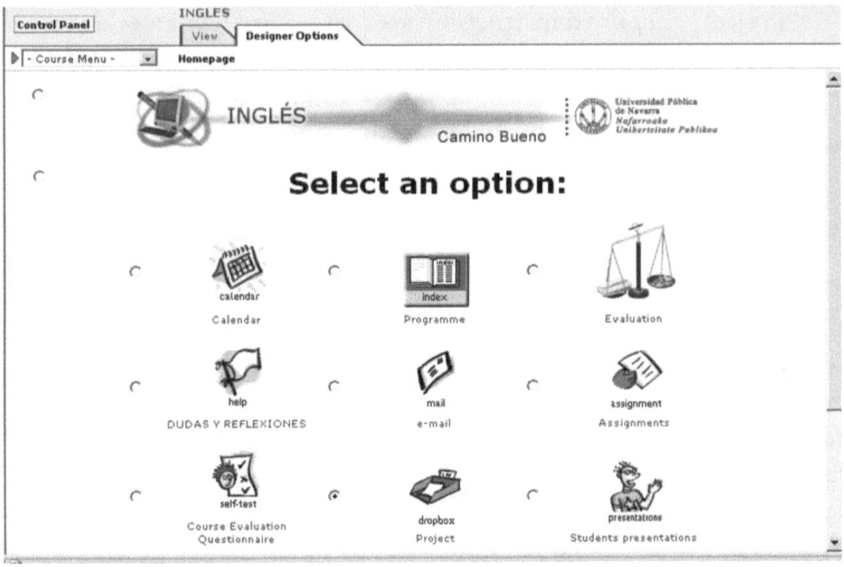

Figure 2. Main page 2005/2006.

The second change took place inside the folder "Calendar", which became a page of suggestions and included specifications of which skill should be worked at and the time to be devoted to it.

The third important improvement was the reorganization of all the material inside "Modules" and "Programme" into "skill" folders. Consequently, there were "Grammar", "Listening", "Reading", "Speaking", "Pronunciation", and "Vocabulary" sections and a new element called "Translation" was also added. Each of these components held all the material related to that skill from previous years.

Fourthly, the forum was divided into grammar doubts and reflection on learning. The first was used because the instructor redirected there all the questions about grammar done both in class and through e-mail. Consequently, students' use increased and at the end, both instructor and peers asked and answered lots of questions there. The second did not work so well because it was not given any class time and students found it hard to reflect on their own learning process. As it has been reported in other studies, reflection on language learning seems to be the hardest for students (Polisca, 2006).

2.3. The Classes

All the classes were held in a computer lab to use WebCT. At the university, two big labs with capacity for 50 and 56 students respectively, and around twenty smaller ones with a capacity varying from twenty to thirty computers are available.

The first year, the theory classes consisted of explanations of the main grammar points and exercises or tasks to practise them, followed by a problem-solving activity designed and directed by the teacher. However, this system was not very effective as students unable to follow the explanation in English and, consequently, the exercises or the problem-solving activity tended to talk and noise distracted people who wanted to work. The second year, students had to read the explanations beforehand and come to class with doubts. Even though this system was a bit more effective, we decided to introduce PowerPoint presentations in 2005/2006. The theory classes were held in the bigger labs and students were asked to see the PowerPoint Presentations included in the grammar section of WebCT beforehand. Further links to pages of theory and others with explanations in Spanish were also obtainable. In class, they chose exercises from the links provided in the corresponding section, which were graded from pre-intermediate to advanced. At the end of the class, the appropriate solution section was made visible. The role of the teacher in this hour was the role of facilitator or mentor, mainly encouraging lower level students and solving particular doubts.

The practice hours, which were two-hours long, were held in smaller labs and the groups were separated by speciality. The first year of the project, what to do in each class was decided by the teacher so students only had the choice of level or pace. The second year, more freedom was given as to what to do and in what order from specific material, and the students seemed more satisfied. The last year of the project, students selected what to do – from all WebCT and even from other sources – and at what level, and the only role of the teacher was to specify which skill had to be developed. One week, the two practice hours would be devoted to listening and vocabulary, and the following session to speaking and pronunciation. Both the readings and the translations were done out of class and only problematic parts or some sections were discussed in it.

With more material in WebCT, the choice broadened and a wider variety of tasks could be chosen from. The only condition was the practice of specific skills – at least at some point – to make sure work included an even quantity in all the skills. This last arrangement meant that more material should be available for selection. In our case, the amount of material was sufficient for choice, and the option of looking for more material if it best suited individual needs was also provided. Nevertheless, it should be mentioned that this apparently positive factor might mean an overload of work for some very responsible students who want to do everything.

2.4. Evaluation

The evaluation of the subject was based on an oral component from the recordings done in class and from a PowerPoint presentation in the last week making up 10% of the grade; a written project, another 10% of the grade; work done in class, which was controlled by the records kept on WebCT and by collecting some exercises from selected students in class, 15% of the grade; and a final exam, which included reading, listening, vocabulary, grammar and pronunciation, 65% of the grade. A proficiency test was also administered the first week of each course. The quantitative data analysis in the next section is based on the students' grades and the pre-test scores every year of the project (see Table 1 for the data).

An end of course questionnaire was also administered to analyse the students' reactions to some components of the course. The questionnaire consisted of eighteen items and included:

- eight rating questions related to the content of the course and to the use of WebCT. The former rated satisfaction level, learning, work done, relation between learning and work done, and learning and assistance to class. The latter ranked the usefulness, organization and ease of use[6] of WebCT,
- two yes/no questions about whether it was better to use or not to use WebCT, and whether the course fulfilled the needs of the students of that degree,
- four further questions asking students to state the three most necessary aspects: most useful for professional life, most difficult and best covered in the course,
- and four open-ended questions asking about the changes that could be introduced to improve WebCT, suggestions to ameliorate its organization, explanations of the way it fulfilled or not the needs of the students of their subject, and statements on what they would maintain and what they would change in WebCT.

The analysis of some of the data from the questionnaires and the changes introduced based on them will be discussed in the following sections.

3. Teacher's perceptions

3.1. Advantages

There are numerous advantages to using WebCT in *English for Agriculture.* First, it means more motivation because students choose what to do and when so their participation in the learning process is more active. This way of working promotes the individualization of learning

6 These factors have been identified as very important for the use of WebCT. If students find it useful, well-organized and ease to use, usage will increase and they will also show a better attitude towards it (Ngai et al., 2007).

as it suits individual levels, interests and styles of learning. It helps students to become autonomous, as they have to make their own decisions about their learning and the way they work. They also 'learn to learn' by exploring the different possibilities they have and become active decision-makers in their own process of learning. Furthermore, they discover many sites and ways to improve their skills on-line, which will help them continue their learning after they leave university and so support the process of lifelong learning. Moreover, it promotes the development of new competencies, above all digital competence, which is a highly valued skill in the labour market.

WebCT allows more speaking practice as students record their interactions with foreigners, with whom they have to communicate in English, and they also record their interactions among themselves. This gives all communication a purpose, as they can listen to themselves and their performances and review them. At the same time, it allows the teacher to control what they are doing, as one of the problems we had was their reluctance to do the speaking practice in English unless the teacher was next to them. With the recording of the speaking tasks and activities, they know the teacher can listen to all the interactions. The teacher also provides feedback on errors in some of the speaking practices. WebCT offers a safe environment to try out communication, as it is very similar to but less threatening than real face-to-face communication. It is also very positive for listening and grammar exercises, as students can work at their own pace and spend as long as they need in any task or exercise.

Another of the strengths of using WebCT is the easy marking of exams, which is automatically done by the computer and the records it keeps of students assignments, pages visited and work done so that summative and formative evaluation become easier and feasible with very high numbers of students per class. It also makes it possible for students unable to come to class to follow the course from other sites.

3.2. Disadvantages

The biggest disadvantage for teachers is the overload of work involved in setting up the site. In fact, the teachers could not introduce the material in one year and numerous changes were introduced every year because of students' statements in the end of course questionnaires. Setting up a site should be done step by step, as it has been done in other institutions (Frank & Barzilai, 2004).

Re-organizing a site using WebCT is also costly in terms of time and the course menu option does not have a clear structure either. At the same time, having the option of placing material in the site and adding to it every year may mean that there is too much material there and sometimes teachers underestimate the time involved in doing some tasks. Furthermore, very responsible students should be discouraged from trying to cover all the material that has been placed in WebCT as some of them feel insecure unless they have done so.

Even though WebCT provides a safer environment to practise and try out new language and like all ICT leads all students to produce more language than it is possible in a traditional classroom (Beauvois, 1992; Pinto, 1996; Von der Emde, Schneider & Kotter, 2001), it makes creating a community of learners more difficult. As our classes were held in a physical setting where we were together and students knew each other beforehand, the community was already created. However, the effect of isolation should not be underestimated. As teachers, we felt that we had to make an extra effort to create rapport in class and that it would have been very easy to leave students working on their own without interacting with them and that would have enhanced their feeling of isolation.

Students demand much more individual attention when they abandon their passive role as recipients of information and become active in the learning process. This can lead to two problems. First, too many students want the attention of the teacher for explanations and for guidance. The teacher cannot attend all the requirements at the same time so students have to wait, have to ask their peers or are left unattended because of lack of time. Consequently, they may feel there is lack of feedback, lack of attention or lack of interest in their learning process on the part of the teacher. At the same time, the fact that it is impossible for the teacher to attend all the demands may force students to trust their peers and to collaborate closely with them, which is a very positive outcome both as a learning tool and as a valuable skill in the labour market. As Dovey (2006, p. 396) affirms, collaboration implies "the collective leveraging of knowledge distributed among participants and technologies, a skill regarded as vital to the contemporary workplace". The second problem is to establish a balance between promoting their independence and thus their capacity to learn autonomously and their need for feedback and support. This is a problem that does not exist in the traditional class as students' role is just to listen, and there is usually very little interaction, and for students needing a lot of guidance and for analytic type learners this lack of attention at some point may influence their satisfaction with the course.

Technical problems are another important disadvantage. Teachers using WebCT should learn to cope with and admit technical problems and should try to become expert users, relax and always have an alternative activity at hand in case technology fails. To plan alternative activities is a must in this kind of blended learning class.

Lastly, a great disadvantage is the short time allotted to the course. On the one hand, some students resist this new way of working as they see it increases their responsibility and, furthermore, they do not feel as secure about what they will be asked in the exam. Forty-five hours is the minimum time it takes to make them start getting involved in the process of autonomous learning and then the course has finished. We have the feeling that many students never get the full potential out of it, and in fact, it has been reported that the best results in learner autonomy are achieved after the first year in blended courses with ICT (Polisca, 2006).

3.3. Attainment: data based on the students' grades and pre-test scores obtained in every year of the project.

Table 1. Mean and standard deviation in pre- and post-test.

	Pre-test		Post-test	
Year	Mean	SD	Mean	SD
2003/2004	4.09	0.65	5.6	0.53
2004/2005	4.5	0.92	6.26	1.15
2005/2006	4.02	1.09	6.30	0.97

Attainment in the course is satisfactory as can be seen in the mean scores obtained by students in the pre-test and the test. As is shown, their grades increased with the use of WebCT in these courses and the standard deviation seemed to be lower.

4. Students' perceptions

Prior to analysing students' perceptions of the course using WebCT, three factors should be borne in mind to place the students' opinions in context. First, English is a compulsory subject for students whose major is not languages so although some students like English and are motivated, many resent the fact that they are forced to pass a subject such as English. Second, an important part of the evaluation is a test and they feel very insecure about their performance in the test because they do not have a book or notes that, learnt by heart, will assure them a pass. Third, a different number of students answered the questionnaire each year: 65 in 2003/2004, 55 in 2004/2005 and 75 the following year.

4.1. Advantages

As perceived by the students the strengths of the platform are its usefulness, its organization and its ease of use (Table 2). It should be noted that organization of the platform increased its value of very good/excellent after the content section was organized by skills and more links were added to the main page. They also considered the relation between learning and assistance to class very positive. Therefore, even though the majority of the subject was based on a virtual platform and independent learning, this seems to suggest that students value the role of the teacher as facilitator and mentor and that both the teacher and the class are perceived as necessary. Another factor that could explain this positive perception is that the majority of work was done in pairs or in groups. This may indicate a high appreciation of this type of work.

Table 2. All values in percentages.

		Very badly/Badly	Correctly	Well/Very well
Organization of WebCT	2003/2004	15.2	50.1	34.7
	2004/2005	26.7	56.5	16.8
	2005/2006	10.2	42.3	47.5
		Very difficult/ Difficult	Not very difficult	Easy/very easy
Ease of use	2003/2004	38	20	42
	2004/2005	30.3	24.6	45.1
	2005/2006	19.6	21.5	58.9
		None/Little	Good	Very good/ Excellent
Usefulness of WebCT	2003/2004	40.6	45.5	13.9
	2004/2005	35.7	50.8	13.5
	2005/2006	20.3	52.7	27
Learning & assistance to class	2003/2004	8.4	71.3	19.3
	2004/2005	4.4	73.1	21.5
	2005/2006	16	58.2	34.9

Both the negative and the middle values for satisfaction with the course, learning and the relation of learning to time invested in the subject and use of WebCT increased, while the Very good/Excellent value decreased (Table 3). The four factors increase in negative value may be due to the increase in content in WebCT and the subsequent overload of work some students felt there was. Another possible explanation is that those students would feel safer in more controlled environments with more guidance and as close monitoring and guidance decreased their satisfaction levels also decreased. These two explanations are supported by the answers of students to the open ended questions.

Table 3. All values in percentages.

		None/Little	Good	Very good/ Excellent
Satisfaction with course	2003/2004	15.8	60.2	24
	2004/2005	18	65.4	16.6
	2005/2006	15.5	75	9.5
Learning	2003/2004	20.2	70	9.8
	2004/2005	14.1	69.6	16.3
	2005/2006	13.9	70.7	15.4
Learning & time	2003/2004	20	60.4	19.6
	2004/2005	8.7	65.3	21
	2005/2006	11.3	58.6	30.3
Learning & use of WebCT	2003/2004	37.3	48.1	14.6
	2004/2005	35.6	50.2	14.2
	2005/2006	27.8	59.7	12.5

Students also considered WebCT should be used so they were aware of the benefits this kind of platform can represent for language learning and autonomous learning and it should be noted that the value has increased over the years. As more teachers at the institution have started using WebCT, students have begun to appreciate its possibilities. However, they did not feel so positive about the fulfilment of the needs of the students of their subject. As we will see in the analysis of the open-ended questions, they did not provide general guidelines as to how to adapt to their needs better and in fact, it might be a matter of level of English and expectations, as we will discuss later.

Table 4. All values in percentages.

		No	Yes
Should WebCT be used	2003/2004	45.2	54.8
	2004/2005	40.6	59.4
	2005/2006	24.6	75.4
Fulfils the needs	2003/2004	54.6	45.4
	2004/2005	46.5	53.5
	2005/2006	38.4	61.6

From the open-ended questions in the end of course questionnaire, we can conclude the most useful aspects of the platform for students were the listenings, as the majority of the students considered the possibility of doing the listenings at their own pace to be the biggest benefit. They also considered the different levels in grammar and the possibility of doing the things they selected from the material in WebCT as very beneficial. Furthermore, most of them mentioned the recordings of the speaking activities and tasks, and the possibility of listening to themselves as a great improvement. Other parts of the course mentioned as improvements were the pronunciation practices and the possible improvement it induced. Students also stated the PowerPoint Presentations would be very useful for them in the future, and, moreover, being able to see their performance had contributed to the effectiveness of their presentation skills more than written advice.

4.2. Disadvantages

The biggest disadvantage students detected was the workload. As stated in the questionnaires, they perceived the amount of work to pass the subject a lot or too much (see table 5). This perception probably permeated their rankings in other areas, as the quantity of material and things to be done was perceived as overwhelming in some cases. Probably this is due to the students' misconception that to pass the subject everything on WebCT had to be done. Jager (2006, p. 45) also considered that "users may easily become overpowered, because of the vast range of options offered to them."

Table 5. All values in percentages.

		Very little/Little	Enough	A lot/Too much
Workload	2003/2004	10.3	50.3	49.4
	2004/2005	9.2	41.5	49.4
	2005/2006	0	20.2	79.8

The answers to the open ended questions in the questionnaire showed changes over the three stages of the project. In 2003/2004, students demanded more material in other areas apart from listening and grammar and self-tests to check their progress. As more material was introduced, in 2004/2005, the request was for a better organization of WebCT, a division of the material by skills and not modules, and more direct links in the homepage. They also asked for more self-tests and a clearer schedule of assignments together with a place to post them. In the year 2005/2006, students requested lower level listenings and more vocabulary work. As that year most of the readings had to be done outside class, we suspect their claim for more vocabulary was due to the fact that many of them had not done the reading component.

Two more disadvantages mentioned every year are their perception that they would work better on paper and, in fact, they print a lot of the material, and the fact that when working in the Web instead of using a book, distractions increase. Similar findings are reported in Chenoweth, Ushida & Murday (2006).

Some of the shortcomings stated by students are difficult to solve because of their relation with administrative or skills factors. The first factors considered are administrative decisions related to the curriculum such as the credits assigned to the subject, the level set and the compulsory character of the subject. The second is the claim for classes devoted to WebCT and computer tools usage. Having a folder in the Introduction folder with instructions has not solved these problems. Apparently, students with problems in WebCT usage are also not very skilful computer users. The fact that they also seem very dependent on teacher guidance, and consequently, do not try to look for solutions on their own aggravates the problem. Other studies such as Burguess (2003) confirm these problems.

Lastly, dependence on traditional modes of learning also appeared in some students' statements requiring only work on reading, translation, grammar and vocabulary sections, and English classes "as they have always been".

5. Conclusion

As a conclusion, we should give an answer to five questions:

a) Can WebCT contribute to language learning?
b) Can it contribute to the teaching of Languages for Specific Purposes at tertiary level?
c) Can it help to solve some of the problems of large classes at tertiary level?
d) Can it contribute to offering new methodologies for the European Common Space for Higher Education?
e) Can it contribute to the development of new skills demanded by the labour world?

After our effort and our teaching using WebCT for over three years, the answers to the previous questions should be positive. Our experience has shown us that using WebCT promotes motivation, as students have the choice of working on what interests them and in their preferred style of learning. It also increases the exposure to both authentic oral and written texts, and the tasks, and especially the exchange, provide meaningful language use. Deciding what to do, having different options and not being directed also increases autonomous learning, or at least, establishes good conditions for it.

As for the second and third questions, WebCT offers the opportunity of using specific language and of seeing how the professionals use language. Furthermore, it allows interaction with those professionals and so the purpose and the specificity of that language increases. It also solves the problem of individualised learning in big classes as students can work individually or in small groups on their own activities and tasks, and at their own pace and level, and that way the problem of different proficiency levels is overcome. Moreover, it permits the development of speaking skills and promotes more language production than would be possible in a traditional class or in group discussions. From the positive answers to these last two questions, it must be concluded that WebCT fulfils all the objectives pursued at the beginning of the project.

Regarding the fourth question, WebCT offers a learning space that caters for individual interests, different levels of knowledge and different styles of learning and gives practice in learning to learn. Moreover, it makes close monitoring of the work done by students possible and, consequently, it is very adequate for student-centred methodologies at tertiary level.

And lastly, WebCT promotes the improvement of computer skills, communication skills, problem-solving skills and co-operative working, as most of the work is done in pairs or in groups.

The fact that we found out that different organizations and the layout of WebCT greatly affected students' perceptions should not be ignored either, and therefore we would like to conclude with some advice about setting up our site in WebCT that we would have found valuable, in an effort to try to lessen what Von der Emde et al. (2001, p. 210) mentioned, "the enormous commitment of time required to develop and adopt new technologies, especially because return on that investment of time is often not immediate".

First, we would advise all teachers not to try to set a site in a year. They should start by using some components and add to them every year. Teachers should also try all the tools even if they think they may not work because sometimes there are surprising outcomes to trials. Teachers should be aware that the best way to set up WebCT is to include as many links in the main page as possible and that organizing it by skills is better than by modules. Self-tests are also necessary for students to check progress and to know what the final test will be like. Something else to bear in mind is that assignments and due dates should be clear and constant reminders are needed. An important aspect is to be able to foster students' autonomy, even though at the beginning some resistance is bound to appear. Conacher et al. (2004, p. 21) highlighted that "well-meaning efforts to transfer decision-making responsibilities from the teacher to the learner may equally well be interpreted by the learner as an abdication of responsibility on the part of the teacher". The role of the teacher also changes so teachers have to be able to let go of the control they normally have of their classes. It is usually very difficult to stop being the authority and the transmitter of knowledge in a class to become a facilitator, a mentor, and a helper in the process of learning. However, this change is necessary if autonomy is to be promoted.

Summing up, our experience has been a very positive one, even if we have found some disadvantages and we have felt that students were overwhelmed by their new role and by a lot of material. We think our project has been successful and we will continue introducing innovations into the site, and trying to meet our students' needs. We believe blended learning is the future "and even in a less structured form, this type of combination has the advantage that it allows conventional teaching to branch out in many different directions according to the learners' interests and learning styles, without this branching out implying the use of a haphazard flurry of materials and activities" (Conacher et al., 2004, p. 23).

References

Beauvois, M.H. (1992). Computer-assisted classroom discussion in the foreign language classroom: Conversation in slow motion. *Foreign Language Annals*, 25 (5), 455–464.

Bueno, M.C. (2004). Un examen de inglés para ingenierías técnicas informáticas en WebCT. In Sanz Sainz, I., & Felices Lago, A. (Eds.) *Current trends of languages for Specific Purposes in an International and Multicultural Context.* Granada: Universidad de Granada, 435–441.

Burgess, L.A. (2003). WebCT as an e-learning tool: A study of technology students' perceptions. *Journal of Technology Education, 15 (1)*, 6–15.

Chenoweth, N.A., Ushida, E., & Murday, K. (2006). Student Learning in Hybrid French and Spanish courses: An overview of language online. *CALICO Journal*, 24(1), 115–145.

Conacher, J.E., Taalas, P., & Vogel, T. (2004). New language learning and teaching environments: How does ICT fit in?. In Chambers, A., Conacher, J.E., & Littlemore, J. (Eds.). *ICT and Language Learning: Integrating Pedagogy and Practice.* Birmingham: University of Birmingham, 9–33.

Condie, R., & Livingston, K. (2007). Blending online learning with traditional approaches: changing practices. *British Journal of Educational Technology*, 8 (2), 337–348.

Dovey, T. (2006). What purposes, specifically? Re-thinking purposes and specificity in the context of the new 'vocationalism'. *English for Specific Purposes*, 25 (4), 387–402.

Felix, U. (1998). *Virtual Language Learning: Finding the Gems among the Pebbles.* Melbourne: Language Australia.

Felix, U. (2000). Learning on the Web – who does it, why and how? Paper presented as poster as part of the History of CALL exhibition at CALICO and EUROCALL 2000. Retrieved May 1, 2007 from http://users.monash.edu.au/~ufelix/lote.htm.

Fortanet, I., Palmer, J.C., & Ruiz, M.F. (2005). De general a específico: Carencias comunicativas orales detectadas por el profesorado de lengua inglesa. In Hernández, E., & Sierra, L. (Eds.). *Lenguas para Fines Específicos (VIII). Investigación y Enseñanza.* Alcalá de Henares: Universidad de Alcalá, 63–75.

Frank, M., & Barzilai, A. (2004). Designing course web sites for supporting lecture-based courses in higher education – some pedagogical aspects. *International Journal of Instructional Technology and Distance Learning*, 1(12), 37–50.

Jager, S. (2004). Learning management systems for language learning. In A. Chambers, Conacher, J.E., & Littlemore, J. (Eds.). *ICT and Language Learning: Integrating Pedagogy and Practice.* Birmingham: University of Birmingham, 33–47.

Leloup, J.W., & Ponterio, R. (2001). On the Net. Sites for Soar(ing) Eyes. *Language Learning and Technology* 5/1. Retreived May 14, 2007 from http://llt.msu.edu/vol5num1/onthenet/default.html.

Martínez, A., Bellés, B., & Ruiz, N. (2004). Using an Internet Resource Guide in the ESP classroom: A comparison of pair and individual work with students of Computer Science. In I. Sanz Sainz & A. Felices Lago (Eds.). *Current trends of languages for Specific Purposes in an International and Multicultural Context*. Granada: Universidad de Granada.
Mishan, F. (2004). A task-based approach to Webauthoring for learning. In A. Chambers, J.E. Conacher & J. Littlemore (Eds.). *ICT and Language Learning: Integrating Pedagogy and Practice*. Birmingham: University of Birmingham, 121–143.
Nelson, T., & Oliver, W. (1999). Murder on the Internet. *CALICO*, 17(1), 101–114.
Ngai, E.W.T., Poon, J.K.L., & Chan, Y.H.C. (2007). Empirical examination of the adoption of WebCT using TAM. *Computers and Education*, 48, 250–267.
Pan Sanchez, R.M. (1988). *Glosario de Terminos Técnicos Agrícolas/Glossary of Technical Agricultural Terms Spanish-English, English-Spanish*. Pamplona, Spain: Gobierno de Navarra.
Pierce McMahon, J. (2004). Why join ICT into the ESP curriculum at the tertiary level in Spain?. In I. Sanz Sainz & A. Felices Lago (Eds.). *Current trends of languages for Specific Purposes in an International and Multicultural Context*. Granada: Universidad de Granada.
Pinto, D. (1996). What does "schMOOze" mean? Non-native speaker interaction on the Internet. In M. Warschauer (Ed.). *Telecollaboration in foreign language learning. Proceedings of the Hawai'i Symposium*. Honolulu: University of Hawai'i Second Language Teaching and Curriculum Centre, 165–184.
Polisca, E. (2006). Facilitating the learning process: An evaluation of the use and benefits of a Virtual Learning Environment (VLE) – enhanced Independent Language-learning program (ILLP). *CALICO Journal*, 23 (3), 499–515.
Rocklin, T. (2001). Do I dare? Is it prudent? *National Teaching and Learning Forum Newsletter*, 10(3).
Von der Emde, S., Schneider, J., & Kotter, M. (2001). Technically speaking: Transforming language learning through Virtual Learning Environments (MOOs). *The Modern Language Journal*, 85 (2), 210–225.
Warschauer, M. (2000). The changing global economy and the future of English teaching. *TESOL Quarterly*, 34 (3), 511–535.
Warschauer, M. (2001). The death of cyberspace and the rebirth of CALL. *CALL in the 21st Century*. IATEFL CD-ROM.

Antonella Elia

Can a Collaborative *Wiki Weblish Dictionary* Project Help Academic Writing of ICT Language Learners?

1. Introduction

Nowadays many language teachers have enthusiastically embraced the world of collaborative opportunities that the Internet has offered. First Web generation of synchronous and asynchronous tools, such as e-mail, forum and chat are, by now, familiar to many teachers and they continue to be fundamental media for classroom exchanges.

Recent innovations, belonging to the second Web generation, such as blogs, wikis and VoiP may be less familiar but they are rapidly proliferating as they offer powerful opportunities for online collaboration to teachers and learners. This is due to the e-learning 2.0 which aims to utilise the spontaneous and informal learning approach potential in daily situations. As Bonaiuti claims (2006, p. 42), "the history of the Internet can be interpreted as the success of non conventional forms of collaborative learning characterized by ideals of freedom and spontaneity".

The use of online interaction has become more widespread in formal academic situations. As numerous students participate in electronic discourse, the Faculty of Languages at L'Orientale in Naples is trying to develop linguistic awareness and competence among the students of English and a proper use of linguistic registers in different communicative contexts.

The workshop which will be presented in the following sections is part of a Humanities Computing course. Its main purpose is to improve motivation and ICT language awareness, by familiarizing learners with the current Internet trends expressed in the Weblish, the unconventional language used online by netsurfers. Weblish, also referred to as Netlingo or NetSpeak Jargon, is characterized by the use of an informal spoken-written register, where inattention to the spelling and grammatical rules, the use of all-lowercase letters, infrequent punctuation, the widespread employment of abbreviations, acronyms and emoticons, are just some of its new distinctive trends.

Students of our faculty are considered frequent netsurfers. The language centre of our University offers them the opportunity to communicate freely in English with other foreign students using the equipment in the self-access area. Exploiting the previous (chat, email, mailing lists) and the new social technology offered by the Web 2.0, the linguistic goal which we aim to reach is to stimulate language learners to be in contact through e-tandem exchange programs with other foreign students in order to practice their written and oral language skills. Nevertheless, our students are rigorously trained in proper writing techniques and academic conventions in traditional English classes.

This paper is focused on the following research questions: if students get accustomed to using Weblish, is there any danger that some of its slangy aspects will creep into their academic writing? Will this be a hindrance in the development of the academic English writing skills of our students? Will they have difficulties in identifying and using formal and informal registers properly?

This paper will provide an overview on common Wiki features explaining, first of all, how it works. The socioconstructivist pedagogy which it embraces will be illustrated and, after having shown the basic principles which identify it as a collaborative community of practice, some ideas and activities which can be used in an e-learning setting will be provided (section 2). Weblish, a new variety of ICT language, and its origins will be presented; its word formation process and the use of new spelling techniques will be explained. Does Weblish represent a threat for learner's academic English writing skills or can awareness reduce the danger that its informal features 'creep' into it? All these aspects will be discussed in section 3.

Wiki Weblish Dictionary, an experimental workshop held at our University, will be presented in section 4. An explanation will be provided as to how collaborative commitment to the wiki project can positively affect students' metalinguistic awareness and language learning process. In addition, how the *Wiki Dictionary* has spurred students' active research role on the Web while carrying out assigned tasks will be explained. Conclusions will be presented in the final section.

2. What is a Wiki?

Wiki is an online environment which is naturally suited for collaborative projects. Whereas blogs can be highly personal, wikis are intensely communal. Once an exclusive domain for 'open source' software enthusiasts, nowadays many teachers are making wikis the central agora of their courses, as they promote a more casual and flexible form of class discussion than blogs and forums (Read, 2005).

The *WikiWikiWeb*[1], founded by Ward Cunningham, appeared on the 25th of March 1995 on the Web, two years before the birth of the first blog. Cunningham also invented the software name based on the Hawaiian term *wiki wiki*, meaning 'quick'. Moreover, he was the author of the *the Wiki Way* (2001) the first book dedicated to the subject.

Wikipedia[2], a multilingual web-based free-content encyclopedia, written collaboratively by volunteers, was launched in January 2001 by Larry Sanger and Jimmy Wales. It is, at present, the largest wiki project in the world with approximately 7.9 million articles in 253 languages, 1.91 million of which are in the English edition.

1 *WikiWikiWeb* http://c2.com/cgi/wiki.
2 *Wikipedia* http://www.wikipedia.org.

Since the beginning of this new millennium, the use of *Peer to Peer* (P2P) technology has spread rapidly. Pros and cons offered by wiki technology are synthetically outlined in the table below (fig. 1).

PROS	CONS
• Open source free and easy to use	• Minimalist page
• Open editing environment	• Lack of control on content organization
• Excellent tool for co-authoring projects	• Lack of accountability on the information offered
• Hypertextual architecture with data-based pages	• Lack of a fixed format
• Free and not prestructured content organization	• Vandalism
• Informal and spontaneous communication tool	• Spamming
• Plain text storage	• Effect of confusion for the high number of hypertextual links amon pages

Fig. 1. Wikis: Pros and Cons.

A characteristic of wiki software is the ease with which pages can be created and updated. Most wikis are open to the general public without registration. Nevertheless, private wiki servers can sometimes be protected requiring user authentication through login and password in order to be safeguarded against malicious behaviour (page deletion, vandalism and spamming).

While for years the standard was the *Wiki Markup Language*, original syntax of the *WikiWikiWeb*, currently the formatting instructions vary considerably. Simple wikis allow only basic text formatting, whereas more complex ones have support for tables, images, formulas, or even interactive elements.

Some wikis, such as Wikipedia, do not require the user to know wiki syntax, as they provide a *WYSIWYG*[3] editing, that translates graphi-

3 *WYSIWYG* (pronounced 'wizzy-wig' or 'wissy-wig') is an acronym for *What You See Is What You Get*. The term is used in computing to describe the likeness between the appearance of edited content and final product.

cally entered formatting instructions (such as bold and italics), into the corresponding html tags. Wiki software can be downloaded free of charge on the Internet. The reason for this is that the wiki code is available under the *GNU*[4] General Public Licence, so the code is freely available to be reviewed and adjusted by developers. Most wikis, which offer by default a search engine, are a true hypertext medium with non-linear navigational structure. This is made possible by *WikiLinks* which connect different wikipages. Links across different wiki communities are possible using a special link pattern called *InterWiki*. New wiki pages are usually constructed by simply creating the appropriate links on a topically related page. A link opens an 'edit' window, which allows users to enter the text for a new page. This simple editing mechanism generally ensures a high level of connectedness.

Wikis have two different writing modes. The first one is known as *document mode*. When used in document mode, contributors create collaborative documents by adding their contributions to the wiki document. Multiple authors can edit and update the content of the document and gradually the content becomes a representation of shared knowledge or beliefs of the contributors (Cunningham & Leuf, 2001).

The second writing mode is *thread mode*. Each document has an associated *discussion page*[5] where contributors carry out discussions by posting signed messages. Others reply to the original message and so a group of threaded messages evolves *(ibid.)*. It is a sort of virtual agora which assures the accuracy of the information to be found in the main document, thanks to the unanimous approval of the content by the participants in the discussion.

4 *GNU* is a license created by the *Free Software Foundation*. The purpose of the GPL is to grant any user the right to copy, modify and redistribute programs and source code from developers that have chosen to license their work under the GPL.

5 A *discussion page* (or *talk page*) is used in wiki collaboration to talk about ways to improve the content of an official wiki page. Each wiki page has a corresponding discussion page. They are intimately related, forming a combined whole, although for technical reasons they are stored in the web server's database as separate table rows.

2.1 Wikis and socio-constructivist pedagogy

While there has been a boom in interest in e-learning in the last decade, current e-learning systems are mainly focused on content delivery. E-learning systems anchored in the behaviourist tradition are making interesting progress on modularity and standardization of content in learning objects, but they are not seeking to improve pedagogies by supporting rich socio-constructivist scenarios (Schneider et al., 2002).

A high number of online courses are set up as *Instructional Management System* (IMS) or *Web Course tool* (WebCT). They do not support the creation and recreation of content so much as they reproduce traditional classroom interactions and roles. Even though socio-constructivist pedagogy is very effective in education, there is a lack of widely used supporting tools, even if the new educational scenarios of Web 2.0 e-learning can support, at very reasonable costs, online communities of practice.

A typical constructivist approach, based on Vygotsky (1962), is structured in the following phases: *Look* (discovery), *Discuss* (interaction), *Do* (production), *Deposit* (sharing) and *Feedback* (discussion of results). Since then, the importance of the 'project' idea is fundamental and reconfirmed in the most recent virtual socio-constructivist scenarios.

A Wiki-based learning environment is a promising host for constructivism, whereby learning is a search for meaning; therefore, learning must start with the issues around which students have to construct meaning actively. Meaning requires understanding wholes as well as parts and parts must be understood in the context of wholes. Therefore, the learning process has to focus on interrelated concepts, not isolated facts, since education is inherently interdisciplinary. The purpose of constructivist learning is for an individual to construct his or her own meaning, not just memorizing the right answers and repeating someone else's theories.

Wikis do not provide IMS but free environment that might generate more satisfactory teaching and learning. The structure of wikis grows from within, shaped by people working with content.

2.2 Wiki as Community of Practice

Wiki provides an excellent collaborative environment, since it represents a perfect model to build *Communities of Practice* (CoP). Communities of Practice are based on the assumptions that learning is fundamentally a social phenomenon as people organize their learning around the communities which they belong to.

Wenger (1998, pp. 55–64), defining the concept of practice, which is the basic issue of his theory on community, uses three fundamental concepts: *negotiation* of meaning, *participation* and *reification*. *Negotiation* refers to the process of dynamic construction of meaning which does not exist autonomously, but is the result of a continuous interaction with the world. *Participation* is the belonging to social communities and the involvement in social projects. *Reification* refers to the process which shapes our experiences producing objects which concretize each experience in what he defines as *thingness*.

The process of learning and membership, also in wiki communities, is indivisible because learning is intertwined with community membership. Knowledge is inseparable from practice and, using Wenger's terms, they are translated in a process of *negotiation, participation* and *reification*. Since it is not possible to know without doing, as by doing we learn, the ability to contribute to a community creates the most powerful learning environment.

Many claim that any *Content Management System* (CMS) offers the possibility to operate in a simpler, more effective and more secure way than any other e-learning 2.0 environment. While CMS continues to be widely employed, wikis have just started to be experimentally used as new and flexible online learning settings also in Italy. Although their teaching and learning applications are not yet very well-known in our country, the specific peculiarities of these e-learning 2.0 environments are already producing their positive effects in online language teaching.

2.3 Some wiki-learning activities

As Wiki is social in nature and is an open editing website, it is an excellent webtool which supports learner centred collaborative activities and is widely used for language learning purposes. It enables learners to share authority and empower themselves with the responsibility of building on their initial and basic knowledge. In particular, wiki, as e-learning 2.0 setting, can be used to (Augar et al., 2004):

- improve student writing skills;
- exchange ideas with classmates;
- encourage students to constantly revise their work, instead of turning in a paper and forgetting it forever;
- produce documents that reflect the shared knowledge of the learning group;
- enable the interwiki exchange of ideas and facilitate group interaction;
- facilitate the distribution and classification of information (e.g. dictionaries, encyclopaedias, etc.).

A precious source of information is *The Georgia Tech Wiki,* known as *CoWeb* (or *Swiki*)[6]. It is a catalogue of very innovative and useful learning activities developed by teachers.

The catalogue is split into three sections, corresponding to the potential uses in class: *Distributed Information* (where teachers and students share information, and the *CoWeb's* role is to ease the collection and distribution of that information); *Collaborative Artefact Creation* (where students work to create an artefact, e.g. a collaborative paper, and the *CoWeb* is used to gather the pieces, assemble or coordinate the work); *Discussion and Review* (where the *CoWeb* serves as a place to review papers, ideas, designs and critique/discuss them).

Beyond the well-known Wikipedia project edited in 253 different languages (http://www.wikipedia.org), the *21st-century Teaching and*

6 *A catalog of CoWeb uses* (2000) Collaborative Software Lab. College of Computing Georgia Tech http://guzdial.cc.gatech.edu/squeakers/coweb-catalog.pdf.

Learning Project, built around a wiki (http://www.tamucc.edu/wiki/TFCTL/HomePage) at Texas A&M University is worth mentioning. Dan Craig's website (http://danielcraig.wikispaces.com) is also a very interesting educational wiki; it is dedicated to CALL (Computer Assisted Language Learning) topics. Among the numerous wiki projects on the Web the *EduTech Wiki* (http://edutechwiki.unige.ch/en/Language_learning) also deserves our attention. It is a wiki which is dedicated to Educational Technology, built at TECFA (http://tecfa.unige.ch/), an educational research and teaching unit at University of Geneva.

3. Weblish: A new variety of ICT language

Digital writing style has been affected by the electronic channel since the use of the keyboard implies a mediated and slower form of communication compared to face to face communication as well as the restricted available space delimited by the monitor width.

Nowadays, the number of net surfers is exponentially growing. They interact online, by the use of a spoken-written language, the Weblish, which is one of the most creative domains of contemporary English. What makes Weblish so interesting as a form of communication is the way it relies on characteristics belonging both to speech and writing. This dynamic language reflects the rapid development of new concepts and the birth of "high-speed" communicative needs. Teenagers, the most frequent users of instant messaging and other forms of simultaneous online communication, have been the chief proponents and users of this emerging style. Tracking this development is an interesting way of linguistically documenting the progression of the ICT language which is evolving on a national and international level. Like most jargon, internet slang aggrandizes authors and readers, causing them to appear to have specialized knowledge of a complex medium. As Mcluhan (1964) said more than forty years ago the "medium is the message", hence also the Internet, as a global and interactive medium affects our linguistic production.

Today all mass media, especially the Internet, have an important role in creating and establishing neologisms. Coinage of new words is strictly connected with innovations in society. It tends to occur more often in cultures which are rapidly changing and which can ensure easy and fast propagation of information. A large number of neologisms have emerged in the ICT domain. Net programmers and hackers have coined new words for their new world, as they need to invent novel ways to say old things, as well as ways to say new things that do not yet have adequate references. Online discourse has broken the conventional linguistic code, creating and altering the traditional language in use.

The Weblish currently spoken by net surfers on the Web has its origins in the technological vocabulary once used only by computer programmers and hackers. Thus, the matrix of Weblish can be found in the hackers' *Jargon File*[7]. It is a collection of slang terms used by various subcultures of computer hackers for fun, social communication, and technical debate.

Hackers, as a rule, love wordplay and are very conscious and inventive in their use of language. Linguistic inventions and coinage of neologisms in most subcultures of Western countries are largely an unconscious process. Hackers, in contrast, regard slang formation and use as a game to be played for conscious pleasure. Their inventions display an almost unique combination of language-play enjoyment with an educated and powerful intelligence. Electronic media adapted well to the dissemination of this new slang. The results of this process give perhaps a uniquely intense and accelerated view of a linguistic evolution in action. It is written in a page of the *Jargon File*[8] website:

7 The *Jargon File* is a glossary of hacker slang. Originally, *Jargon File* was a collection of hacker slang used only by IT experts of technical cultures such as the MIT AI Lab, the Stanford AI Lab (SAIL), and others of the old ARPANET communities.

8 *Jargon File*, version 4.4.7 http://catb.org/esr/jargon.

> It is usually claimed that low-context communication (characterized by exactness, clarity, and completeness of self-contained utterances) is typical in cultures which value logic, objectivity, individualism, and competition; by contrast, high-context communication (emotive, elliptical, heavily coded, nuance-filled, multi-modal) is associated with cultures which value subjectivity, consensus, cooperation, and tradition. ICT linguistic domain is themed around extremely low-context interaction with computers and exhibits primarily "low-context" values, but on the other hand, it cultivates an almost absurdly high-context slang style.

Thus, *Jargon File* challenges the traditional linguistic and anthropological assumptions, being a miscellaneous of "low-context" versus "high-context" language and culture (Hall, 1976).

3.1 Linguistic features of Weblish

The Weblish dictionary workshop, which will be presented in the next section, is a project part of a Humanities Computing course held in our faculty of languages. It has been delivered in a blended formula. The informative pre-workshop session has been held in class, while collaborative dictionary tasks were carried out by students in the university computer lab or through remote connections.

The general aim of the pre-workshop session was to "indoctrinate" students in Weblish linguistic features. In this way, language learners acquired a theoretical framework to refer to during their collaborative work.

Weblish distinctiveness certainly lies in its lexicon where many word processes take place, including several ludic innovations. The majority of linguists classify Weblish as dynamic jargon. Linguistically, the most interesting feature is its morphology. Scholars have developed a taxonomy for classifying different types of word formation (Adams, 1973; Bauer, 1983; Crystal, 1995). The volume of new words coming into Weblish through the construction of a specialized dictionary is an opportunity to see their classifications in action.

Composites	• Prefixes • Suffixes • Compoudings
Shortenings	• Acronyms • Initialisms • Clippings
Blendings	
Shifts	• Functional shifts • Semantic shifts
Loans	
New Creations	

Fig. 2. Word formation process.

During the workshop, to explore the most common new word-formation processes in the Weblish, Algeo's (1999) categories have been considered as the main point of reference (fig. 2–3). His theoretical framework has spurred both awareness and linguistic reflection.

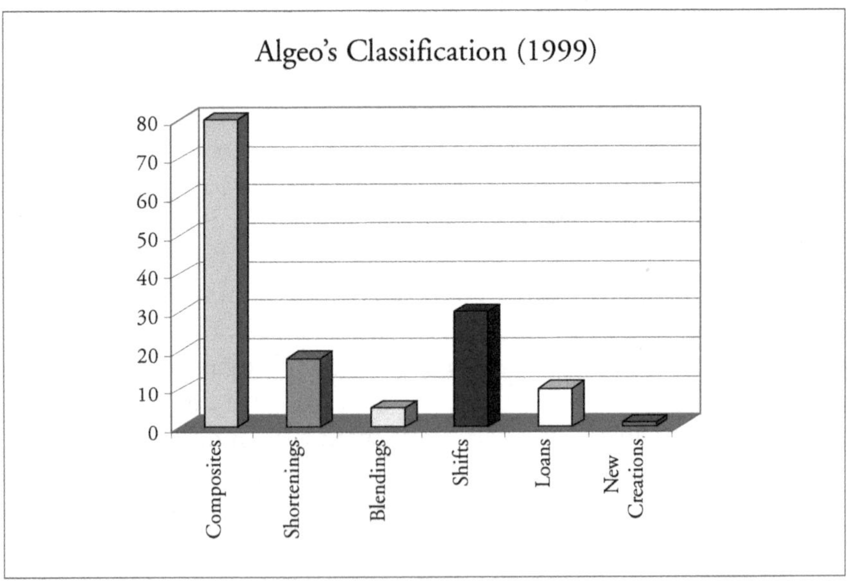

Fig. 3. Algeos's word formation classification.

With reference to Algeo's classification, Weblish has revealed that a recurrent word-formation process is the use of composites and particularly of affixation (prefixes).

Typical Weblish prefixes which have been found by students in ICT lexicon are: *cyber* -(cyberculture, cybercrime, cyberstyle), *e-* (e-learning, email, e-commerce, e-cash), *techno-* (technophobia, technostress, technobabble), *tera-* (terabyte), *giga-* (gigahertz), *mega-* (megahertz), *multi-* (mltimedia), *nano-* (nanotechnology), *micro-* (microcomputer), *hyper-* (hyperlink), *inter-* (Internet), *anti-* (anti-virus-software), *auto-* (automated), etc. Typical examples of suffixes which have been found in Weblish are: *-ware* (software, hardware, shareware, freeware), and *-ize* (computerize). Another popular Weblish formation process is compounding, e.g. *egosurf* (ego + surf), *hotlink* (hot + link), *laptop* (lap + top), *screensaver* (screen + saver), etc.

Shortenings are also commonly used in Weblish. Full forms of the words are rarely found. Emails, chats, forums, blogs and wikis are riddled with shortenings. As David Crystal states (2001, p. 85) "to use an abbreviated form is to be *in the know* part of the social group to which the abbreviation belongs". Shortenings, very recurrent in Weblish, are made up of acronyms, initialisms and clippings. Acronyms are pronounced as a single word; they are usually written in lower case letters, are governed by phonological rules, and tend to have a vowel in the middle of consonant clusters: e.g. *FAQ* (Frequently Asked Question), *MUD* (Multi-User-Dungeon), and *URL* (Uniform Resource Locator) are some of the most frequent *TLAs* (Three Letter Acronyms) found by students on the Web. On the other hand, initialisms, usually written in capital letters, have sometimes a full stop between letters and each of them is pronounced (e.g. *XML, TLA, IT, CD, DVD, HTML, LAN,* etc.). Initialisms make up a large part of Weblish jargon. They are not restricted to words, but can also imply clauses, e.g. *WDYS* (what did you say?), *CIO* (check it out), *RDM* (read the manual), etc. A moderate use of acronyms and initialisms is generally recommended; otherwise, the message could be incomprehensible to *newbies* (web or computer beginners). The use of clippings is also typical of Weblish, e.g. *net* (network), *com* (commercial), *admin* (administrator), etc. Weblish also makes a remarkable use of blendings e.g. *emoticon* (emotion+icon), *netiquette* (net+etiquette), *netizen* (net+citizen), *blog* (web+log), etc.

Semantic shifts are also noteworthy. Many words used in net jargon are taken from regular English and then applied to new ideas or protocols. Thus, to *surf* (to move around the Internet), *icon* (small picture on computer screen), *bug* (computer or program error), *flame* (an insulting or unfriendly email) are nouns and verbs which already exist in English but have assumed new connotations. Functional shift is another frequent linguistic phenomenon observed in the Weblish. It consists of changes in grammatical classes. Thus, words can carry out new functions in speech; nouns are turned into adjectives, verbs into nouns, nouns into verbs, etc. Some examples are provided below (fig. 4).

(noun) backspace	(verb) to backspace	(to wait, to hold on)
(noun) 404 error	(adj.) 404	(unavailable, not around)
(noun) geek	(verb) to geek	(to talk technically)
(noun) Google	(verb) to google	(to search the Internet using the Google Search engine)

Fig. 4. Examples of Functional Shifts.

Loans are also very common in Weblish. Many English terms are universally used on the net. The words *Internet* and *cyberspace* are used all around the world.

Furthermore, it is not unusual to find new creations on the Web. Some examples of neologisms are shown below (fig. 5).

teenagers	screenagers	(younger generation of mouse potatoes)
verbiage	webbiage	(excessive use of web tools and design)
nanosecond	ohnosecond	(a minuscule fraction of time in which an important file is deleted)

Fig. 5. Examples of New Creations.

During the pre-workshop session, students have also been informed of the distinctive graphology of Weblish which sometimes unconsciously creeps into their standard written English. All orthographic features have been affected. For example, the status of capitalization varies greatly on the Web. There is a strong tendency to use lowercase everywhere on the net (e.g. i want) (Elia, 2006). The 'lower-case default mentality' means that any use of capitalization is a marked form of communication. Using *all-caps* is a way Net users have found to bring voice to their written communication. Messages wholly in capitals are considered to be 'shouting' and usually avoided. Emotional expressions make use of varying number of vowels and consonants (yayyyyyyy) and repeated interjections (Yes!!!!, WHAT????). However, punctuation sometimes tends to be minimalist or completely absent; a lot depends on the user's personality (Elia, 2006).

An example of Weblish creativity is the use of emoticons. They are found sprinkled throughout electronic communication to denote feelings such as happiness, or to express sarcasm or humour. Most Net users consider them as a part of their vocabulary, even if they do not fall into traditional grammatical rules.

In conclusion, it is believed that teaching students ICT word formation processes and the new linguistic practices on the Web, can help them in spurring their metalinguistic reflection, in correctly carrying out their project tasks and, finally, in developing a conscious use of Weblish in suitable contexts.

3.2 Is Weblish a danger for Academic writing?

An interesting study (Valenza, 2003) has demonstrated that 70% of teenagers use instant messaging (IM) or chat, 83% of 18–19 year old use IM (instant messaging and chat), and 56% of 18–19 year old prefer the Internet to the telephone. Younger generations are undoubtedly familiar and comfortable with the use of Weblish.

Krohn (2004) shows that e-mail recipients who are *traditionalists* (born before 1946) and Baby *Boomers* (those born between 1946 and

1964) do not send e-mails with emoticons. *Generation Xers* (those born between 1964 and 1980) may send e-mails with some of the most common emoticons, while *Millenials* (born after 1980) make a generous use of them in their online communication.

Does Weblish degrade or enrich the English language? Points of view vary. Boyd (2005) reports that a speaker at the "Language on the Internet" symposium declared that "this rapidly, spreading digital dialect of English is doing more good than harm". Moreover, according to Peterson (1999) Weblish fosters creativity and one's own style. On the other hand, critics claim that Weblish, ignoring English grammar rules, has a negative effect on the quality of formal linguistic production. North (2003) finds that text is an example of a "uniquely human ability to adapt language according to the interdependent variables of a given situation (context, activity, relation to communicators)." On the other hand, Rovner (2003, p. 28) asserts that "once proper language is learned, it is not unlearned." He claims that it is essential to become familiar with Weblish because even if we do not actively use it in CMC, our potential interlocutors may, thus it is necessary to understand what they want to communicate.

There has always been a certain resistance to language change in our culture, especially among educated people, who regard any deviation from the standard as "unnecessary sloppiness, laziness or ignorance". Aitchison (1991) suggests that for modern speakers of English, linguistic conservatism is due to our descent from the 18th-century purist view that Latin is inherently superior, and as such we should shun any further "decay" in our own language trying to make it as close as possible to Latin.

What is the effect of Weblish on the students of English of our faculty? If students are so fluent with it, can some of its slangy aspects infiltrate and influence the proper development of their academic writing skills? Will students have difficulties in identifying formal and informal registers? The purpose of the *Weblish Dictionary* project, which will be presented in the next section, tries to avoid all the above mentioned negative effects.

4. *Wiki Weblish Dictionary* Project

In traditional English lexicography, individual dictionary editors have had ultimate control over the selection, meaning, and illustration of words and extensive collaboration with contributors is limited. Web 2.0 technologies have easily permitted exchanges between a user and a database allowing the birth of a new type of dictionary online: one that is built by the collaboration of contributing end-users, engaging users who are not trained lexicographers in the actual editing of dictionary entries.

Besides the renowned *Wiktionary* (http://www.wiktionary.org/), a multilingual, Web-based project to create a free content dictionary, available in over 150 languages and run by the Wikimedia Foundation, another well-known example is the *UrbanDictionary* (http://www.urbandictionary.com/), a popular online slang dictionary. It is one of the best cases showing how traditional lexicographic principles are joined with Web communication technologies providing a context for collaborative engagement and meaning making. *UrbanDictionary* shares many features and functions with traditional printed dictionaries. Moreover, it captures what most traditional English dictionaries fail to, as it records ephemeral everyday spoken language and represents popular views of meaning.

By relying on the language users to select and define words for a dictionary, *UrbanDictionary* has more than one million words and it has had a fundamental effect in influencing both access to and formulation of the lexis. Inspired by the *Wiktionary* and *UrbanDictionary* model, but with an explicit and additional language educational purpose in mind, the project which will be presented in this section has the following specific goals:

- familiarize the students with the new Internet linguistic trends which follow new rules and conventions;
- develop student awareness in a proper contextual use of Weblish and empower their competence in the use of different registers and varieties of English;

- expand their virtual lexicon knowledge and the proper use of trendy Weblish while favouring the rules and traditions which must be the main point of reference in their academic writing;
- improve their motivation in studying and learning a foreign language through authentic and online searching activities;
- familiarize them with the use of wiki software and with the new co-authoring opportunities offered by Web 2.0;
- stimulate their active and participatory commitment through a collaborative construction of an experimental dictionary project.

The experimental *Wiki Weblish Dictionary Project,* which lasts 25 hours, has involved 30 students of English in their second year at university. It is part of a Humanities Computing course. The main purpose of the workshop has been the compilation of a comprehensive guide to Weblish built collaboratively by students on a wiki (http://www.wikispace.org). The *Wiki Weblish Dictionary* is made up of an "A to Z" listing of Internet and CMC entries, with a dictionary style treatment of its terminology complete with definitions, contemporary usages and Italian translations.

The *Wiki Weblish Dictionary* is an evolving online reference work containing an alphabetical list of words and expressions not generally acceptable in formal and academic contexts.

Definitions are completely and collaboratively written online by students. Thus, the dictionary is completely based on their contributions.

Access to the wiki is not free. The wiki space admission has been protected to avoid the participation of external users and to track learner commitment. Like Wikipedia, and other open source environments, the *Weblish Dictionary* is a never ending work in progress, thus, dictionary entries can always be changed and subjected to further refinement.

The informative pre-workshop session, where the teacher has had a central pedagogical role (see section 3.1), has been limited in this second phase only to group organization and coordination. The teacher has to silently check individual and collaborative student work and is authorized to intervene only in case of conflicts to arbitrate *flame*[9] and *edit wars*[10]. Students are organized into 5 groups made up of 6 members each. In order to create a sense of responsibility within their independent work groups, a supervisor has been selected by the members of each group to coordinate the peer to peer work.

During the pre-workshop session students were informed that each member had to edit at least 20 new entries. Thus, the 26 letters of the alphabet were divided among the 5 groups (each group was responsible for a range of 5/6 letters: A–E; F–G; K–Q; P–T; U–Z). Further subdivision of the group work was allowed, but it was autonomously decided and coordinated by each group supervisor.

As already stated, the teacher's organization of group work was essential in guaranteeing a successful start-up of collaborative work and, moreover, in assessing student individual commitment, which has been tracked through the *page history*[11] (fig. 6).

Nevertheless, once the group work has taken off, class interaction has been free and student collaborative exchanges have found a natural and independent balance.

Students *googling* the Web and consulting the numerous available English websites (e.g. *Netlingo Dictionary*, *Urban Dictionary*, *Internet slang dictionary*, *online technical glossaries*, etc.) have implemented the number and improved the quality of the bilingual dictionary entries.

The mechanism of consensus is fundamental in any wiki environment, whatever its specific purpose. Student interaction in discussion pages has been very intense and sometimes extremely passionate, but collaborative work has been prevailing, as politeness and respect of

9 *Flaming* is the hostile and insulting interaction between Internet users.

10 An *edit war* is when two or more contributors repeatedly revert one another's edits to an entry. For *revert* is meant any change to an entry that partially or completely goes back to any older version.

11 All wiki editable pages have an associated *page history*, which lists all changes made to the page in reverse-chronological order.

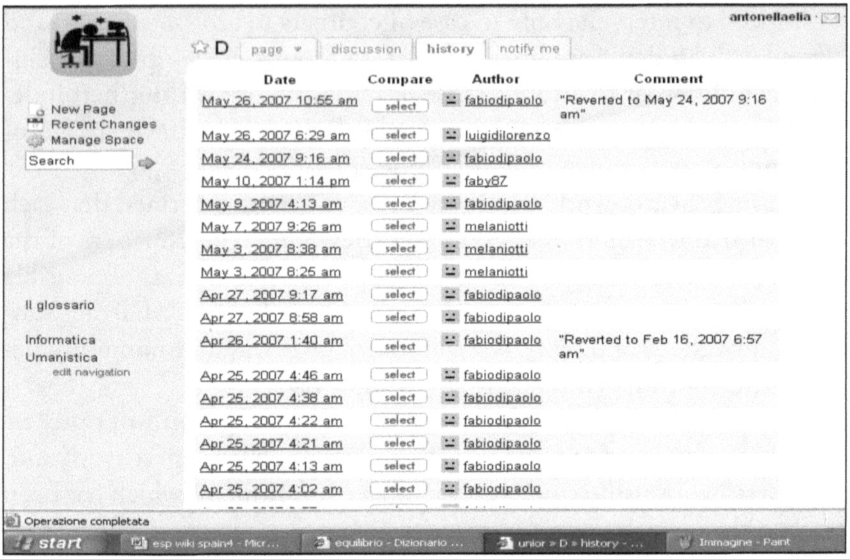

Fig. 6. Example of a Page History.

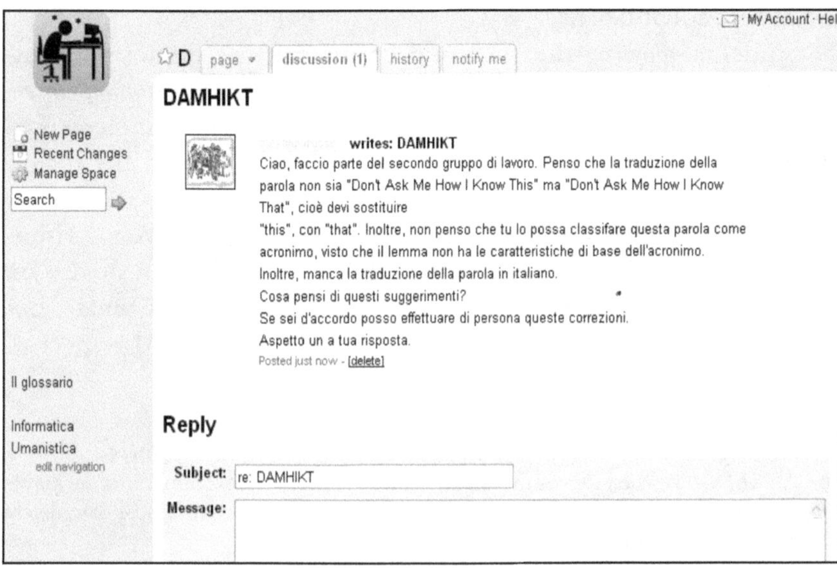

Fig. 7. Example of a Discussion Page.

Wikiquette [12] conventions was generally observed. It has helped them to work harmoniously with their classmates. Thus, basic rules were followed (such as *assume good faith, avoid deletions whenever possible, edit, discuss, be polite, sign and date posts to talk pages but not entries, work towards agreement, do not ignore questions*, etc.).

Treating others with respect is the key to an effective collaborative work also in the specific case of a coauthored dictionary. An example of a discussion post is shown (fig. 7).

Newly submitted entries immediately appear on the site. Collaborative work allows a peer to peer assessment which identifies new added entries as "well done" or not.

Thus, in case of controversial submission, when students do not agree on content, translation or explanation of given terms, entries can be modified and improved only after a general consensus has been reached in the associated discussion page.

During the dictionary compilation, students have to follow the *Editing Guidelines* which have been previously published by the teacher in a dedicated wiki page. New terms had to be grouped and classified by students in one of the following three categories.

Slang	Informal language from mainstream English or non-technical subcultures (bikers, rockfans, surfers, etc.)
Jargon	Without qualifier, denotes informal 'slangy' language peculiar to or predominantly on the web
Techspeak	The formal technical vocabulary of programming, computer science, electronics, and other fields connected to technology

Fig. 8. Weblish categories.

12 The word *Wikiquette* comes from *Etiquette*. It is a neologism, the contraction of 'wiki+etiquette'. It expresses the conventions of politeness and the informal rules which have to be followed. These rules are slightly different in the variety of online communities (newsgroups, web forums, chat, blogs and wikis). The term implies civic responsibility and participation. In case of participation, the best thing to do is to *'lurk'* before writing (to familiarize oneself with the local conventions) and to read the *FAQ* (Frequently Asked Questions).

The jargon/techspeak distinction is a very delicate operation. Generally speaking, any term that communicates primarily by a denotation well established in textbooks, technical dictionaries, or standard documents is considered techspeak. Nevertheless, a lot of techspeak words originated as jargon, and later migrated into techspeak. At the same time, a lot of jargon expressions come from overgeneralization of techspeak terms.

When students edit a new dictionary entry, they should have the following structure in mind, which includes (fig. 9):

• Term	(in alphabetical order)
• Category	(Slang, Weblish Jargon, Techspeak)
• Italian translation	
• Explanation	(meaning of the word has to be provided)
• Word function in speech	(noun, verb, adjective, clause, etc.)
• Type of word formation	(compounding, blending, acronym, initialism, etc.)
• Context of use	(an example where the word is used in context)

Fig. 9. Structure of a dictionary entry.

Example of an entry is shown (fig. 10) below.

Term	EAK (Eating at Keyboard)
Category	Weblish Jargon
Italian Translation	"Sto mangiando alla tastiera"
Explanation	E' un acronimo utilizzato nelle chat, nelle email e nei forum. Si impiega per comunicare al proprio interlocutore che si sta mangiando mentre si è impegnati al computer
Word function in speech	Clause
Type of word formation	Acronym
Context of use	Sorry for my delayed response, I'm EAK!!!

Fig. 10. Example of a dictionary entry.

At the end of the workshop, Weblish dictionary counted exactly 997 entries. This means that students have enthusiastically added twice as many entries as the compulsory minimum required (in total, there should have been only 500 entries).

The Bilingual (English/Italian) *Wiki Weblish Dictionary*, as already stated, is a project in progress, a linguistic and social experiment, which does not claim to be authoritative or balanced. The first dictionary edition was produced in the academic year 2006–7. It will undergo new editing, expansion and a qualitative improvement in workshops which will be held in future academic years.

It is hoped that it will become a valuable web source in the future not only for students of English and Humanities Computing at our university but also for those interested in looking for information on Internet language.

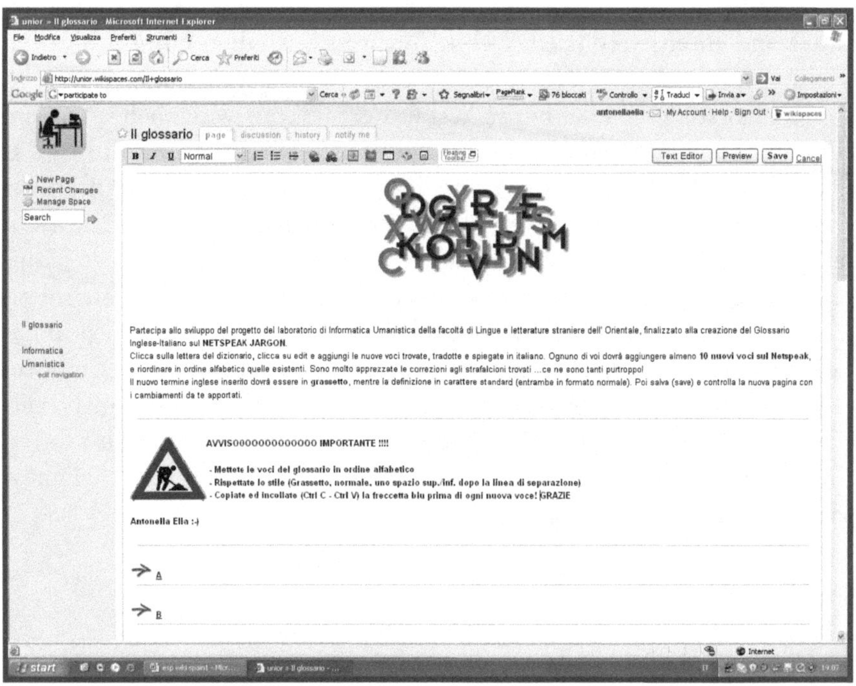

Fig. 11. Weblish dictionary homepage.

4.1 Preliminary results on the effects of Weblish Dictionary

At the conclusion of the workshop a questionnaire was submitted to the students of Humanities Computing. An initial brain storming and warm up session held at the beginning of the workshop revealed that our university students are very familiar with Weblish linguistic conventions, but sometimes have problems in distinguishing between formal and informal registers when writing in academic English. At the end of the workshop, students were asked to fill in the questionnaire (fig. 12). An analysis of their answers revealed that 15 out of 30 students regularly use the Internet for more than 5 hours per day (5 students – 4 hours, 6 students – 3 hours, 3 students – 2 hours and only 1 students – 1 hour per day). Only 5 students claimed that they always and intensively used Weblish expressions when communicating online.

Italian students mainly use Weblish expressions with their e-tandem English language partners and foreign friends in online communities as its use is considered very trendy. Eight students (out of 30) often use Weblish, but not always; 7 students occasionally, and 10 do not use it at all. Although most of our students frequently surf the net (since 20 students out of 30 are online at least 5 hours per day) and are members of international online communities where Weblish is a popular jargon, 70% of them do not think that netlingo and CMC (Computer Mediated Communication) can affect their academic writing. Nevertheless, 10 students out of 30 replied that their teacher of English found informal and colloquial traces and Weblish expressions in their academic writing (reports, compositions, summaries, etc.).

1. How much time do you spend online everyday? (searching, chatting, blogging, participating in forums, wikis, etc.)?
   ☐ more than 5 h. ☐ 5 h. ☐ 4 h. ☐ 3 h. ☐ 2 h. ☐ 1 h.
2. Do you use Weblish expressions when you communicate online?
   ☐ always ☐ very often ☐ occasionally ☐ never
3. Do you think "virtual CMC" can affect your academic writing in English?
   ☐ yes ☐ no
4. Does your language teacher find informal expressions in your academic writing?
   ☐ yes ☐ sometimes ☐ never
5. After the workshop, did you find any difficulty in distinguishing between the different types of written registers required in different situations?
   ☐ yes ☐ no
6. Do you think that your active and collaborative participation in the Weblish dictionary project has improved your linguistic awareness of different registers and their use in proper context?
   ☐ yes ☐ no

Fig. 12. Questionnaire.

Eighty percent of the students claimed that, after the workshop, they had improved their skills in recognizing the proper register to use in different contexts of communication (e.g. when they chat informally online with friends, when they write more formal emails to professors requesting information, or when they write an academic report). The same percentage of students claim that their active and collaborative participation to the *Weblish Dictionary* project has consistently improved their linguistic awareness of different registers and lexicon and syntactical structures to avoid in academic writing. This indicates that, with or without a consistent exposure to Weblish, most of the students have no difficulty in differentiating Weblish from academic and formal writing. Students participating in the workshop have developed a new linguistic awareness which has led them to an automatic code switching in the proper use of online/offline, formal/informal registers to use in different communicative contexts.

5. Conclusion

A proper training, maturity and use of co-authoring writing tools, such as wiki, can lead to an active comprehension of different registers and can develop a higher sensitivity towards proper code switching in writing. Based on the preliminary results of the questionnaire submitted, it may be claimed that while many students frequently use Weblish in CMC, they are generally reluctant to alter their offline writing style in order to conform to the new online linguistic style. Furthermore, they are able to use proper registers in different contexts.

Wiki, used in this educational project, has offered new and challenging opportunities as it has promoted a socio-constructivist scenario in a linguistic and technological learning project. At the end of the workshop students have demonstrated new metalinguistic awareness and expertise in distinguishing the appropriate register to use in online chatting or formal composition, thus considerably avoiding the danger of using online lingo in academic writing.

The use of wiki has offered a chance to maintain the Internet spirit in education, which is threatened by the philosophy of e-learning systems which promote very expensive, closed and proprietary platforms. Wiki has been a precious environment in developing the *Weblish Dictionary* project. Thanks to the workshop, students have been active participants and protagonists of their culture, collaboratively building their own technical knowledge and linguistic competence.

Their collaborative work has allowed the construction of an "A to Z" listing of the Weblish lexicon, made up of almost 1000 entries. The terminology has had a dictionary style treatment complete with definitions, contemporary usages and Italian translations.

To conclude, the results of a first survey, made through a conclusive questionnaire submitted to the students at the end of the workshop, has shown that learner collaborative commitment to the construction of the *Wiki Dictionary*, has developed a dynamic understanding of Weblish and a conscious usage of it. Moreover, it appears that the active research role of students in the workshop has positively affected their language competence. This will probably reduce the danger that they will become so fluent in Weblish that some of its "slangy" aspects will have a negative effect on their standard and academic English writing.

If language awareness is actively cultivated today and in the future, the widespread popular dystopic mythology that accuses the Internet and Weblish of being the main causes of the disappearance of Standard English will probably be a remote and unachievable scenario for the new born digital generation as well.

References

Adams, V. (1973). *An Introduction to Modern English Wordformation*. London: Longman.

Algeo, J. (1999). *Cambridge History of English language*. Cambridge: Cambridge University Press.

Atchison, J. (1991). *Language change: progress or decay?* Cambridge: University Press.

Augar, N., Raitman, R., & Zhou, W. (2004). Teaching and learning online with wikis. In R. Atkinson, C. McBeath, D. Jonas-Dwyer, & R. Phillips (Eds.), *Beyond the comfort zone: Proceedings of the 21st ASCILITE Conference*, 95–104. Perth, 5–8 December.

Bauer, L. (1983) *English Wordformation*. Cambridge: Cambridge University Press.

Boyd, R. (22 March 2005). 'Netspeak' doing more good to English language, experts say. In *Knight Ridder/Tribune News Service*. Retrieved 2 November, 2005, from Lexis Nexis Academic database.

Bonaiuti, G. (Ed.) (2006). *E-learning 2.0: il futuro dell'apprendimento in rete tra formale e informale*. Trento: Erickson.

Crystal, D. (1995). *The Cambridge Encyclopedia of English Language*. Cambridge: Cambridge University Press.

Crystal, D. (2001). *Language and the Internet*. Cambridge: Cambridge University Press.

Cunningham, W., Leuf, B. (2001). *The Wiki Way, Collaboration and Sharing on the Internet*. London: Longman.

Elia, A. (2006). An analysis of Wikipedia digital writing. In *Proceedings EACL Conference*, 11th Conference of the European Chapter of the Association for Computational Linguistics, 16–21. Trento.

Hall, E. (1976). *Beyond Culture.* New York: Doubleday.
Krohn, F. B. (2004). A generational approach to using emoticons as nonverbal communication. *Journal of Technical Writing and Communication,* 34/4, 321–328.
Peterson, A. M. (1999). 'Net-speak': Language in evolution. *Community College Week,* 11/13, 24–25. Retrieved May 19, 2007 from Academic Search Premier Database.
Read, B. (15 July 2005). *Romantic Poetry Meets 21st-Century Technology, With wikis, the new Web tool, everybody's an editor and a critic,* Retrieved 20 May 2007, from http://chronicle.com/free/v51/i45/45a03501.htm.
Rovner, A. J. (2005). *Chat reference and chat speak.* Master's thesis, University of North Carolina at Chapel Hill, 2005). Retrieved 28 October, 2006, from http://hdl.handle.net/1901/175.
Schneider, A., Synteta P., & Frété C. (2002). Community, Content and Collaboration Management Systems in Education: A new chance for socio-constructivist scenarios? In *Proceedings of the 3rd Congress on Information and Communication Technologies in Education,* Rhodes, TECFA, University of Geneva.
Valenza, J. K. (2003). IMing means never having to say you're not there. *Voice of Youth Advocates,* 26/4. Retrieved May 19, 2006, from Wilson Select Plus Database.
Vygotsky, L. S. (1962). *Thought and Language.* Cambridge: MA, MIT Press.
Wenger, E. (1998). *Communities of practice: learning, meaning, and identity.* Cambridge: Cambridge University Press.

The URLs in this paper were valid at the time of the last revision, June 19, 2008.

Philippa Mungra

Online Delivery of a Writing Course: Description of a Blended Language Course Integrated into Medicine

1. Introduction

In the past 15 years, computer-assisted language-learning (CALL) and teaching has burgeoned worldwide, mainly because of improved access to better and more available instructional tools using information technology (henceforth IT). Although the pedagogical gains have been mixed (Salaberry, 2001), the decision to create an on-line course for the final years of English at Rome University Medical School was considered an attractive option, given that students have a large number of clinical hours to complete for internship and thus find it difficult to attend regular language classes. This decision was based on a series of considerations, such as widely-diffused student access to the World-Wide-Web, widely differing levels of prior language competence, time constraints for formal lessons and lack of staff for mentoring language activity (Reinders, 2007). Although the structuring of an on-line course for medical students was a daunting proposition, three factors of implementation were given relevance: student autonomy, integration with subject teaching and time-flexibility for students. This paper describes the structure of the resulting course and discusses some of the factors taken into account in deciding which objectives would be reachable and which elements of the language course should be prioritized.

Teaching at a tertiary level such as in a Medical school requires, among other things, careful attention to integrate content in an ESP course into existing syllabuses in order to achieve what Chambers &

Bax (2006, p. 465) call "normalisation", defined as "a state where computers are fully integrated into pedagogy". Integration with other subjects taught in the degree course is fundamental, but an explicit methodology is still the subject of much debate. One such approach, which we adopted, is the team-teaching methodology course used by Finkel, Brown, Gerber, & Supino (2003) for teaching and testing critical discourse skills of Evidence-Based[1] Medicine (EBM) research publications. In their paper, the student body consisted of native speakers of English, but such a teaching methodology for language in medicine has not, to the best of our knowledge, been applied to speakers of other languages. Besides this, we were interested in seeing whether critical discourse skills could be activated in the production of written professional English among native Italian speakers.

Effective pedagogy requires that learning be carried out in the most stimulating environment and that it builds on prior knowledge and is integrated with other elements of the degree course (Van de Poel, 2004), so we decided to focus our attention on the skill of writing rather than other linguistic competences in an on-line course of academic written English for our students in the 5th year of Medicine. One reason for our selecting writing is that, "through features such as reference to prior research, technical lexis and familiarity with particular argument forms, writers work to establish a coherent context and enrich propositional meanings" (Hyland 2002, p. 7–8).

In an ethnomethodological evaluation of three modules of writing, Warschauer (2002) identifies three models of teaching writing: firstly, a formalist model, rooted in grammar and textually constructed, secondly a process model, in which internal reflection on thoughts and ideas predominate and finally, a social constructionist model of teaching writ-

1 Evidence-Based Medicine or EBM is a school of thought, first enunciated in Canada, which advocates searching the medical literature for the best methodological proof of procedures in order to improve patient care. It also advocates a methodologically strict procedure in the design of a research project. In reading, such methodological procedures are placed in a checklist to determine how valid the study was in both its design and its execution.

ing. In this final model, the author defines the teaching approach as a collaborative apprenticeship, tutorship and the creation of a professional *persona,* especially among young academics (Hyon & Chen, 2004*).* Each of these three approaches has its strong and weak points, but we propose that it is possible and perhaps even necessary, to use all three models at different stages of a language course to achieve maximum language competence in a professional setting. The structure of our language course aims at both integration with other subjects and at the same time flexible use of the three models of teaching writing in an academic setting.

In this paper, we describe a model for an on-line course spread over five years. The preliminary years of language learning, which we will call the pre-course in years 1–4, are described in section 2 and use mainly a formalistic approach with some elements of process pedagogy. This pre-course consists of a series of short modules of lexico-grammar building and reading-skills language teaching and may be considered the process build-up to the more social-constructionist on-line course of the 5th year.

Three exercises from the modules of the on-line course of the 5th year are then described in section 3 to illustrate the social constructionist approach of genre pedagogy, as proposed by Bhatia(1999), Swales & Feak (2004) and Hyland (2002).

2. Description of the modules of the pre-course

Pedagogy in these pre-course modules used task-based activities, except for beginner students in the first year of medicine, who were given an intensive course of lexico-grammar using a formalist approach.

One problem that we observed in prior years is the absence of IT skills in large swathes of the undergraduate medical students. For this reason, we decided that the build-up to the on-line course should include several exercises involving the use of the computer, in order to familiarise

Task

1. Examine the following website: **The HON code for** evaluating health websites at http://www.hon.ch/HONcode/Conduct.html. Compare and contrast the web sites of 2 companies in terrns of the HON code: (Table + 8 sentences of conclusion for your portfolio)

   Frame of reference
   In your write-up on the HON code, identify the 8 guiding principles of this code and evaluate the any two 2 pharmaceutical company sites for their use of the HON code: eg: Allergan vs. AstraZeneca. or AstraZeneca vs AstraZeneca Italia

2. A friend/cousin has been offered a position to be an assistant-photographer for a prestigious magazine, a job that involves travel to several Third World countries. He turns to you for advice about travel in the Congo on safari, to Bolivia Brazil and Peru in South America as well as Bangkok in SE Asia. He knows that he will be travelling to remote areas for the photographic service.

Where would you find information about health risks, vaccination, prophylaxis and other advice to give?

Choose a world area/country and prepare a set of guidelines to give your cousin.

Student writing (vaccination option)

Last month my cousins asked me information about eventual vaccination advised or obligatory to go to Chile. So I try to help him and I have carried out of the searches. From these searches that I have carried out on pub med and on the website of the Ministry of Health, I knew that the vaccine against the virus of the yellow fever is advised. Indeed a yellow fever vaccination certificate is required from travellers coming from endemic areas and travelling to Eastern Island. Here I bringing back the read pages about this argoment.

Figure 1. Rubric of task and example of one student effort to search for public health guidelines for travellers.

students with basic IT skills such as registration at a medical site, the interrogation of a medical database and accessing the electronic library of the university. The IT components of this pre-course are described in the rubric of each of the following exercises in the modules for the 2nd to 4th year using both the electronic platforms of Blackboard and Moodle[2].

2.1 Module for the 2nd year

According to Stapleton, Helms-Park & Radia (2006), L2 students need to be taught how to evaluate websites. Figure 1 (p. 184) shows the rubric of a task in two parts designed to encourage students to learn to evaluate websites in Medicine and one student response. Students were given the option to evaluate two pharmaceutical company websites using the HON[3] code or to search for public health guidelines for travellers. Although weak grammatically, this piece of writing indicates that this student took the initiative to search for information from an authoritative source such as the Italian Ministry of Health.

2.2 Module for the 3rd year

Using Blackboard, students were given a patient scenario for the semester and were asked to summarise the clinical case working in groups and to formulate queries and their own reflections about this case in English. The following *Figure 2* is a brief excerpt of questions prepared by two groups of students upon reading the case assigned. This response amply demonstrates the usefulness of this task in helping the formation of the professional *persona* (see also Appendix 2). Group activity was

2 Both software platforms Blackboard and Moodle are available for instruction at the University of Rome. Moodle is an opensource platform available at http://moodle.org/.

3 HON refers to *Health On the Net* and is a set of 8 criteria for checking the reliability and completeness of health websites. It can be accessed at www.HON.ch/.

found to facilitate both analysis and writing and served to aid and encourage weaker students.

Student 1 Why has anybody ever diagnosed the infection caused by Streptococcus, which brought to endocarditis?Why did doctors privilege the familiar history, instead of making a colture? Considering that usually the values of Troponine T, CKMB, aspartate aminotransferase, alanine aminotransferase are not normal when there is a bacteria infection, why are only Troponine T levels high? Is it possible that the next reduction of Troponine T is due to the somministration of antibiotics, made during the admission?
Student 2 1. What does the literature say about the possibility to take a patient with acute endocarditis to surgery or to treat him with antibiotics and delay surgery? Which is the incidence of recurrent infection in patient treated with antibiotics before surgery and in patients treated directly with surgery? 2. What does the literature say about the choise to perform preoperative coronary angiography? Which are indications for coronary angiography that the patient have to present?

Figure 2. Student questions upon reading the case assigned for the semester by lecturers of internal medicine.

Another on-line task consisted of the evaluation of a set of ten abstracts of Research Articles (or RAs) and Randomised Clinical Trials (or RCTs[4]), based on the same patient assigned for the semester. Variations of different types of RCT abstracts were examined in English, while the same abstracts were exploited for Pathology and Surgery. The rhetorical model used for evaluation of the quality of the publications was based on a series of critical EBM[5] questions, listed in column 1 of *Table 1*, in grey. The questions served to elicit information about the purpose, structure, study design, clinical outcomes and other factors necessary for a good RCT. A selection of student responses to five abstracts out of ten is presented in the other columns of Table 1. This question-answer format was designed to aid in understanding the structure of the text and

4 In medicine, a research article (RA) having a prospective design with patients randomised to two alternative treatments and followed-up for several months is called a Randomised Clinical Trial or RCT.

5 Evidence-Based Medicine. see footnote 1.

to facilitate comprehension, leading to a critical evaluation of the methodological quality of the RA or RCT. Students were then invited to search PubMED[6] for other similar abstracts pertinent to this same case.

Column 1	*Student Responses to questions based on the critical analysis of abstracts*				
1. What is the topic?	*genetic assay*	*CardioVascDisease*	*CVD risk*	*Screening colonoscopy*	*CVD*
2. How was the study designed?	Prospective study. genes but not patients	RCT double blind	prospective cohort community	RCT trial	RCT
3. For what purpose?	*risk* correlation for association of *causation*	risk to identify *prognosis*	*risk to* identify *prognosis = cross sectional*	Colon rectal cancer's *prevention*	*Risk* to identify *prognosis*
4. Was there a treatment or intervention ?	no	Rofecoxib vs. placebo	No, only time	Removal of Small polyps	Aspirin vs. placebo
5. Was a cohort selected? How was it selected? Criteria of inclusion & exclusion?	yes. tamoxifen treated.	yes all with adenoma	no? but Framingham cohort which was free of CVD at baseline	no	no
6. What groups are being compared? Is there a gold standard?	low dosage vs. intermediate vs. high	Rofecoxib vs. placebo	middle-aged vs. elderly male & female	Male & female control group vs. Screening group	Aspirin vs. placebo
7. What is the primary outcome being studied?	recurrence or nodes	thrombotic events	hypertension	Small polyps	Gastrointestinal bleeding requiring transfusion
8. The secondary outcome?	gene expression	other CV events, RRisk		Colon rectal, cancer, adenomas	
9. Is the intervention conclusive beneficial harmful or uncertain	Not applicable because no intervention	conclusive, Harmful	uncertain.	uncertain	beneficial
10. What statistical tools are used	Kaplan Meier & Cox	Hazard ratio, Confidence Interval	% & p	%	%&p RRisk,CI
11. Was there a follow-up? for how long?	no	3 yrs	none indicated	10 yrs	39.9-28.8 months

Table 1. Student responses for critical analysis of abstracts of RAs or RCTs. Column 1, with a grey background, shows critical analysis questions. In the table, only 5 of the 10 abstracts are shown. These were limited to two medical topics: risk of Cardiovascular disease (CVD) or screening by Colonoscopy.

6 PubMED is the publications database of the NLM (National Library of Medicine) which forms part of the National Institutes of Health (NIH). The retrieval system, launched in 1965, in Bethesda, Md. USA. allows public consultation in Internet since 1993 at http://www.nlm.nih.gov/.

2.3 Module for the 4th year

Using Moodle, students were introduced to the linguistic moves in five subgenres of review articles in Medicine (Mungra, 2006). They were assigned to retrieve and read one review article of a disease or pathological condition pertinent to their course of study for that year: rheumatology, immunology or cardiology. The review articles could be chosen from the subgenres: narrative reviews, systematic review, meta-analyses, consensus conference statements or professional guidelines of the broad area or of specific pathologies. A question-answer format similar to that used in Table 1 was applied. Students were required to identify the sequence of moves in a review article of their choice. They were also encouraged to analyse narrative reviews or guidelines of the pathologies of the semester.

Having had this largely formalist task-based linguistic preparation using process-pedagogy, the writing course proper was then introduced.

3. Description of the writing course: Three online exercises

This section describes three tasks for student writing with specific prompts designed to stimulate, revise and apply their knowledge about moves in academic genres. Genre-based instruction has now been recognised as a valid method of teaching reading and writing (Bhatia, 1999; Hyland, 2002) and the ulterior purpose of moves analysis is to sharpen critical thinking in different professional genres. The genres chosen for this course were primarily intended to develop and foster skills in communication in a future professional setting. Thus, the first genre chosen, letters – discussed in section 3.1 – permit students to create a fictional professional *persona* to exploit it in interpersonal interaction between correspondents. The second genre seen in section 3.2 is the abstract (RA or RCT). This is an authentic text and has been extensively studied in the 3rd. year of the pre-course. The writing task of the abstract was limited to a re-construction of the method actually used by researchers and is a reflection of the ability to extract information and re-create a logical scientific procedure, much used in Evidence-Based Medicine. Finally, in section 3.3 the third genre is the argumentation genre, which is a classic of the scientific literature and gives scope to student ingenuity and inventiveness, within the constraints of scientific thought.

3.1 Letters in a professional setting

Based on the genre approach suggested by Bhatia, (1999), Flowerdew (2002), Hyland (2002) and Magnet & Carnet (2006), we drew students' attention to moves of this genre, followed by a question-answer lesson to shape a text thereby furnishing a schema or scaffold for the students to use in the creation of their own text. In this module, students were offered the choice of three scenarios: writing to a friend, to a colleague about a patient or writing to a research colleague who is an older and a well-known international figure. Power relations, polite forms and textual characteristics (Halliday & Hasan, 1985) were considered during the lesson and reinforced in the comments to student writing, of which three examples are shown in *Figure 3* below. The linguistic parameters which constitute academic register were discussed.

Example 1: letter to a friend

Elena P
Carlo Magno Street
00199, Rome

Dear Elena,

I'm writing you to let you know what blackboard is: a site where teachers put their lessons every day so that we can always bring ourselves up to date about what we did in the morning. They tell us everything we should know about the program of our course, if the lesson will be done or not, if there are any problems with exams and other things

like these. We can also keep in touch with our colleges and do works like this on internet. Blackboard helps me to have always the news I need at the university and helps me to study, too.
The only problem is that I don't have internet at home so I have to ask my friend to tell me what new every day and another problem is that sometimes can happen that internet doesn't work so that we have problem to get on blackboard.
I suggest you to start and use it.
Let me know how you feel about it.

Kisses Maria

Example 2: letters of referral

Doctor Hans Derrik
Marcchionne Strasse 14
S-H725 Berlin

Dear Colleague,
I would inform you that on the 15th July 2005 I visited one of your patient, Coca Koller.
The patient aged 65, afficted with CVD and Diabetes, arrived to our E.R. referring an omolateral emitemporal emianopsy and an emiparesys at the right side of the face.
He also reported dysfagia, dysartria and high grade headache localized on the left frontal region.
We immediately supposed the presence of a cerebral ischemic sufference, then we treated him with eparin 100mg/die e.v. and mannitol 200g e.v..
We also required cerebral CT and NMR exams to exclude or confirm the presence of a stroke attack.
Mr Koller was kept under observation for 24 hours and with our relief his conditions gardually got better.
Therefore our diagnosis was of a TIA, as the negativity of the strumental analyses had confirmed.
Actually the patient conditions are stable and the syntomatology has completely regressed.
Mr Koller will be discharged in a week and we suppose he will be able to return to Munich by car. We think you should follow him closely and do more diagnostic test. perhaps a MRI or 24-hr Holter.
If you would like to have more informations, you could contact me by e-mail at the following address:
pincopallino@uniroma1.it
Sincerely yours,

Example 3: to a senior professor

Dear professor Tanzilli!

I am terribly sorry to disturb you in a moment as this because I know that you are very busy among clinic research and lessons.
Therefore to do it brief I come to the point:
I would like to ask your permission to use your publication/abstract on "Enoximone coupled to very low dose dobutamine echocardiography detects myocardial viability in akinetic and dyskinetic post-myocardial infarcted areas." appearing in Am J Cardiol. 1999 of Aug 1; 84(3): 264–9.
I wondered me if it were possible to know better the criterions of inclusion and exclusion used in your publication.
Considering that the patients with heart attack STEMI but not Q induce modifications of the of the cardiac wall motility I ask why you have not included them in your study.
I hope that you does not consider this as a not appreciation of your immense job.
Thank you for your kind attention and cooperation.

3.2 Reconstructing the research method of an abstract

This exercise consisted of the completion of an abstract, from which the methods section had been removed. Using moves analysis and applying research study design from clinical methodology training done in the 3rd year, students were invited to reconstruct the methods used by researchers on the basis of information deduced from the rest of the abstract. They were expected to indicate how the patients were recruited and subdivided, what treatment was used and how the data were analysed. *Figure 4* is a screen shot of one group's writing while *Table 2* shows other groups' writing, with tutor comments.

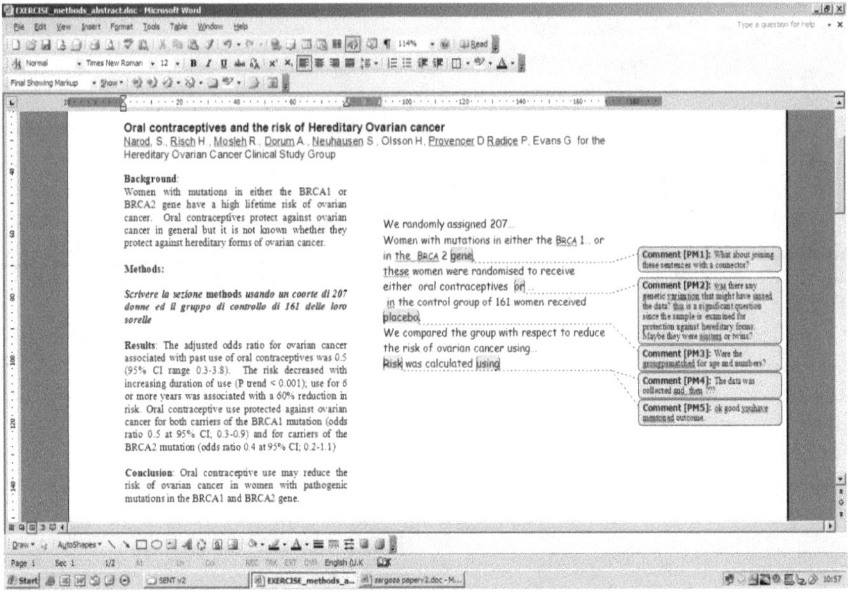

Figure 4. Screen shot of student work from exercise 3.2 on the reconstruction of the methods section of a abstract, with tutor margin comments. Other student writings and tutor comments are seen in Table 2.

3.3 Argumentative writing

There were two parts to this activity: first, summarizing salient information followed by the second step of evaluation and taking a stance. Following Kavaliauskienė (2006), we applied some important criteria or steps in the scaffolding for writing an effective summary as follows:

1) appropriate layout comprising three parts – an introduction, main information, and conclusions,
2) a reduction of 20–25% of the text,
3) no verbatim copying,
4) application of ABC rule (Accurate, Brief, Clear),
5) polishing grammar or spelling errors.

		COMMENTS & CORRECTIONS
1	A research was made on a group of 207 women with mutations in either the BRCA1 or BRCA2. They were given oral contraceptives. A control groups was made up of 161 women which were sisters of the main group. EC	A control groups were they given oc and why? who (persons) not which(things) so, what next was done?
2	There was a study group of 207 women with mutations of BRCA1 and BRCA2 gene under treatment with oral contraceptives and it was possible to see a consistent reduction of the risks. Use for six or more years, in fact, reduced the possibilities of ovarian cancer of the 60% as in carriers of the BRCA1 mutation than in carriers of the BRCA2 mutation. FM	why *study* group? what was this treatment forresults what are you comparing here?
3	Clinicals undertake a study with 207 women and they chose as control groups 161 of their sisters. A part of these women used oral contraceptives The main point for clinicals was to individuate in which women with BRCA1 and BRCA2 the risk to develop an ovarian cancer was decrease by use of oral contraceptives VC	Who or what are "clinicals"? The passive is more appropriate. What part, head or arms? Do you mean purpose, not point? to identify not individuate. Do you want to see in which women the risk was decreased?
4	We assembled a cohort of 207 women, 100 of which carriers of the BRCA1 mutation and 107 carriers of the BRCA2 mutation. They have been treated with oral contraceptives for a long time (more than 6 years). We compared them with a control group composed by 161 women who were the sisters of the cohort women – they had the same mutation but they didn't have to use oral contraceptives. FN	method errors incomplete procedure. What did you do with the data?

Table 2. Student writing of methods section of the abstract exercise in Figure 4 with tutor comments.

The second step was the effective argumentation consisting of

6) a generalization (not narration) of the diagnosis with the event that furnished proof of the correct diagnosis, followed by
7) a statement of author stance and supporting proof.

The patient in question was Alexander the Great, published in the New England Journal of Medicine.[7] Students were given the abstract and a choice of possible diagnoses and were required to choose and argument their case. Instructions on argumentation and possible ideas were discussed during the lesson. *Figure 5* shows the rubric and two examples of student writing in answer to the module:

7 Oldach DW, Richard RE, Borza EN, Bcnitcz RM. 1998. A mysterious death. N Engl J Med. 338: 1764–1769.

Rubric: You are required to choose a clinical diagnosis and defend it. Using 3 steps, state your opinion, argument your opinion (bringing evidence in support of or excluding) and then state possible loopholes.

Example Student 1.
The patient was an important conqueror in the past. He had fought a lot of battles conquering many nations. For his fame, many people envied him and wanted his death. Since this patient, always, presented his symptoms after drinking alcohol, I think that wine was poisoned with arsenic. In fact it was an efficace tool used in the past by professional assassins. Even if arsenic was used to treat several disease such as agues, periodic headaches and syphilis, the ingestion of large quantities of it could cause severe abdominal pain, hemorrhagic gastroenteritis and hepatic necrosis (symptoms presented by the patient). Moreover a progressive neuropathy could ruin patient's life or the patient could develop pulmonary edema, hypotension and shock that leaded him to death.

Example Student 2.
We think that this patient had an alcholic hepatitis after the consumaption of 6 liter of wine and so it explains fever , pain in the right upper quadrant and generalizated fatigue.
Besides we believe that the patient was infected by a form of typhoid fever causeted by the penetrating trauma to the right chest, complicated by hemo-pneumo thorax. We believe infection by Sthapilococcus epidermidis or Candida or Negative Gram. An other hypothesis is that this man was infected by his homosexual partner, because he is bisexual, and so our patient was affected from syphilis, as if the synthomatology is missing of skin and mucous lesion.
This two question can be independent one the other, and we think that this man is dead because of infection with syphilis.

Figure 5. Argumentative writing by two student groups on the case of Alexander the Great.

Both students summarised the case and took a stance in formulating a possible diagnosis and both used the first person to articulate their respective positions. Both used syntactically important forms such as the conditional and modal verbs. They were both able to bring proof from the text to support their statements, in much the same way that a professional doctor might support his/her hypothesis of a diagnosis. The use of the first person, singular and plural, passives and connectors in both exercises indicates student reflection on the theme of evaluating diagnostic options as well as a budding professional *persona*.

3.4 Additional information on course administration

Table 3 shows the week-by-week sequencing of the modules in the online course. After an initial run-in period of 2 weeks, during which students were allowed to practise using Blackboard and course enrolment so as to get used to the electronic platform, the first module was introduced. This was a revision module with exercises on editing, identifying errors, grammar, pragmatic and stylistic improvements of given texts, register and meaning as well as the interpersonal aspect of the genre such as writing instructions for paramedical staff such as laboratory technicians or nurses. The combination of on-line access to the Blackboard modules was punctuated by a few formal lectures (referred to as lessons), is referred to as Blended Learning (Balirano & Castaldi, 2003). Students were allowed to work in groups and had to deliver the completed exercise within 48 hours before the next lesson. During the lesson itself, attention was paid to error analysis, misinterpretations and stylistic improvements of student output and suggestions for improvement were made. We then presented the new module and any general directions or restrictions were announced. Details of the contents of each module are given in Appendix 1.

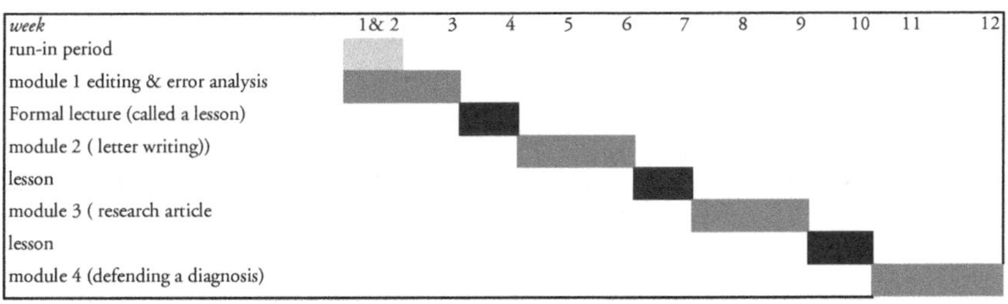

Table 3. Time frame of Blended course: run-in period (light grey), online modules (darker grey) and lesson (black). Details of the course content are given in Appendix 1.

At the end of the course, an anonymous questionnaire was filled out by students and handed back to instructors. The questions with student responses are shown in *Table 4* and students were asked to show their agreement by using a Likert scale of 1–5. The responses were grouped as 1–3 and 4–5 to show marginal or active agreement respectively.

Indicate your agreement using a Likert scale of 1 to 5 *1 = do not agree ….. 5 = Indeed I agree*	*Likert scale grouping* *1–3*	 *4–5*
I understood what the authors were trying to say	1	15
I verified some important information	8	9
I plan to discuss this information with others	5	12
I plan to see more information of this topic	3	14
This information is likely to be integrated in to my studies	3	14
Autonomous on-line study has helped my reading accuracy	4	13
my reading speed has improved	5	12
I am able to interpret all the data/graphs correctly	4	13
I feel more confident in reading and interpreting the scientific literature	2	15

Table 4. Student response to end-of-course questionnaire.

Of 35 questionnaires handed out, about 50% were returned with responses. From Table 4, of the 17 responses, 13 responses (76.5%) fell into the more positive Likert scale of 4–5, while only 4 were more negative in their evaluation to the questions on the usefulness of the online course.

4. Discussion and assessment of teaching-learning experience

The previous sections of this paper described a model of blended learning for English. In this course of blended learning, the modules containing the tasks described were put in Blackboard and made available to students. Such on-line access was punctuated by formal lessons, dealing with error analysis, feedback and improvements to tasks submitted. An assessment of the benefits and disadvantages of this teaching model for a language course follows.

4.1 Use of Blackboard and IT skills.

After five years of use, we have found that Blackboard is user-friendly since it allows the tutor to return an assignment with comments either as a page or as a link to the student's email address, as can be seen from the screen shot in *Figure 6.* The ease of making, saving and sending comments with Blackboard is a very useful feature for tutors since corrections and textual evaluation constituted a very large part of tutor activity. For example, extensive tutor comments were necessary in another task on the grammatical correctness of question forms, which can be seen in Appendix 2 and returning comments to the students would have been very difficult if not impossible, without this feature in Blackboard.

Feature allows for sending by email

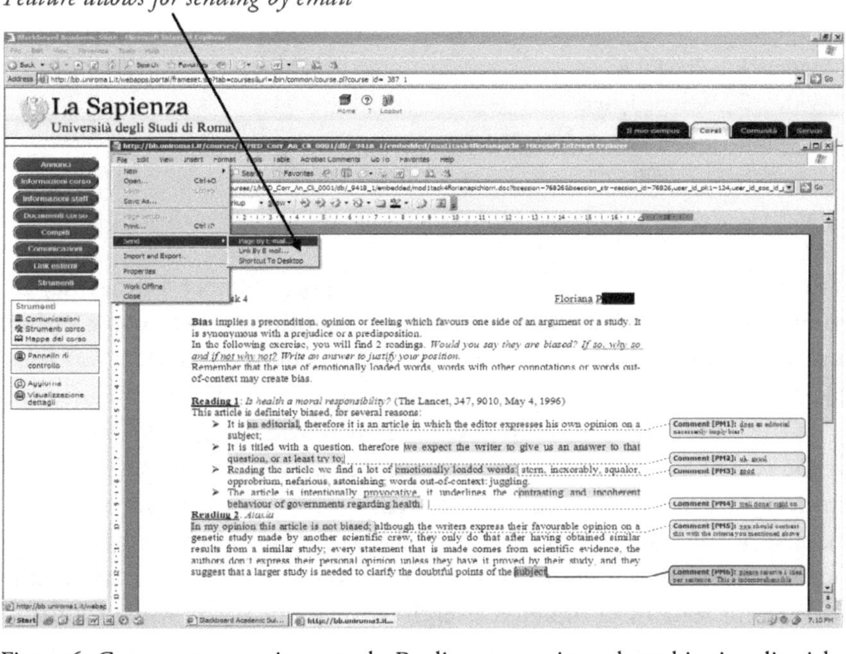

Figure 6. Comments on written work. Replies to questions about bias in editorials. Blackboard allows tutor to comment on written work and return corrected version by email, as seen by the feature indicated by the arrow.

Although tutors have found Blackboard user-friendly, students initially had some difficulty with it since roughly 30% of all student usage was to query the helpdesk, according to data from the Blackboard Manager, presented in Table 5. In order to minimize this querying the helpdesk, we found it important to give students a run-in period of two weeks at the start of the course.

With respect to the broad aims of the three different modules of the 5th year course, over 43% of usage, according to the Blackboard Manager, was to access exercises for the revision module 1. Usage dropped dramatically to roughly 6% by the time the module 3 on argumentation was available. Perhaps these variations in percentage use are physiological but it would be interesting to compare usages in other courses.

Forum	*Hits*	*Use*
Helpdesk	169	28.64%
Module 1 self editing	254	43.05%
Module 2 Writing letters	134	22.71%
Module 3 Argumention Alex the Great	33	5.59%
Total	*590*	*100%*

Table 2. Usage of Blackboard for English (data downloaded from the Blackboard Manager).

The main student complaint was about having to meet a deadline, although a few (5%) had positive comments about having to work within a time schedule for the first three modules. The module that was least liked was the open writing – having to chose and defend a diagnosis.

Given the general pattern at University where exercises are not given at the end of a class lecture, the assigning of exercises to be pasted in the student forum by a deadline was initially viewed with suspicion by the class and was criticised by some faculty as being too much like giving homework at high-school. However, the judicious use of 0.33 of a credit for having sent in completed exercises for each of the three modules soon overcame student resistance and the avalanche of student replies and comments in the Blackboard forum for English soon convinced other faculty to adopt a similar *iter.*

Blackboard was used not only statically for giving information about grammar or lexis or material covered in class time or for notifying students about deadlines but an attempt was made to use many of the interactive features such as the forum for communication with students and for returning corrected assignments as well as entering the grades earned. The usage rates were high – 61.03% all student access was for the discussion area used by English.

The problem of a high tutor workload for an online course is a serious drawback since the work-load is not only heavy but also intensive during the 12 weeks of this course. However, this disadvantage could be remedied by assigning mentors or former students to assist in correcting assignments – a procedure to be tried in the future. This would be beneficial not only for the new students but also for the mentors themselves, since according to Beatty & Nunan (2004), students' learning was independent of a constructivist setting and is fostered by collaboration between students to create a learning environment.

4.2 Language Learning in an online course: assessment of types of tasks

During the first module of the writing course, many students indicated that the error analysis of their own grammar and syntactic mistakes as well as reinforcement of moves in the different genres were useful exercises because of the revision of lexico-semantic and pragmatic linguistic elements which seemed to them to improve their reading skills. Although some of this material had been covered before in earlier years, not surprisingly, students seem to understand and evaluate the scientific literature better, having a better cognitive understanding of the subject matter.

In the letter-writing module, the formulation of opinions, criticising and making suggestions to colleagues as well as the recognition of power relations in the academy are predominantly Process-oriented. The hidden aim of these exercises was to raise consciousness about the issues of register and especially of interpersonal role-relationships between the writer and his hypothetical interlocutor/reader. This exercise drove student to focus on pragmatic issues such as register and in particular formality and politeness, as indicated by Swales & Feak (2004) since these are two factors which often make the non-native speaker appear to lack polish (Schauer, 2006).

The exercise on the reconstruction of a scientific abstract module was perhaps the most interesting of those in this module because it stimulates reading skills of authentic medico-scientific material, essential for a medical professional. Several professional informants, all working researchers, have indicated that in their own reading, one of the first evaluations made of a newly-published research paper is its methodological soundness, its research design and its conformity with EBM[8] standards. Thus, from the point of view of a scientist, this linguistic exercise reflects what a working scientist unconsciously does while reading in his/her subject area. The abstracts used in this task were all authentic papers from which the methods section had been removed. Prior to this, during their 3rd year of the pre-course, (see exercise in section 2 above) students had been taught how to evaluate abstracts using a schema of moves called IMRD[9] structure (Swales,1990; Nwogu, 1997; Lorés, 2004). Students were aware of this scaffolding and knew of the series of elements that should be present in well-written abstracts, but now they had to activate this knowledge in writing sentences containing information deduced from the other parts of the abstract. This exercise may be considered a process activity but it also involves higher order cognitive processes.

The final exercise presented in this model involves evaluating patient data, formulating a diagnosis and defending it – all processes typical of the medical professional. This activity involves two important cognitive-linguistic-communicative processes: the first is deductive reasoning combined with the art of summarizing information and the sec-

8 Evidence Based medicine/see footnote 1.

9 Frequently used in abstracts, IMRD or IMRaD represents the four-part structure of a RA or RCT and consists of Introduction, Methods, Results and Discussion, typical of a laboratory-based science report.

ond deals with formulating written evaluations with supporting evidence. These are two high-order cognitive activities and require application of the scaffolding steps inherent in the composing strategies used in the previous task within a content-based environment. Although only about 6% of students actually did this exercise, this was a considerable improvement on previous years. The use of a dialogic procedure involving question-answer format as well as tutor comment, the support of group activity and the judicious use of assigning credits for work handed in on-line, induced many students to try this exercise. In the lesson immediately preceding this module, we found it important to pay attention to grammar items such as conditionals, modal verbs, hedges, cohesion devices and connectors. Specific examples on how to formulate these communicative functions were reviewed and students were warned that they would be graded on these items.

4.3 Didactic effectiveness of Model

Writing in a professional context such as the model proposed in this course aims at not only refreshing passive cognition of lexico-grammar and syntax, but also activating this passive knowledge in a professional setting. The choice of tasks reflect the kinds of activities medical professionals actually do, such as searching the literature and evaluating websites to arrive at "best practise", writing letters of hospital discharge or evaluating the methodological soundness of a new publication. The tasks employed not only language-based skills but also content-based skills and incorporated social or professional realities. Thus, the choice of exercises closely follows the norms suggested by Bhatia (1999) that tasks must have 4*P*s: *purpose*: such as institutionalized community goals and communicative purposes; *products*: textual artifacts or genres; *practices*: discursive practices, procedures and processes and finally the *players*: discourse community membership. In science, especially in academe, a writing course built along our model also allows students to organize their thinking and identify their discoursal selves (Eik-Nes, 2004) and to insert a budding professional *persona* into the Community of Practitioners (Wenger, 1998; Mavor & Trayner, 2001).

A blended course consisting of online access punctuated by frontal lessons such as we used in this course, allows for active student input which facilitates problem-shooting in teaching (Balirano & Castaldi, 2003). The sequence of assignment-deadline-lesson has fostered extensive student input and we concur with Selfe (2003) that there is more student effort in planning the piece and revising activities. Class discussion was also very active and revolved around syntax and pragmatics, unusual among medical students. Using their own written work, students would discuss and decide on issues such as complex sentences, when to use the 1st person or passives in scientific writing, the scaffolding of moves in writing expository argumentative text as well as stylistic issues like transitions, thematic progression, clear intratextual references and other similar narrative conventions.

Having student assignments before class has facilitated text analysis since exercises such as summarizing and retell of a patient suggested by Pica (2002) or comparisons of text with and without connectives, such as those suggested by Van Gelderen & Oostdam (2002), permitted explicitness in teaching stylistic improvements and allowed us to show how the reader may interpret alternative meaning.

Although scarce, data on student feedback should be designed in a more rigorous manner than the questionnaire we gave. Orally, student comments were positive for learner autonomy and empowerment, for authenticity of the exercises and helpful collaboration from and with colleagues. One student remarked that the exercises on register for e-mail and letter-writing were most helpful when making plans for an exchange internship at a Mexican hospital. Such writing activity exemplifies what Bhatia (2002, p. 3) calls the

> many communication based curriculum contexts [...] which can be used as analytical resource to understand and manipulate complex inter-generic and multicultural realisations of professional discourse, which will enable learners to use generic knowledge to respond to novel social contexts and also to create new forms of discourse to achieve pragmatic success as well as other powerful human agendas.

5. Conclusions

In a review of technological tools for language teaching, Salaberry (2001) questions the pedagogical benefits of many of these new tools and suggests that pedagogical effectiveness should be tied to three factors: a thorough understanding of the nature of the technological tools and what they can or cannot do, proper integration in the regular curriculum and finally the appropriate use of human and material resources. This experience with an online course, such as we have described above, allows major integration of clinical subjects and language by permitting students to choose topics driven by their own academic interests. The use of professional scenarios for each of the tasks has helped raise our Italian students' awareness about the existence of a professional *persona* that needs to operate in an international or trans-national forum with colleagues and interns. Such approach proposed by Canagarajah (2002), fully exploits the strengths of CALL and collaborative learning.

An online course offers several advantages. For students, there is timetable freedom for clinical time with patients and electronic access for English reading-writing tasks on demand. Online courses using our model may offer additional advantages such as collaborative learning, building group coherence, sharing information-processing ideas and mentoring (Paran, Furneaux & Sumner, 2004). Tutors too, are sure they are reaching most of their students and can thus insist on student assignments with a deadline by offering credits as a proverbial carrot-and-stick.

One area of concern is the potential for plagiarism inherent in the use of electronic files for assignments especially in the cut-and-paste feature. From an ethical point of view, some may argue that it is not a good habit to encourage students to cut-and-paste since it might facilitate bad habits of plagiarism – a problem raised by Hirvala (2005) but we believe it to be useful in that it allows students to focus on more cognitively demanding exercises like identifying lexical or interpersonal features such as supporting argumentation in their writing or citing moves in long stretches of text while reading or writing. We believe that it is good to inculcate in students the correct format of citing authors or scientific works.

Many of the writing tasks were put into a student portfolio for a global assessment of student effort for the final grade of this course. Although the production of a portfolio may be considered a practical evaluation tool, such an evaluation procedure raises doubts about how much language activation is actually achieved in a genre-based course using tasks which are mainly consciousness-raising ones. We were also concerned about whether the portfolio emphasised a product-based approach to teaching rather than a process-focused approach. These doubts require clearer assessment tools and might be answered by more rigorous, extensive and careful assessment of student writing and by motivation studies. Undoubtedly much remains to be done but despite its shortcomings, a writing course built along these lines may go some way in achieving the objectives of furnishing linguistic skills which are current and potentially useful for a budding professional.

References

Balirano, G., & Castaldi. F. (2003). Blended Learning and TEFL perpectives in the multilingual enviromnent: towards a holistic approach. In: R. Wilkinson (Ed.) *Integrating Content and Language: Meeting the challenge of a multilingual higher education. Proc. ICL Conference* (pp. 218–226). Maastricht: University of Maastricht Press.

Beatty, K., & Nunan, D. (2004). Computer-mediated collaborative learning. *System* 32, 165–183

Bhatia, V. K. (2002). Applied genre analysis: a multi-perspective model. *Ibérica* 4, 3–19.

Bhatia, V. K. (1999). Integrating products, processes, and participants in professional writing. In C. N. Candlin & K. Hyland (Eds.), *Writing: Texts, processes and practices* (pp. 21–39). London: Longman Group.

Canagarajah, S. (2002). Multilingual writers and the academic community: towards a critical relationship. *Journal of English for Academic Purposes* 1(1), 29–44.

Chambers, A., & Bax, S. 2006. Making CALL work: Towards normalization. *System* 34, 465–479.

Eik.-Nes, N. (2004). e-Technologies in Engineering Education: Learning Outcomes Providing Future Possibilities. *Proceedings of the 2002 eTEE Conference*. Vol. P1, Article 5. Retrieved 14 May 2007 from: http://services.bepress.com/eci/etechnologies/5

Finkel, M., Brown, H.A., Gerber, L., & Supino, P. (2003). Teaching evidence-based medicine to medical students. *Medical Teacher*, 25(2), 202–209.

Flowerdew, J. (2002). Genre in the classroom: a linguistic approach. In: Ann. M. Johns (Ed.) *Genre in the Classroom: Multiple Perspectives* (pp. 91–102). Mahwah, NJ: LawrenceErlbaum.

Halliday, M.A.K., & Hasan, R. (1985). *Language, context and text: aspects of language in a social-semeiotic perspective*. Oxford: Oxford University Press.

Hirvala, A. (2005). Computer-based reading and writing across the curriculum:Two case studies of L2 writers. *Computers and Composition 22*, 337–356.

Hyland, K. (2002). *Teaching and Researching Writing*. Applied linguistics in Action Series (Series Eds. C.N. Candin & D.R. Hall). Harlow, England: Longman-Person.

Hyon, S., & Chen, R. (2004). Beyond the research article: University faculty genres and EAP graduate preparation. *English for Specific Purposes* 23, 233–263.

Kavaliauskienė, G. (2006). Testing Literacy at Tertiary Level: A Case Study. *Journal of Language and Learning* 3 (2), 300–311.

Lorés, R. (2004). On RA Abstracts: From Rhetorical Structure to Thematic Organization. *English for Specific Purposes* 23(3), 280–302.

Magnet, A., & Carnet, D. (2006). Letters to the editor: still vigorous after all these years? A presentation of the discursive and linguistic features of the genre. *English for Specific Purposes* 25, 173–199.

Mavor, S., & Trayner, B. (2001). Aligning genre and practice with learning in Higher Education: an interdisciplinary perspective for course design and teaching. *English for Specific Purposes* 20, 345–366.

Mungra, P. (2006). Macrostructure and Rhetorical Moves in Secondary Research Articles: the Meta-Analysis and the Systematic Analysis. In M. Gotti & Françoise Salager-Meyer (Eds.), *Advances in Medical Discourse Analysis: Written and Oral contexts.* (pp. 331–355). Bern: Peter Lang.

Nwogu, K.N. (1997). The Medical Research Paper: Structure and Functions. *English for Special Purposes* 16/2, 119–138.

Paran, A., Furneaux, C., & Sumner, N. (2004). Computer-mediated communication in distance MA programmes: the student's perspective. *System* 32, 337–355.

Pica, T. (2002). Subject matter content: how does it assist the interactional and linguistic needs of classroom learners? *Modern Language Journal* 86, 1–19.

Reinders, H. (2007). Big brother is helping you: Supporting self-access language learning with a student monitoring system. *System* 35, 93–111.

Salaberry, M.R. (2001). The use of technology for second language learning and teaching: a retrospective. *Modern Language Journal* 81, 39–56.

Schauer, G.A. (2006). Pragmatic Awareness in ESL and EFL Contexts: Contrast and Development. *Language Learning* 56(2), 269–318.

Selfe, D. (2003). Techno-pedagogical explorations: Toward sustainable technology-rich instruction. In P. Takayoshi & B. Huot (Eds.), *Teaching writing with computers: An introduction* (pp. 17–32). Boston: Houghton.

Stapleton, P., Helms-Park, R., & Radia P. (2006). The Web as a source of unconventional research materials in second language academic writing. *Internet and Higher Education*, 9, 63–75.

Swales, J. (1990). *Genre Analysis: English in Academic and Research Settings.* Cambridge: Cambridge University Press.

Swales, J. & Feak, C. (2004). *Academic Writing for Graduate Students* (2nd edition). Michigan: University of Michigan Press.

Van de Poel, K. (2004). Improving the academic writing skills of language students. – the Scribende Project. In: R. Wilkinson (Ed.) *Integrating Content and Language: Meeting the challenge of a multilingual higher education. Proc. ICL Conference.* (pp. 242–250). Maastricht: University of Maastricht Press.

Van Gelderen, A. & Oostdam, R. (2002). Improving linguistic fluency for writing effects of explicitness and focus of instruction. *L1-Educational Studies in Language and Literature.* 2, 239–270.

Warschauer, M. (2002). Networking into academic discourse. *Journal of English for Academic Purposes* 1, 45–58.

Wenger, E. (1998). *Communities of practice: Learning, meaning, and identity.* Cambridge: Cambridge University Press.

Appendix 1: Outline of Writing Online course in Blackboard

Run-in period for registration. Please let me know your group. After closing date, I shall assign people to a group, if they have not chosen a group. Group leader and assistants are expected to put work into forum for the group. I generally read the forum and assignments on a Monday and try to comment by Wednesday. So assignments are due on Monday morning at 0900 (CEST) Central European Standard Time

didactic purpose

Module 1: OBLIGATORY for all: review of grammar

- Errors and self editing
- Expanding and contracting
- Bias in writing
- Instructions to a technician on how to make a blood smear.
- question forms

Didactic purpose:

- Grammar, nouns and articles
- Going from notes to sentences & viceversa
- Taking on the role of reader
- Giving clear instructions

3 weeks then I close the module and course availability. No more guests; or you're in or you're out!!!! Group must work together and put assignment in forum. 2 HR LESSON ON WEDNESDAY ON ERROR ANALYSIS OF GRAMMAR

Module 2: Genres & Analysis of information

- Abstract on intolerance to cow's milk
- Case: Alexander the Great
- Editorials

Didactic purpose:

- write methods – extrapolating information
- Convince reader: arguing a case for
- Opinions & flow of information in editorial

2 WEEKS THEN 2 HR LESSON.

Module 3: letter writing : do both letters

- Text letters 3 choices (to a friend, to a prof and to a colleague)
- Email writing

Didactic purpose:

- Asking for something. Role and social order
- Netiquette.doc (also see my book)

2 WEEKS THEN LESSON

Module 4: Free writing: Opinions and Argumentation module

do 3 out of the 4 exercises: individual activity after group consultation. (Put 2 exercises into your portfolio)

- Case: choose a diagnosis and defend it.
- Breast cancer: reflections on how the new paradigm of the redevelopment of breast cancer might affect thinking on the development of new therapies: read 5 publications on the topic
- Creative writing on an emotional episode in your life
- Nosocomial triage: read an abstract on a proposed scheme for quickly determining risk and evaluate the usefulness; write evaluation of triage. How do other emergency departments do triage? You can add a literature search on triage standards.

Didactic purpose:

- The pros and cons of argumentation
- Opinions
- Paragraph structure
- Admitting SWOTs
- Planning a piece
- The mechanics of writing task – creativewriting.doc
- revision *literature search* in PubMed on this topic

For your credits, you must insert the original exercise and your improvements and corrections of the modules into your *portfolio of work*. I will leave module 4 available until end of course and will give you another week after the end-of term to hand in all your work.

Appendix 2: clinical questions formulated by the students with tutor queries and comments in **bold** on stylistic and register changes

- showing L1 interference
- Teaching formal academic register
- Question forms.

1) Which are the instructions for the surgical intervention in s. anginosus endocarditis cases?
What indications are there for surgery in those cases of….
Use "there is/are" because you want to indicate that "indications" exist, but you don't know what they are.
"Which" implies that you can't find them in the set of "instructions"
Which are the risks of a surgical intervention in *S. anginosus* endocarditis cases? (Lorenzo) **same comments as above**
2) ~~Which~~ **What** are the complications of the s. anginosus endocarditis? (Emiliano)
3) What do you know about vancomycin? Is ~~the~~ therapy with vancomycin and gentamicin more effective than the one using only vancomycin? (Antonella) **ok**
4) Why is ~~the~~ **a** tissue valve more effective than the mechanical prothesis in this case? And which are the requested parameters to define it? (Paola) **Remember when you use a noun for the first time, it should carry the indefinite article.**
5) Which are the most attested ?? techniques for an intracardiac abscess diagnosis? (Michela)
6) What are ~~the~~ Duke-criteria? What ~~about their use~~ **are they used for** and attestation ? in endocarditis diagnosis? **ok** (Valentina)
7) What is the difference between endocarditis due to beta-hemolytic streptococci and the endocarditis due to streptococcus milleri? (Elisa) **ok but I think you want to know "What clinical features distinguish… you should choose the right verb.**
8) Which ~~could~~ **might** be the cause of the persistent fever in association with infective endocarditis?
(Anna Laura)
9) Which ~~are the~~ factors ~~that~~ increase the risk of s. anginosus endocarditis? (Angela)
10) How have the principles of valvular surgery in endocarditis changed since the first reported surgery in 1965? (Martina) **ok**
11) Which ~~could be~~ other causes of endocarditis **might there be**? (Serena)

Jarosław Krajka

Promoting Discovery Learning in English for Academic and Professional Purposes: Implementing Concordancing Procedures in Online Courses

Introduction – defining corpora for ESP/EAP

Together with the development of new areas of study and much greater specialisation of knowledge, ESP teachers more and more frequently face the challenge of teaching a foreign language to the students of highly specialised disciplines. This growing demand for ESP teaching in a wider range of areas is in clear contrast with the offer of ESP teaching materials provided by ELT publishers. Consequently, lack of properly developed commercial materials confronts many ESP teachers with the urgent need of finding and adapting appropriate teaching resources. At the same time, the multitude of target language input available in the electronic format on the Internet opens interesting instructional opportunities for ESP teachers, enabling browsing, evaluating, retrieving and adapting texts and recordings from their specialist areas as classroom materials.

Corpora and concordancing have been widely used in ELT, also to assist teachers in making informed choices about curriculum development, vocabulary selection and lexical testing. However, these tools are not always of full relevance for ESP contexts, as the corpora available for searching usually fail to represent specialist areas adequately. On the other hand, promoting active learning through exposure to "raw" linguistic data produced by concordancers helps to increase the inductive reasoning skills, enabling students to formulate rules on their own and retain them for a longer period of time.

Let us look first at what a corpus is. Crystal (1991) defines it as "a collection of linguistic data, either written texts or a transcription of recorded speech, which can be used as a starting-point of linguistic description or as a means of verifying hypotheses about a language". In a similar vein, Sinclair (1991) adds that corpora are made of naturally occurring language, while Krishnamurthy (2001) indicates that genuine communicative situations are recorded without any editing to create corpus contexts. McEnery and Wilson (1996) enumerate four crucial characteristics of a corpus: sampling and representativeness, finite and fixed size, machine-readability and standard reference. Four other criteria indispensable for a body of texts to be met to be labelled a corpus are, according to Sinclair (1996), considerable quantity, authenticity, plain text simplicity for data storage and documentation of full details about the constituents of a component (annotation) kept separately from the document itself.

The aim of the present chapter is to describe an attempt at the implementation of concordancing procedures to promote discovery learning, both using ready-made corpora resources and custom-made ones, in Moodle-based online courses. The Moodle-based ICT training course for ESP focused heavily on the use of corpora and concordancing to promote discovery learning. We will start with a brief overview of the opportunities and drawbacks of concordancing-based discovery learning approach, pointing out some possible applications of corpora in teaching various language skills. A substantial part of the paper is constituted by the description of the steps executed to introduce concordancing procedures to online students in a Moodle-based learning environment.

Online corpora for ESP and EAP – from ready-made resources to teacher-made materials

The availability of ready-made corpora for widespread and unlimited pedagogical use by ESP teachers has greatly increased recently, together with the popularisation of the Internet and the open source software movement (Tribble, 1997). The proliferation of corpora resources demands careful categorisation and classification, to ensure proper understanding of the strengths and limitations of the specific tools both by teachers and learners. The selection of a particular resource for an ESP context, according to Aston (1996), should take into account and balance the following three criteria:

> [...] the extent to which the texts contained in a corpus should be limited to the particular domain of ESP (corpus specificity); the number and length of the text samples it should contain (corpus size); and the extent to which these mirror the universe of discourse which the corpus aims to capture (corpus representativeness).

An extensive list of publicly available corpora resources, both pertaining specifically to particular areas of ESP and of general language learning applicability, can be found in the Appendix.

A viable alternative for ready-made corpora resources can be custom-made collections, compiled by ESP/EAP teachers with the use of online texts in response to the specific requirements of a particular teaching context (Lee & Swales, 2006). Such 'do-it-yourself corpora' will be an indispensable solution when students' needs cannot be satisfied by the above-listed ready-made resources, when representative corpora contain relatively little coverage of specialist areas or text types (Tribble, 1997), or when the teacher aims at enhancing the classroom with the language of a particular domain, geographical area or register. When analysing the issue of the selection of sources for corpus compilation, Curado (2006) quotes Hunston (2002, p. 16), saying that "the selection of sources should reflect the communicative exchanges that take place in the target context of research and work". In other words, the corpus should constitute a balanced view of materials, ranging from formal writing (e.g., technical reports and instruction manuals) to informal conversational messages (discussion forum postings).

Obviously, the selection of sources, their balance resulting in the representativeness of a corpus (Biber, Conrad & Reppen, 1998) or, on the contrary, the overrepresentation of a certain genre, text type or register are the result of the needs of the class and the didactic purposes for the exploitation of a mini-corpus. Thus, the teacher may decide to create a corpus for the English for Archaeology class that will be as representative as possible, trying to balance the subareas, text genres and levels of formality, if the general language development of ESP students is the main goal. On the other hand, with a clear focus shared by most students in a group, e.g., Polish drivers planning to work in the public transportation system in the UK and Ireland, the teacher might use other sources, more focused on the specific area of interest, such as the websites of drivers' trade unions, traffic regulations, bus operation manuals, to get a focus which is narrower and more targeted at specific needs of students.

Promoting discovery learning with corpus consultation procedures – opportunities and drawbacks

Discovery learning, involving students to a much greater extent in the process of decision making and rule formulation in inductive reasoning, be it in the area of grammar or vocabulary, is an essential characteristic feature of a learner-centred classroom. The shift from teacher-centredness to learner-centredness of activities involved in the language learning process is clearly one of the preconditions for learner autonomy. As defined by Benson (2001, p. 47), learner autonomy is "the capacity to take control of one's own learning," on the following possible levels: learning management, cognitive processes and learning content. With the three dimensions being mutually influential, smooth progression from one to the other is essential for the successful growth of autonomy. Inductive reasoning, or inferring principles and generalisations from the linguistic data given (discovery learning) is an example of the learner autonomy approach developed on Benson's (2001) cognitive processes level. Promoting learner discovery in the instruction of diverse language skills and elements should ensure deeper processing of knowledge and its restructuring and individualisation, which, in turn, influences better retention and retrieval.

Out of many different features of a successful language learner, contemporary methodology strongly highlights "a willingness to experiment" as an essential step towards fostering strong intrinsic motivation and developing a positive attitude towards second language learning (Harmer, 1998, p. 10). Obviously, this particular feature, and a resultant inclination (or resentment) towards promoting active exploration of texts and examples to arrive at generalisations is largely dependent upon the learner's individual characteristics, an individual learner profile. Thus, the learners who can be characterised as "inductive", "active" and "sequential" (Felder & Henriques, 1995) as well as possessing more mathematical-logical intelligence (Gardner, 2002) will be much more open to discovery learning procedures than their peers of a more deductive, reflective and intrapersonal nature, who might find activities of this particular nature difficult to execute on a non-linguistic basis. This calls for careful diagnosis of learners' characteristics and skilful implementation of inductive learning procedures, to maximise the learning benefit and minimise the appearance of negative feelings towards language instruction.

The concordancing procedures, especially when based on a properly selected corpus, can constitute a significant teaching aid both in teacher preparation for classes, in their self-development as well as in building students' language awareness ('direct' corpus use – Leech, 1997). The provision of a large amount of linguistic data in the form of KWIC (Key Word In Context) concordancer output creates a learning environment conducive for inductive reasoning, discovering rules and finding recurrent patterns.

The promotion of active learning in a corpus-based learning environment is ensured due to the fact that concordancing interjects authenticity (of text, purpose, and activity) into the learning process, as students assume control of that process and their competence is built by gaining access to the facts of linguistic performance (Johns, 1988). Another point made by Cobb (1999) is that knowledge encoded from data by learners themselves will be more flexible, transferable, and useful than knowledge encoded by experts and transmitted to them by an instructor. Successful independent learning is triggered also by noticing a word in several contexts, which extends the knowledge of that word beyond standard coursebook formulation (Cobb, 1998).

However, even though the conditions for active learning can be created by the provision of concordancing procedures, the development of the learner's competence may be thwarted by vast and often confusing lexical information, with many unknown, short and incomplete contexts (Cobb, 1998). Similarly, lack of proper training in corpus use (Stevens, 1995) or misunderstanding of the inherent characteristics of corpus data (Stevens, 1995, Dellar, nd.) may lead learners to false conclusions and discouragement in the use of the tool. Thus, proper training guided by the teacher as a facilitator (Stevens, 1995) seems to be necessary for learners to formulate queries independently in order to observe subtle patterns in language.

Concordancing-based activities for ESP teaching

The implementation of any teaching tool or procedure – not only corpora and concordancers – in a particular teaching context needs to take into account psychosocial considerations (learners' and teacher's perceptions of the tool and the process), logistical considerations (the availability of computer lab with a display device for concordancing sessions, the copying provisions for the preparation of corpora-based teaching materials) and administrative considerations (the accordance of a particular corpus or the discovery learning approach in general with the overall training philosophy, ultimate teacher objectives and the like).

Having determined these, one could reflect on the mode of use, which is where Leech (1997) distinguishes between the direct and indirect use of corpora in teaching: teaching about corpora, teaching the use of corpora and using corpora to teach are said to represent a direct use of corpora, while reference publishing, materials development and language testing are indirect applications (Leech, 1997).

The reflection on which areas of language instruction can be subjected to discovery learning procedures, particularly with the use of ready-made or customised corpora for ESP/EAP, could probably be interminable, leading to the formulation of a number of training activities and approaches in most areas of the learning process. However, there are some areas where such concordance-based tasks can be of most immediate use, which can be enumerated as follows:

1. Grammar:
   - the use of concordancing for presentation of new language points (Hasselgård, 2001), assisting the induction of grammatical rules with concordance output on contrastive issues (e.g., the use of 'for' and 'since');
   - constructing true/false, right/wrong or correct the errors tasks to be verified with the use of concordance queries (see, for instance, Lextutor's "Check grammar against corpus data" activity, http://www.lextutor.ca/grammar_tester/);
   - corpus-based investigation of certain grammatical forms which may cause problems with use in order to demonstrate a greater range of applications in a fuller context (St. John, 2001);
   - investigating how particular language features are used, by examining concordances of them and comparing frequencies (Aston, 1996).

2. Vocabulary:
   - vocabulary-based concordance sheets, classroom projects and task-based learning-filling gaps (Tribble & Jones, 1990; Chen, 2004);

- corpus-based enquiries to investigate the differences between words commonly confused or misused (Krishnamurthy, 2001).

3. Reading comprehension:
   - assisting inferring new words from the text with additional, carefully selected examples (Cobb, 1999);
   - making predictions about the content of the text and activating schemata in the pre-reading stage by concordancing selected words to observe the most prototypical contexts of usage.
4. Writing:
   - improving the awareness of register by using a concordancer as a look-up tool to check the register of particular words to be potentially used (or misused) in a writing piece;
   - learner-made comparisons of their personal corpora with publicly available collections to enhance language awareness and improve writing skills (Krishnamurthy, 2001).

Introducing ESP students to online concordancing-based discovery learning – technical considerations for Moodle-based online learning courses

Addressing the question of implementation of concordancing procedures in Moodle-based online courses needs to take as its starting point the reflection on this particular Learning Management System, which of its functionalities could facilitate guiding learners to proper exploitation of corpus consultation procedures for language learning. It is important to note that any online curriculum set in the context of a Learning Management System will have to strike a balance in the use of teacher-, learner- and computer-controlled activities (e.g., assignment vs. journal vs. lesson), executed individually and demanding collaborative learning (e.g., lesson vs. forum), in order to prevent the predominance of solitary human-computer interaction.

When addressing the issue of learner training in corpora use in the distance / blended learning context, we developed a Moodle-based module on corpus-based linguistics within the course "Information and Communication Technology for ESP teachers". It was believed that if future ESP teachers are guided through the gradual process of acquiring concordancing skills as learners, it will be more feasible for them to undertake the same training procedure with their prospective students. The training, delivered in the blended learning mode, encompassed face-to-face tutorials, self-study reading and quiz taking, and individual assignments submitted to the instructor for evaluation. An important part of the course was the reflection on the work of other students, which was published once evaluated positively, as well as using student submissions as materials for further training. It seems that thanks to student teachers' involvement, their motivation to work is significantly enhanced through increased sense of authorship. The same training can be replicated by ESP teachers in their classes, with learners gradually introduced to the concepts and procedures of corpus linguistics, to harness the concordancing tools for individual reference. The following types of activities and learning paths were developed in this Moodle-based course:

1. *Presentation* of the features of a concordancer, made as a downloadable self-paced PowerPoint presentation with teacher narration and gradual introduction to the characteristics of a tool (e.g., developed with an easy-to-use tool such as Online Concordancer, http://www.edict.com.hk/concordance). Posted in a Moodle course as a downloadable resource, linked to a forum available for students to enquire about the tool.
2. The loose presentation of the interface and procedures from the previous step is followed by a *lesson* module, dividing both basic theoretical knowledge and practical concordancing procedures into chunks, each presented on a page and checked with a question at the bottom. Completing a lesson successfully is a means aiming at ensuring mastery of the procedures in an online course.

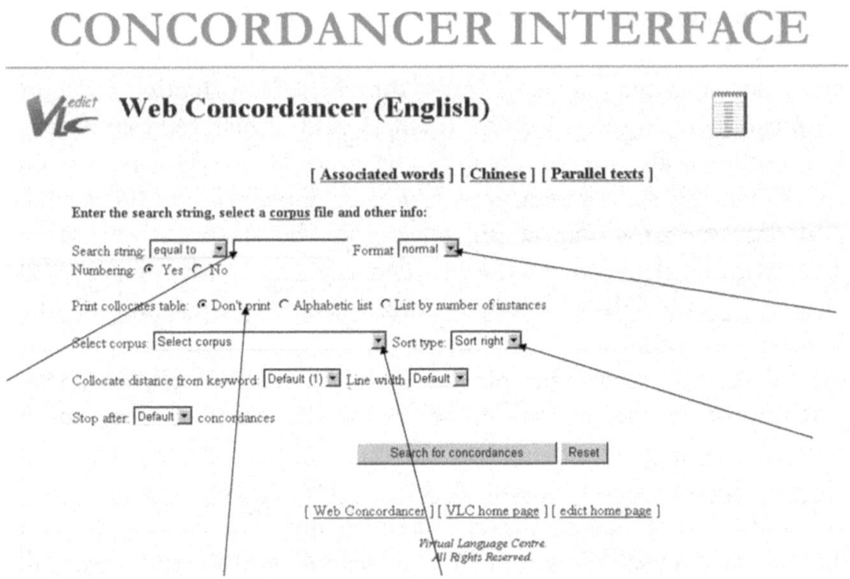

Figure 1. A part of the presentation of the concordancer interface.

3. A learner *assignment* (unscored), asking questions about particular collocations/uses of selected words from the ESP/EAP lexicon, together with clear guidance on the resources to consult and the procedures to use. Developed in a Moodle course as an assignment, with answers to be prepared in the online or off-line mode and submitted to the instructor for feedback.
4. A whole class *forum*, with learners encouraged to think up vocabulary puzzles connected with the recent material or submit their genuine lexical problems, encouraging other learners to submit solutions together with the description of the procedures for using concordancing to solve them (in learners' L1, if necessary). Structured as an open forum, with obligatory subscription of all learners, with or without posting grading, depending on instructional needs.
5. A *journal*, kept privately by learners either in L1 or L2, to reflect on the learning experience provided by concordancing tasks, and responded to by the teacher. Structured as a journal, either scored or

unscored, with limited or unlimited time availability, depending on to what extent the ESP/EAP teacher needs to discipline students to work or wants to leave them greater independence for learning at their own pace.

6. A scored *quiz*, summing up the concordancing skills and knowledge, containing a variety of question types (e.g., true/false, short answer, matching, to mention just a few). A properly developed quiz needs to exploit hyperlinking (e.g., by giving learners a concordancing task to perform in an online concordancer) and multimedia insertion (e.g., screenshots of online concordancers with arrows added to ask learners about particular features of the interface).

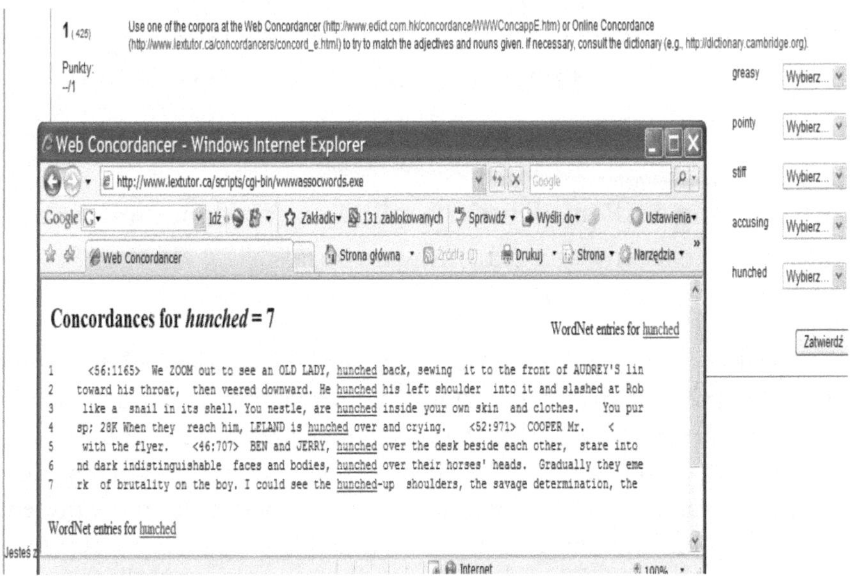

Figure 2. A sample question in a concordance-enhanced quiz.

Another interesting opportunity might be the exploitation of the Moodle Corpus module, an optional part of the Moodle Learning Management System, available for download at http://sourceforge.net/projects/moodleconc. According to the original developer (Henderson, 2005),

Moodle Corpus module was to contain a concordancer, list manager and item viewer, with the options of generating frequency lists and KWiC lines, with links to the source files, support for Boolean and regex searches, and the ability to exclude specific files in the student interface. As for teacher functionalities, it was intended to be a facility to dynamically create and edit multiple corpora, each consisting of a chosen number of text files, the ability to set permissions for each corpus – so that it is or is not available to students – the ability to add to the corpus from content within Moodle, direct text input or file uploads (Henderson, 2005). The module was worked on intensively in 2005 (see the ongoing discussion at http://moodle.org/mod/forum/discuss.php?d=35630); however, it was abandoned at a certain point by the original developer. According to Moodle users, the Corpus module (moodleconc) works with Moodle versions up to 1.5.3, no longer supporting 1.8.1, for instance (Kraus, 2007).

Introducing ESP students to online concordancing-based discovery learning – a training proposal

The problems involved in the use of concordancing, the tool not essentially designed for language learning and producing data in the output that is not easily accessible for learners to interpret, call for skilful incorporation of the software in the language classroom. Thus, in the curriculum development procedure for the course described in the present paper we took into consideration the important guidelines stemming from previous research into learner training in corpus consultation procedures, as summarised below.

Kennedy and Miceli (2001) propose adopting the "apprenticeship model" of classroom concordancing (Johns, 1988), which aims at promoting learning by example and experience. The authors suggest corpus-based activities that are carried out gradually, with the teacher giving directions and asking additional questions, while students work in small groups and later report to the whole class, using problem-solving and treasure-hunting activities.

In the same vein, Kennedy and Miceli (2001) isolate the following steps for corpus investigation: formulate a question, devise a search strategy, observe the examples to select the relevant ones, draw conclusions, identify relevant combinations and use them in target sentences.

The frequent argument against the use of learner corpus consultation is that the complexity of the tool prevents it from being used with low level learners. Cobb (1999) addresses this issue, claiming that a concordance-assisted language program should follow the steps below to be relevant to less proficient students:

- identify which words to investigate;
- provide a means for learners to take away lexical information in hard copy;
- build in motivation for considering each word in several sentence contexts.

In the course described in the present paper, the learner training consisted of the following stages, each covered in a single class, with varied materials and activities, both for in-class and self-study work:

1. *Introduction to basic concepts of corpus linguistics* – defining a corpus and a concordancer, analysing sample concordance output, making a distinction between corpus lookup and dictionary lookup, highlighting different types of corpora.
2. *Using a concordance-enhanced dictionary* (*NetDictionary*, http://www.edict.com.hk/lexiconindex/) *to expand vocabulary knowledge* – during text-based activities students are instructed in how to extend their knowledge of the new words encountered in the text with a concordancer.
3. *Using ready-made concordancers with selected texts in formulating and testing hypotheses about grammar* (e.g., Online Concordancers, http://www.lextutor.ca/concordancers/ or Web Concordancer, www.edict.com.hk/concordance) – in grammar instruction, the teacher guides

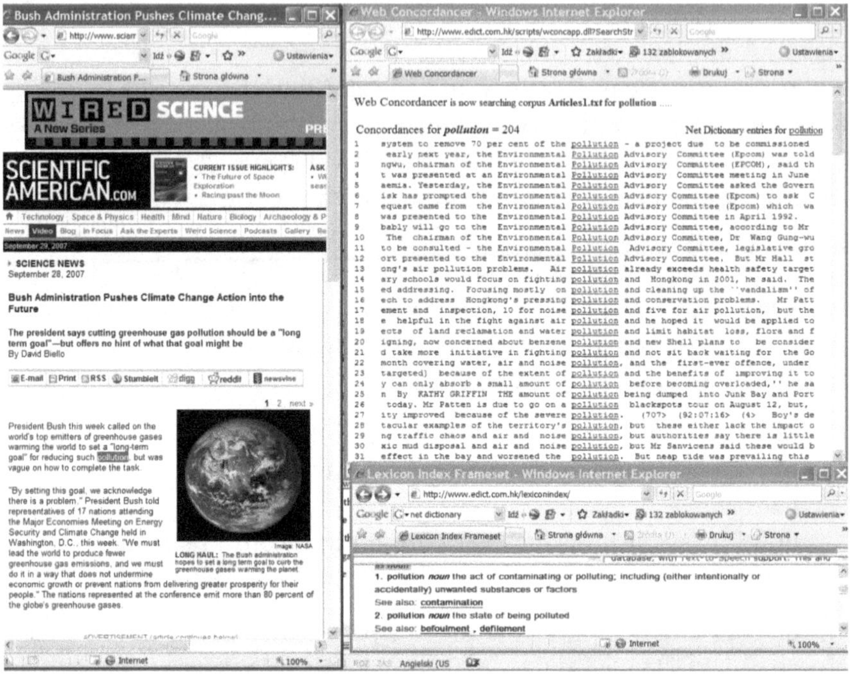

Figure 3. Looking up words from a new text in a concordance-enhanced dictionary.

students to the free concordancers to verify pairs of correct/incorrect statements. Students learn to use different corpora with the search strategy explained by the teacher.

4. *Contrasting the coverage of corpora (a literary text corpus, a representative corpus, a teacher-made ESP corpus)* – the teacher uploads a custom-made ESP corpus to the Online Concordancer interface (http://www.edict.com.hk/concordance/ConcUpload.htm). In the whole-class tutorial, learners are guided to make concordance searches about the recently learnt ESP vocabulary in a non-ESP general corpus (e.g., literature corpora or Brown Corpus at Web Concordancer, www.edict.com.hk/concordance) and a custom-made ESP corpus, to make generalisations about the coverage of various corpora.

5. *Using a teacher-made ESP corpus with a concordancing tool to enhance the awareness of register* – the teacher prepares two parallel files with texts representing different registers (e.g., magazine articles vs. EU legislation from a specific ESP area), which are later added to a single corpus. Then students are guided to follow particular search procedures with a concordancing tool to check the use of the same words in two different areas of language use, evoking the full context of the source file.
6. *Increasing the awareness of concordancing procedures to exploit word formation* – the teacher-made ESP corpus is used in various searches taking a root word and applying prefix or suffix search, to build word families and formulate generalisations on word formation rules.
7. *Using an ESP corpus for vocabulary matching activities* – the teacher provides students with a matching exercise (joining verbs and nouns or adjectives and nouns) within the specialised area. Students try to do the task on their own and then use the associated words concordancing procedures to verify their matches and increase the awareness of collocations.
8. *Using a teacher-made ESP corpus to make reference for students' language use* – students use the teacher-made ESP corpus on their own, browsing it with a simple concordancing tool (e.g., ConcApp) to find instances of specialist vocabulary they used incorrectly in their essays to assist the process of self-correction.
9. *Encouraging students to browse the Internet to suggest sources of texts for the class ESP corpus* – having acquired the awareness of varied opportunities of enhancing language instruction by corpus-based studies, students are asked to browse the Internet to find sources of texts for inclusion to the class corpus. Students apply their web searching skills and learn how to evaluate the authority of materials.
10. *Introducing learners to the procedures of compiling their own mini-corpora* (Lee & Swales, 2006) – students make one corpus of texts suggested by the teacher or found by themselves and another based on their own essay writing for the ESP classes. Then they conduct searches for the occurrences of the same words, comparing their usage in the reference texts and personal texts.

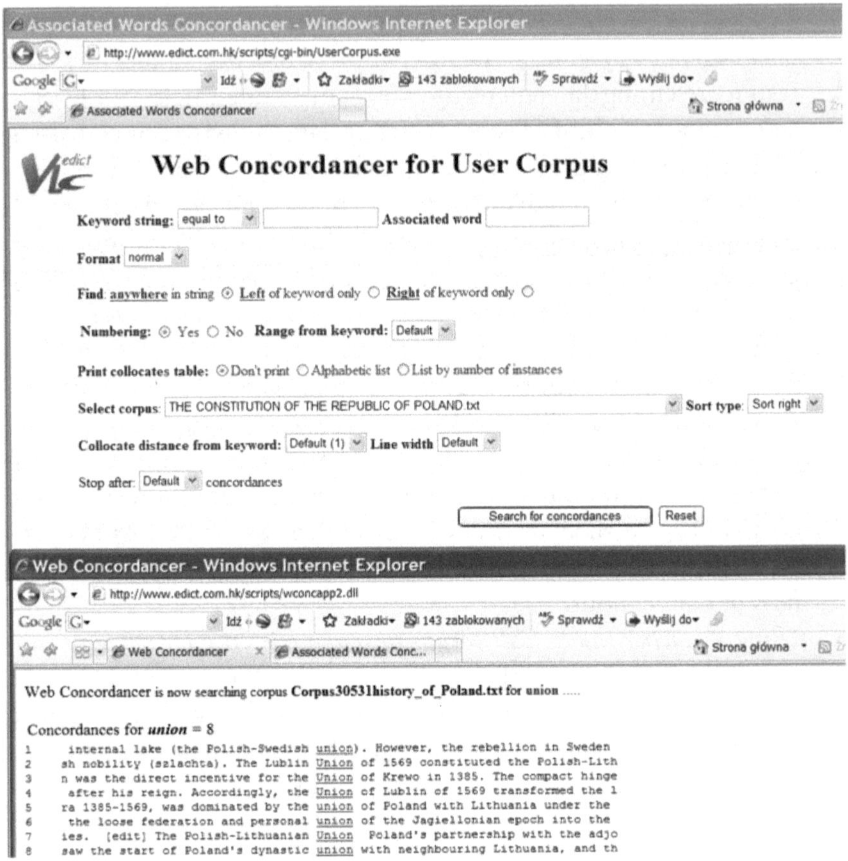

Figure 4. Browsing a custom-made corpus (Constitution of the Republic of Poland) for students of history.

In conclusion, what follows from the experiences of ICT training for ESP students, both prior to the course described above and the actual training effort as outlined in the present paper, is that the incorporation of corpus-based discovery learning work should be done gradually, first exposing students to teacher-prepared ready-made concordance output, for them to learn how to interpret the information. Once this is done, and once such crucial distinctions as simple search vs. associated search, prefix/suffix search, left/right collocates are grasped by students, they can be guided through concordancing tools (such as Web Concordancer, http://www.edict.com.hk/concordance/ConcUpload.htm) with a teacher-made ESP corpus, to finally arrive at the awareness of the procedures to be able to search teacher-made corpora or personal corpora with text analysis tools.

Conclusion

Together with a wide-scale implementation of Information and Communication Technology in English for Specific Purposes instruction, there arises a need to find applications of technology that would allow a successful integration of computer skills and subject knowledge, leading at the same time to the empowerment of learners and improvement in the quality of the learning process. An example of such an area is concordancing, which assists learners in making informed choices about meaning and use of lexical items and grammatical structures. Within the ESP context, due to the frequent shortage of published materials (coursebooks and dictionaries) pertaining to a specialised discipline, the successful integration of in-class corpus consultation, coupled with appropriate corpus selection or compilation, may lead to the improvement of learning skills and greater awareness of the learning process. Gradual introduction of the elements of corpus linguistics in the conscious programme of strategy training should equip learners with the skills replicable in lifelong learning.

The application of a particular technique – here corpus consultation procedures – within the framework of online learning, is to a large extent conditioned by three factors: the characteristics of online learning, the specific constraints imposed by the Learning Management System (here Moodle) and the requirements of the technique itself. As shown above, the attempt to introduce concordancing into an online course will need to be a compromise between what learner training procedure seems to be most efficient in case of corpora use on the one hand and what operations are feasible within Moodle as an authoring environment on the other. Hopefully, with ongoing development of Moodle by the community of users, the future might see new modules and functionalities enabling even more effective learner training.

References

Aston, G. (1996). What corpora for ESP?. Paper presented at a conference on ESP at the University of Pavia, November 1996. Retrieved July 30, 2007, from http://www.sslmit.unibo.it/~guy/pavesi.htm.

Benson, P. (2001). *Teaching and Researching Autonomy in Language Learning.* Harlow: Pearson Education Limited.

Biber, D., Conrad, S., & Reppen, R. (1998). *Corpus Linguistics: Investigating Language Structure and Use.* Cambridge: Cambridge University Press.

Chen, Y. H. (2004). The use of corpora in the vocabulary classroom. *The Internet TESL Journal,* 10 (9). Retrieved May 31, 2007, from http://iteslj.org/Techniques/Chen-Corpora.html.

Cobb, T. (1998). Breadth and depth of lexical acquisition with hands-on concordancing. *Computer Assisted Language Learning,* 12 (4), 345–360.

Cobb, T. (1999). Applying constructivism: A test for the learner as scientist. *Educational Technology Research & Development,* 47 (3), 15–31.

Curado Fuentes, A. (2006). A corpus-based focus on ESP teaching. *Teaching English with Technology,* 6 (4). Retrieved May 31, 2007, from http://www.iatefl.org.pl/call/j_esp26.htm.

Crystal, D. (1991). *A Dictionary of Linguistics and Phonetics.* Oxford: Blackwell.

Felder, R. M., Henriques, E. R. (1995). Learning and teaching styles in foreign and second language education. *Foreign Language Annals,* 28 (1), 21–31.

Gardner, H. (2002). *Inteligencje wielorakie: teoria w praktyce* (Multiple Intelligences: The Theory in Practice). Poznań: Media Rodzina.

Harmer, J. (1998). *How to Teach English. An Introduction to the Practice of English Language Teaching.* Harlow: Longman.

Hasselgård, H. (2001). Corpora and their use in research and teaching. Retrieved May 31, 2007, from http://folk.uio.no/hhasselg/UV-corpus.htm.

Henderson, S. (2005). Concordancer module. A message sent to Moodle / Lang Teaching / New Proposals for Development discussion forum, December 4, 2005. Retrieved July 30, 2007, from http://moodle.org/mod/forum/discuss.php?d=35630 (available having set up a Moodle account).

Hunston, S. (2002). *Corpora in Applied Linguistics*. Cambridge: Cambridge University Press.

Johns, T. (1988). Whence and whither classroom concordancing? In T. Bongaerts, P. de Haan, S. Lobbe, H. Wekker (Eds.), *Computer Applications in Language Learning*. Dordrecht: Foris Publications, 9–33.

Kennedy, C., & Miceli, T. (2001). An evaluation of intermediate students' approaches to corpus investigation. *Language Learning & Technology*, 5 (3), 77–90. Retrieved July 18, 2006, from http://llt.msu.edu/vol5num3/kennedy/.

Kraus, S. (2007). Corpus module with moodle 1.8. A message sent to Using Moodle / Installation Problems discussion forum, July 17, 2007. Retrieved July 30, 2007, from http://moodle.org/mod/forum/discuss.php?d=76140 (available having set up a Moodle account).

Krishnamurthy, R. (2001). Learning and teaching through context – A data-driven approach. *TESOL Spain Newsletter, 24*, 2001. Retrieved May 31, 2007, from http://www.developingteachers.com/articles_tchtraining/corpora1_ramesh.htm.

Lee, D., & Swales, J. (2006). A corpus-based EAP course for NNS doctoral students: Moving from available specialized corpora to self-compiled corpora. *English for Specific Purposes*, 25 (2006), 56–75.

Leech, G. (1997). Teaching and language corpora – a convergence. In A. Wichmann, S. Fligelstone, T. McEnery & G. Knowles (Eds.), *Teaching and Language Corpora*. New York: Longman, 1–23.

McEnery, T., & Wilson, A. (1996). *Corpus Linguistics*. Edinburgh: Edinburgh University Press.

Sinclair, J. (1991). *Corpus, Concordance, Collocation*. Oxford: Oxford University Press.

Sinclair, J. (1996). EAGLES: Preliminary recommendations on corpus typology. Expert Advisory Group on Language Engineering Standards Guidelines EAG-TCWG-CTYP/P. Retrieved August 5, 2007, from http://www.ilc.cnr.it/EAGLES96/corpustyp/corpustyp.html.

St. John, E. (2001). A case for using a parallel corpus and concordancer for beginners of a foreign language. *Language Learning & Technology*, 5 (3), 185–203. Retrieved May 31, 2007, from http://llt.msu.edu/vol5num3/stjohn/default.html.

Stevens, V. (1995). Concordancing with language learners: Why? When? What?. *CAELL Journal*, 6 (2), 2–10.

Tribble, C. (1997). Improvising corpora for ELT: Quick-and-dirty ways of developing corpora for language teaching. Paper presented at the First International Conference: Practical Applications in Language Corpora (1997), University of Łódź, Poland. Melia, J., & B. Lewandowska-Tomaszczyk (eds.), *PALC '97 Proceedings*. Łódź: Łódź University Press. Retrieved May 31, 2007, from http://www.ctribble.co.uk/text/Palc.htm.

Tribble, C., & Jones, G. (1990). *Concordances in the Classroom: A Resource Book for Teachers*. London: Longman.

Appendix – Selected corpora resources for ELT/ESP/EAP:

- full versions of specialist corpora with unlimited access (MICASE Michigan Corpus of Academic Spoken English, http://www.hti.umich.edu/m/micase/; International Corpus of Learner English – Polish section, http://ifa.amu.edu.pl/~kprzemek/concord2advr/search_adv_new.html);
- official demonstration versions of established corpora, usually with only basic keyword search facilities (British National Corpus, http://sara.natcorp.ox.ac.uk/lookup.html; Collins COBUILD Bank of English, http://www.collins.co.uk/Corpus/CorpusSearch.aspx);
- full access custom-made interfaces to renowned corpora developed by researchers (British National Corpus, http://www.lextutor.ca/concordancers/concord_e.html and http://corpus.byu.edu/bnc/; Brown Corpus, http://www.lextutor.ca/concordancers/concord_e.html, http://www.edict.com.hk/concordance and http://www.ldc.upenn.edu/cgi-bin/ldc/textcorpus?doc=yes&corpus=BROWN; Lancaster-Oslo-Bergen Corpus, http://www.edict.com.hk/concordance);
- corpora compiled of selected works of the English literature, such as *Alice in Wonderland, The Lord of the Rings, Call of the Wild* or Sherlock Holmes stories (Online Concordancer, http://www.lextutor.ca/concordancers/concord_e.html, Web Concordancer, http://www.edict.com.hk/concordance);
- corpora compiled of newspaper articles and television news transcripts, also based on current issues of online newspapers (Online Concordancer, http://www.lextutor.ca/concordancers/concord_e.html; Web Concordancer, http://www.edict.com.hk/concordance; GlossaNet, http://glossa.fltr.ucl.ac.be/scripts/gtoday/gtoday.pl; Reuters Corpora, http://trec.nist.gov/data/reuters/reuters.html);
- learner corpora (PICLE Polish International Corpus of Learner English, http://ifa.amu.edu.pl/~kprzemek/concord2advr/search_adv_new.html; Online Concordancer, http://www.lextutor.ca/concordancers/concord_e.html; Web Concordancer, http://www.edict.com.hk/concordance);
- thematic corpora, e. g., of telephone conversations (http://www.ldc.upenn.edu/cgi-bin/lol/swb/speechcorpus?&corpus=swb), business letters (http://ysomeya.hp.infoseek.co.jp/), EU legislation (http://urd.let.rug.nl/tiedeman/OPUS/), culinary, ecotourism, computer and environmental protection texts (http://www.nilc.icmc.usp.br/cortec/ibusca.php), European Parliament session transcripts (Europarl, http://www.statmt.org/europarl/).

The URLs in this paper were valid at the time of the last revision, June 19, 2008.

List of contributors

ELISABET ARNÓ MACIÀ, CARMEN RUEDA RAMOS, ANTONIA SOLER CERVERA. Universitat Politècnica de Catalunya. Spain. <elisabet.arno@upc.edu>

Mª CAMINO BUENO ALASTUEY. Public University of Navarre. Spain. <camino.bueno@unavarra.es>

Mª LUISA CARRIÓ PASTOR. Department of Applied Linguistics. Universidad Politécnica de Valencia. Spain. <lcarrio@idm.upv.es>

ANTONELLA ELIA. University of Naples. Italia. <aelia@unior.it>

ANA GIMENO SANZ. Department of Applied Linguistics, Universidad Politécnica de Valencia. Spain. <agimeno@upvnet.upv.es>

JAROSŁAW KRAJKA. Warsaw School of Social Psychology. Warsaw, Poland. <jaroslaw.krajka@swps.edu.pl>

MARÍA JOSÉ LUZÓN. Department of English Philology. University of Zaragoza. Spain. <mjluzon@unizar.es>

PHILIPPA MUNGRA. University of Rome, La Sapienza, Faculty of Medicine and Surgery. Italy. <philippa.mungra@uniroma1.it>

RUTH TRINDER. Associate Professor at the Vienna University of Economics and Business Administration. Austria. <rtrinder@wu-wien.ac.at>

Giuliana Garzone / Cornelia Ilie (eds)

The Use of English in Institutional and Business Settings

An Intercultural Perspective

Bern, Berlin, Bruxelles, Frankfurt am Main, New York, Oxford, Wien, 2007. 372 pp.
Linguistic Insights. Studies in Language and Communication. Vol. 34
Edited by Maurizio Gotti
ISBN 978-3-03910-889-3 pb.
sFr. 99.– / € 68.70 / €** 70.60 / € 64.20 / £ 48.20 / US-$ 99.95*

* includes VAT – valid for Germany ** includes VAT – valid for Austria

This book explores the intercultural problems related to the widespread use of English in written and oral communication by native and non-native speakers in institutional and business settings. Each chapter looks at a different set of issues emerging from the confrontation of cultures across national, institutional and organizational discourse communities, taking an intercultural or cross-cultural approach. The focus is on workplace settings, both in institutional and business contexts (e.g. politics, public services, media, international corporate communication, advertising, business negotiations, etc.). The theme is all the more interesting today not only in consideration of the sheer magnitude of this phenomenon and its capillary spread, but above all on account of the pervasive penetration of English into professional and workplace contexts as a communication language also for local/internal communication. The complexity of intercultural communication as an object of research is reflected in the variety of the topics explored, the range of settings investigated, and the diversity of methodological approaches taken.

Contents: Giuliana Garzone: Introduction – Paola Catenaccio: Constructing Identities in the Fashion Industry: Building Brand and Customer Image through Press Releases – Delia Chiaro: A Question of Taste: Translating the Flavour of Italy – Marinel Gerritsen/Catherine Nickerson/Corine van den Brandt/Rogier Crijns/Nuriá Dominguez/Frank van Meurs/ Ulrike Nederstigt: English in Print Advertising in Germany, Spain and the Netherlands: Frequency of Occurrence, Comprehensibility and the Effect on Corporate Image – Cornelia Ilie: British, 'Consensus' vs. Swedish *'Samförstånd'* in Parliamentary Debates – Daniela Wawra: On Course for the Next Stage of Success: the Annual Reports of U.S. and Japanese Companies – Kumiko Murata: The Discourses of Pro- and Anti-Whaling in the British and Japanese News Editorials: A Comparative Cultural Perspective – Maria Cristina Paganoni: Recontextualizing Language: Indian Activists and the Recasting of English – Stefanie Zilles Pohle: Offers in Irish English and German Business Negotiations: A Cross-Cultural Pragmatic Analysis – Grahame T. Bilbow: Speaking and not Speaking Across Cultures – Ora-Ong Chakorn: Written Business Invitations: A Cross-Cultural Rhetorical Analysis – Gina Poncini: Communicating within and across Professional Worlds in an Intercultural Setting – Carmen Valero Garcés/Bruce Downing: Modes of Communication between Suppliers of Services and Non-native English-speaking Users: Doctor-Patient Interaction – Cynthia Kellett Bidoli: The Linguistics Conference Setting: A Comparative Analysis of Intercultural Disparities during English to Italian Sign Language Interpretation – Catherine Nickerson: English as a *Lingua Franca* in Business Contexts: Strategy or Hegemony?

PETER LANG
Bern · Berlin · Bruxelles · Frankfurt am Main · New York · Oxford · Wien

FSC
www.fsc.org
MIX
Papier | Fördert
gute Waldnutzung
FSC® C083411

Kolibri 360 GmbH
Ferdinand-Jühlke-Straße 7
99095 Erfurt, Deutschland
produktsicherheit@kolibri360.de